ILLUMINATED LETTERS

ILLUMINATED LETTERS

A Treasury of Decorative Calligraphy

Margaret Morgan

A QUARTO BOOK

First published 2006
A & C Black Publishers Limited
38 Soho Square
London W1D 3HB
www.acblack.com

Reprinted 2006

ISBN-10: 0 7136 7165 3
ISBN-13: 978 0 7136 7165 0

QUAR.BIL

Conceived, designed and produced by
Quarto Publishing plc
The Old Brewery
6 Blundell Street
London N7 9BH

Senior Editor **Jo Fisher**
Designer **Lisa Tai**
Assistant art director **Penny Cobb**
Picture researcher **Claudia Tate**
Text editor **Tracie Davis**
Proofreader **Natasha Reed**
Photographer **Geoff Morgan**
Indexer **Pamela Ellis**

Art director **Moira Clinch**
Publisher **Paul Carslake**

Manufactured by Modern Age Repro House Ltd, Hong Kong
Printed by Midas Printing International Ltd, China

9 8 7 6 5 4 3 2

Health and Safety
Some of the materials used in illumination (plaster gesso, in particular) are toxic and hazardous if not handled properly. Please study carefully the health and safety information supplied on the relevant pages and adhere to good practice at all times. The author, publisher and copyright holder cannot be held liable if this advice is disregarded.

Contents

Introduction

Illumination, expressed simply, is the art of decorating books with colour and gold, the word stemming from the Latin illuminare, "to light up". For centuries, illuminated letters, borders and other decorative elements enriched with gold and brilliant colours have been used to stunning effect, truly lighting up the pages of the manuscripts. The earliest books were intended for religious use, either in church services or for private

▲ **_Rosemary Buczek_**
Panel: 7.5 x 9 cm (3 x 3½ in)
Watercolour paints add a certain luminosity, bringing this letter "S" to life. The image was further enhanced with shell gold.

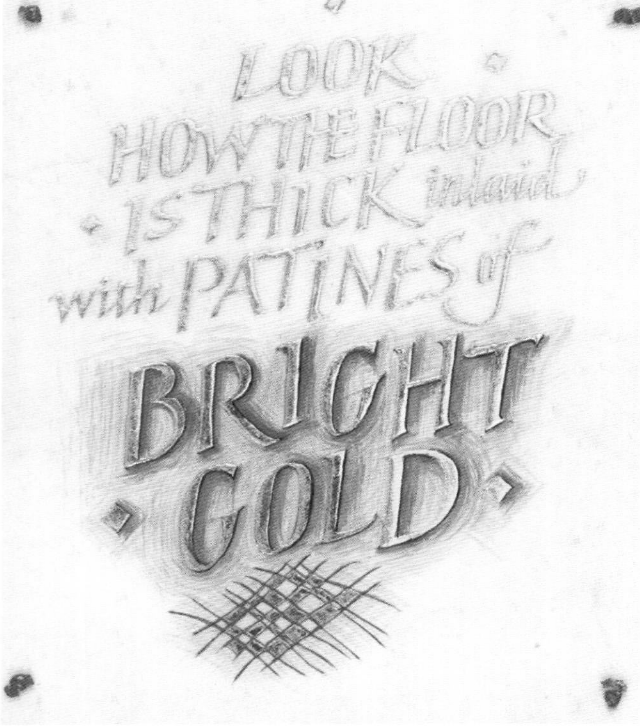

◄ **_Margaret Morgan_**
Bright Gold
Panel: 8.5 x 9.7 cm
(3⅓ x 3¾ in)
Raised and burnished gold lettering written in plaster gesso using metal nibs, with colour added in egg tempera. The calfskin vellum is stitched onto acid-free mount with silk thread.

Marlene Gray
Psalm 46, verse 10
Panel: 14 x 19 cm (5½ x 7½ in)
Gold leaf on gum ammoniac, elegant versals and Roman capitals written in gouache with metal nibs over a mixed watercolour wash on stretched Canaletto paper.

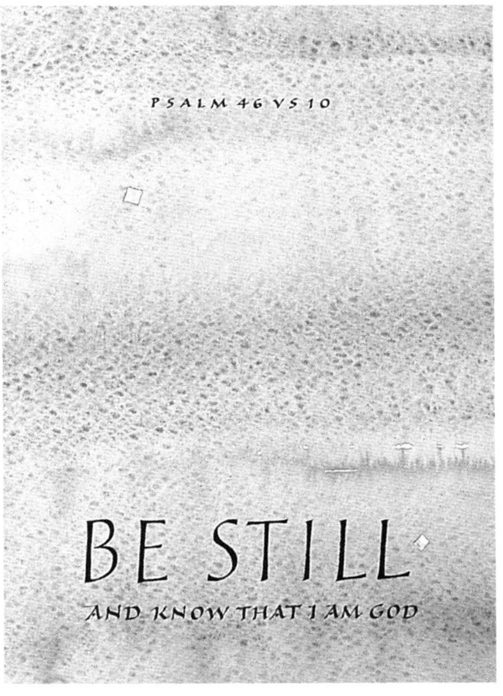

devotions. The fantastic zoomorphic designs of Celtic gospel books and the historiated capital letters of later manuscripts could almost be regarded as medieval visual aids to meditation on the word of God.

This book begins with a chapter on all the tools, techniques and equipment required to produce illuminated letters yourself, knowledge that I have gained over many years of study. It is followed by a chapter on preparing to work, which will take you through all the stages necessary before you can begin illuminating and decorating your own work. Read these chapters carefully and try out the techniques before you begin any of the projects, so that you understand the processes involved and how the various materials behave.

Rosemary Buczek
Panel: 9 x 12 cm (3½ x 5 in)
This decorated "P", illustrated for a hand-bound alphabet book, was painted using watercolour paints. Shell gold was rubbed over the peacock's feathers.

These introductory sections are followed by a unique compendium comprised of complete alphabets and numbers based on six historical styles. They have been devised and adapted from sketches made during my own direct researches with original manuscripts, or gleaned from photographic references in books about illumination.

▼ ***Rosemary Buczek***
Panel: 9.25 x 11 cm (3⅝ x 4½ in)
Watercolour paints were also used to paint this "A". Raised gold (23 carat) forms the square beneath the A, while shell gold has been brushed over the angel's wings.

Each alphabet has a project, which guides you step by step through all the different stages involved, from drafting out to finished letter. The remaining letters are organized into groups by shape and appear in outline form, with large annotated examples to give clear ideas of the colour and decoration style. There are also exemplars of suitable text hands, contemporary with the decorated letters, for you to use in your own work. These exemplar scripts have been adapted for modern use, incorporating letters like W and Z as well as some continental characters, which were unknown to medieval scribes writing in Latin. Similarly, our relatively modern Arabic numerals are

▼ ***Margaret Morgan***
Alphabet Strip
Panel: 33 x 10 cm (13 x 4 in)
24 carat gold leaf on gum ammoniac
Calico stretched over MDF, secured with acrylic gesso primer (for oil painting), and glazed with layers of gouache mixed with PVA medium. Although the gold was laid primarily onto a strip of gum ammoniac, the PVA in the glaze is also an adhesive, and caused the gold to stick randomly across the surface. The letters are brush-painted in black gouache.

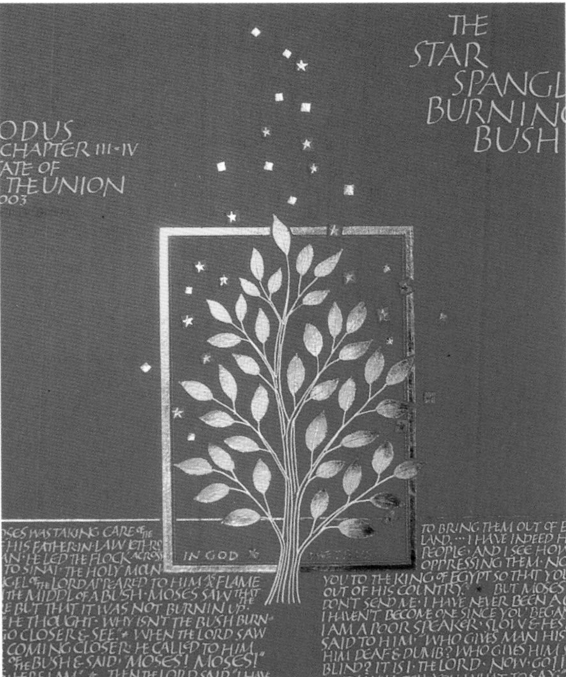

◄ **Peter Halliday**
The Star-Spangled Burning Bush 1 (detail)
Panel: 38 x 52 cm (15 x 20½ in)
The leaves of the bush are gold leaf on a PVA base, with decoration incised into the surface. Text and other decoration in watercolour, on Canson mi-teintes pastel paper.

shown for up-to-date use in preference to the archaic Roman forms.

A love of calligraphy was kindled by italic handwriting lessons at school, which with drawing and painting, have been common threads in my life ever since. Art school training in graphic design, as well as attendance at workshops in calligraphy and illumination, set me on the path to what is now a full-time occupation. Gilding became another passion after a one-day workshop in 1980, and the sheer beauty of polished gold in a piece of work still delights me.

I hope that you will enjoy using this book, which is intended to give inspiration and an idea of what is possible if you have both enthusiasm and patience. Whatever you make, whether it is simple in concept and execution or represents a huge challenge to your skills, even though it is based on a historic style, it will be unique.

MARGARET MORGAN

How to Use This Book

This book takes us through the fascinating history of illuminated letters, with detailed instructions for creating your own artworks. All the necessary equipment and techniques, both traditional and new, are discussed, and six historical styles of illumination are explored and illustrated in detail. A gallery of contemporary pieces completes the book, bringing illuminated letter art into the modern era.

CHAPTERS 1 AND 2
TOOLS AND TECHNIQUES, PREPARING TO WORK

The first two chapters explain how to get started creating your own illuminated letters. Tools and Techniques *introduces the range of tools and materials you will require, and explains all the important techniques you will need to master, from preparing vellum to gilding on plaster gesso.* Preparing to Work *describes how to design and plan your work in order to produce well-crafted finished pieces, with illustrations of tried-and-tested page layouts and a discussion on choosing colours.*

CHAPTER 3
THE ALPHABET DIRECTORY

History

Each section of the Alphabet Directory *begins by putting the work into its historical context, with an explanation of how each style arose and what it was used for. Its particular characteristics are described and images from original manuscripts from the period are included for inspiration.*

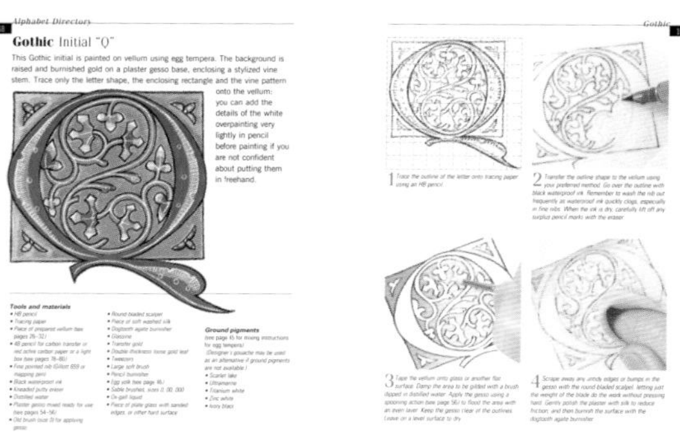

Step-by-step demonstration

Learn how to create your own illuminated artwork in the style of each historical period by following this clear step-by-step demonstration of the illustration of one letter. All the tools and materials required are listed, and references to the relevant technique instructions in the Tools and Techniques *and* Preparing to Work *chapters are provided.*

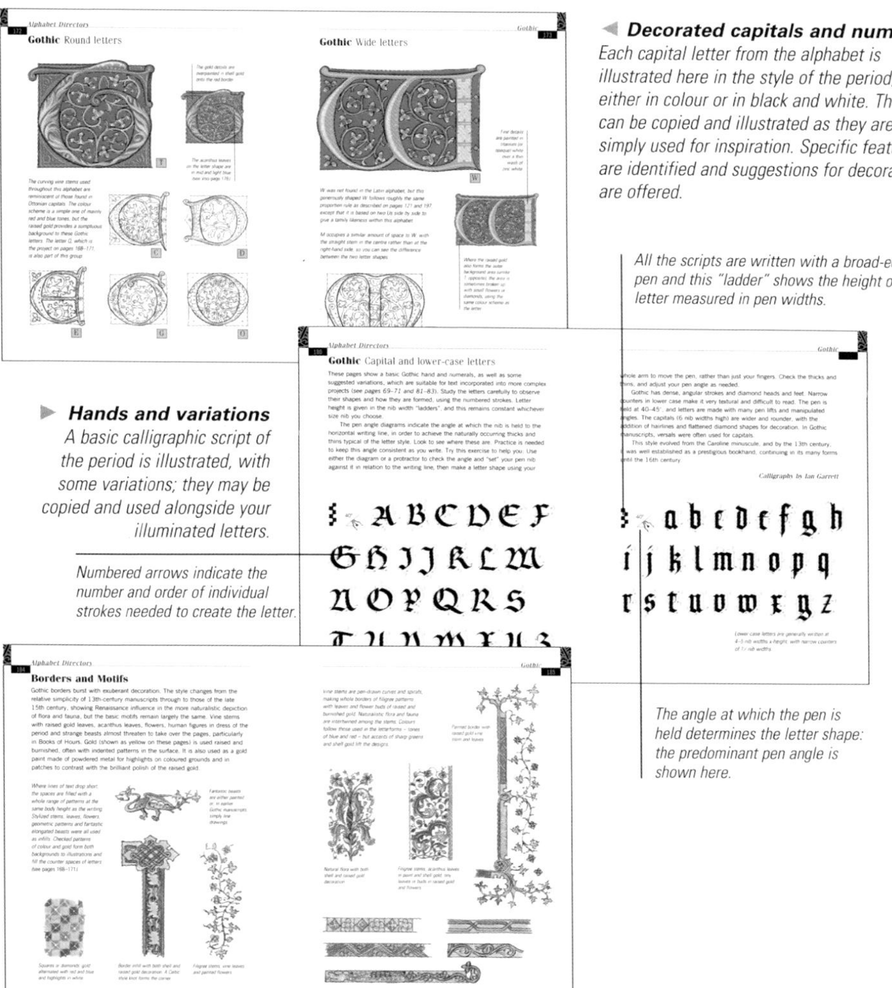

Decorated capitals and numbers
Each capital letter from the alphabet is illustrated here in the style of the period, either in colour or in black and white. These can be copied and illustrated as they are, or simply used for inspiration. Specific features are identified and suggestions for decoration are offered.

All the scripts are written with a broad-edged pen and this "ladder" shows the height of the letter measured in pen widths.

Hands and variations
A basic calligraphic script of the period is illustrated, with some variations; they may be copied and used alongside your illuminated letters.

Numbered arrows indicate the number and order of individual strokes needed to create the letter.

The angle at which the pen is held determines the letter shape: the predominant pen angle is shown here.

Borders and motifs
A selection of borders are offered here to complement your letters and finish off your pieces appropriately. In addition, some of the different motifs from the period are explained and illustrated – these can be incorporated into your own work for an authentic touch.

CHAPTER 4

CONTEMPORARY GALLERY

This inspirational gallery of modern pieces demonstrates the use of both traditional and new techniques in the creation of beautiful, contemporary lettered art.

CHAPTER 1

Tools and Techniques

This chapter provides information on all the tools you'll need to get started and introduces you to the techniques involved, from the preparation of paper and vellum to the different methods of painting and gilding.

Tools and Materials

When you begin to practise the art of illumination, you only require a few basic items: paper, pencils, inks, paint, brushes and a drawing board. You can add to your battery of tools gradually as you increase your confidence and ability. Buying the best equipment you can afford will pay off in the long run, not just in the quality of the results, but also in the pleasure and satisfaction you will find in using good tools.

Detailed information about all the materials as well as the specialized equipment needed for gilding can be found later in this section.

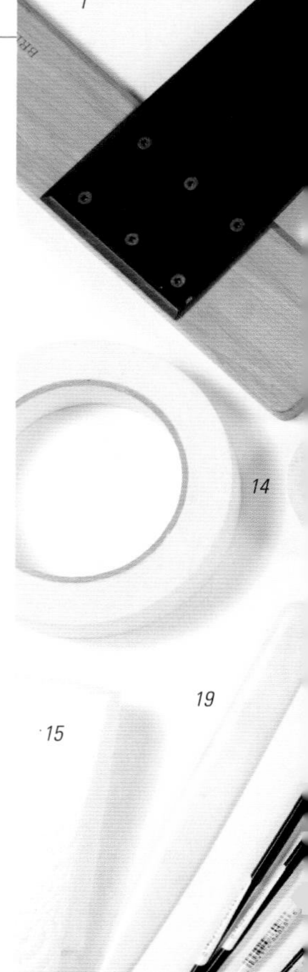

Look after your materials

- Always wash brushes thoroughly in cold water after use. A little liquid soap will help to remove any paint or ink remaining in the bristles. Store bristles upward.
- Do not leave brushes to soak with water over the metal ferrule.
- Rinse pen nibs and reservoirs frequently and dry them off using a lint-free cloth, both during and after use. This avoids any clogging up of ink or corrosion of the nib and ensures clean, crisp marks.
- Replace lids and caps on inks and paints to avoid evaporation and accidental spillage.
- Protect your fingers by pushing knife or scalpel blades into a piece of cork or eraser when not in use.

Basic equipment

The tools you need to tackle any of the projects in this book. Where alternatives are shown (for example, items 6, 14 and 18), you will need only one type to start with.

1 *T-square (parallel rule) for ruling accurate horizontal lines*

2 *Triangle to rule vertical lines as well as angles – available both in fixed (45°, 90°) and adjustable forms*

3 *Plastic ruler for measuring and marking up designs*

4 *Metal ruler or steel straight edge for cutting paper and card accurately*

5 *Cutting mat or a sheet of heavy card to protect work surfaces when cutting out paper and card*

6 *Plastic erasers and kneaded putty erasers for cleaning off surplus pencil marks*

7 *Hard and soft pencils*

8 *Coloured pencils for working out colour schemes in your designs*

9 *Springbow compass used to measure equal distances accurately*

10 *Pencil sharpener to keep pencil leads sharp for accurate drawing and ruling*

11 *Scalpel with different blades for cutting paper and card, also for scraping gesso*

12 Scissors
13 Black or brown waterproof ink for drawing in designs
14 Low-tack adhesive tape or masking tape to secure your work when ruling up
15 Absorbent paper towels or soft lint-free rags for wiping nibs and brushes and mopping up spills
16 Brushes for painting
17 Reservoirs to hold ink or paint for chisel-edged nibs
18 Dip pens for inking in designs

- Drawing board (not shown, see pages 18–19)

Extra equipment

Non-essentials, to be added later.

19 Bone folder for creasing and folding paper
20 Pens for lettering, with a selection of different nib widths
21 Technical pens (optional) with different width points for inking in designs. Cannot be used with paint.
22 Ruling pen that can be adjusted to rule lines of different width in ink or paint
23 Compass and ruling pen attachments for drawing circles in ink or paint
24 Pencil compasses (small and large) for drawing circles

Your Workstation

Good working conditions are important for your comfort and health, especially when you may be sitting down for extended periods. Most importantly, when you are doing such concentrated and close work, you will need to get up from time to time to stretch your legs and get the circulation going. Flex hands and shoulders and turn your head gently from side to side to ease any build-up of muscle tension.

Sit up straight with your feet flat on the floor and your back supported by the chair. Try not to lean forward over your work too much, as this could lead to problems with neck and back pain.

Make sure you have good light, either daylight or from a directed artificial light source.

Sit where the light will not cast shadows over your work area. Have the light from the left for right-handers and from the right for left-handers.

Have a drawing board with the work surface padded for writing (see opposite).

Have a comfortable chair that is the right height for your worktable. One with adjustable height and back support is ideal, but an extra cushion or two may help.

Have a table that is large enough to provide space on one side of the drawing board so that you can lay out tools and other equipment.

Drawing board

- There are sophisticated drawing boards available that have stands to adjust height and angle as well as an attached parallel rule, but initially you do not need anything so complex.
- A piece of plywood or medium-density fibreboard (MDF) is fine to begin with, provided its edges are square and smooth enough for a T-square to move over easily.
- For gilding and painting, you need to work with the drawing board flat, but for writing it needs to be angled against the table edge, with the lower edge resting on your lap.
- Alternatively, you can support the board on a pile of books on a tabletop, with the board taped to the table edge so that it does not slip.

Padding the drawing board

Pad the board surface for writing. The drawing board needs to be padded with several layers of paper, covered with sketching paper, to give a slightly yielding surface for writing comfort. If newspaper is used for padding, this final layer will stop your work (and your hands) from becoming marked with printing ink.

You will need

- *Drawing board*
- *Several sheets of newspaper or white blotting paper*
- *White sketching paper*
- *Masking tape*

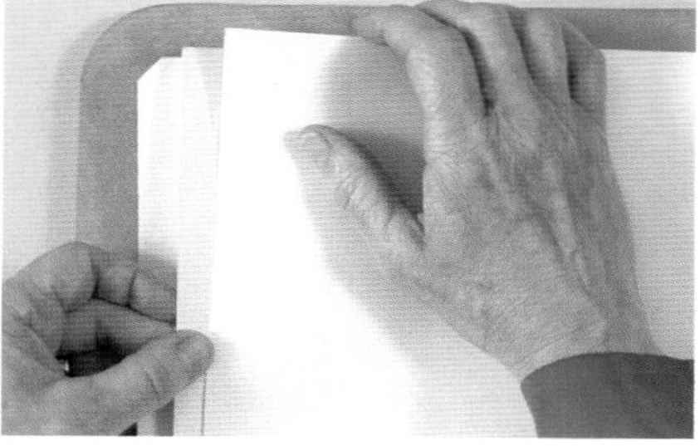

1 *Lay down two sheets of blotting paper or several layers of newspaper (ironed flat and trimmed if necessary) onto the board. Cover with a sheet of sketching paper smaller than the board.*

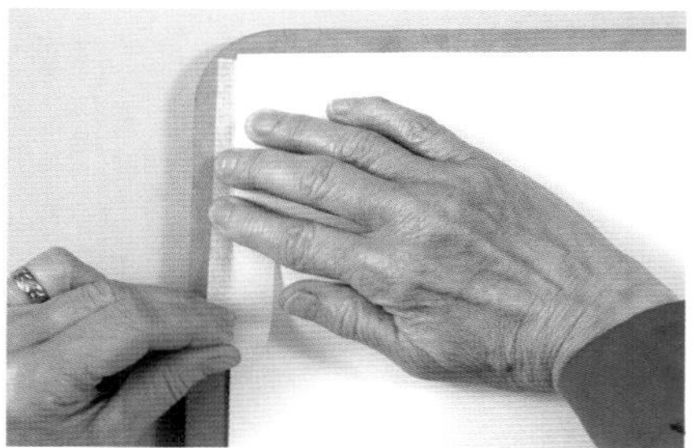

2 *Fix the padding and cover securely with masking tape. If you are going to use a T-square, do not put the tape over the board edges.*

3 *For writing, it is useful to have a guard sheet taped down to protect the work. Cut a strip of sketching paper and attach it with the top edge at writing level (you will need to judge where this is best for you). Put tape only on the sides and leave the bottom open so the paper can be moved up and down.*

Paper

The type of paper you choose will affect the character and quality of your work and, as with any materials, it pays to buy the best that you can afford. Much of your early work in illumination, as you learn the various processes and skills involved, will be on paper rather than vellum, because paper is reasonably priced and readily obtained.

Folding against the grain, there is a certain visible and tactile resistance.

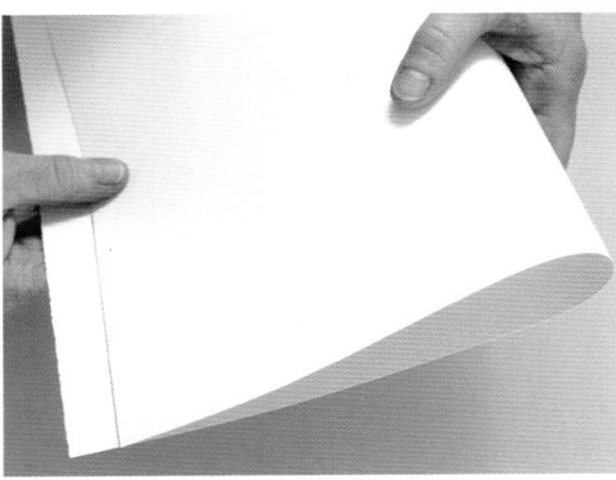

Folding with the grain, there is noticeably less resistance.

Method of manufacture

- **Handmade paper** This is made in a rectangular mould, which gives four deckle (rough) edges. It is expensive and comes in many surface textures and weights.
- **Machine-made paper** This is made on a roller and is less expensive than handmade paper. With four cut edges, it has a consistent surface quality. It also comes in a range of colours.
- **Mould-made paper** Made on a roller, mould-made paper approximates the look of handmade paper. It has two cut edges (where it is cut from the roll) and two deckle edges. Large widths and lengths are available.

There is an enormous range of papers available (*see pages 22–23*), but not all of the colours and textures are going to be suitable for the highly detailed work involved in the alphabets contained in this book. Generally speaking, the harder and smoother surfaces are best for gilding and painting. Use heavier weights, which will not buckle, for large or small panels and use the lighter weights (minimum 160 gsm / 60 lb) in manuscript books. Collect samples of likely papers so that you can do trials of inks, paints and gesso to find those best suited to the purpose. Avoid coated papers, which are made for printing. Some paper may need de-greasing with a light dusting of powdered gum sandarac (available from calligraphic suppliers) to improve adhesion of ink or paint.

WATERCOLOUR PAPER

The best quality watercolour paper is made from cotton fibres that are too short to spin (called linters). Originally, it was composed of pulped linen or cotton fabric (where the term "rag" originates) pressed into a mould, which yielded strong paper with the fibres knitted at random across the sheet.

Hot-pressed (HP) paper This has a hard, smooth surface created by heated glazing rollers. It is eminently suitable for both calligraphy and the finely detailed illumination dealt with in this book.

NOT paper This has a surface that is lightly pressed with cold rollers to give an even texture, but it still has a slight "tooth" or roughness to it. Gilding and painting can also be done on this surface.

Rough watercolour paper This is allowed to dry naturally and not rolled at all, so it retains its highly textured, rugged finish. It is not really suitable for fine detailed work, but is worth experimenting with.

OTHER PAPERS

Cheaper papers (particularly newsprint and some sketching paper) are made entirely of either cellulose fibres (wood pulp) or cellulose mixed with some rag content. Wood pulp papers tend to discolour with age, caused by the chemicals used in production, which give a high acid content.

Layout paper Used for rough work and sketches, layout paper has a smooth, woven surface and is thin enough to see through, so it is ideal for tracing off various stages and refining the design.

Photocopy paper This is a good substitute for layout paper and it is readily available.

Tracing paper A semi-transparent paper that is used for design revisions from layout paper roughs, then tracing and transferring final designs.

Glassine Also known as crystal parchment, this is used in gilding (*see pages 50–51 and 57–60*), but also as an overlay to protect work in progress or when storing finished work before framing.

Sketching paper Less expensive than watercolour paper, this is available in large sheets. It is useful for roughs or first attempts at the various gilding and painting techniques, rather than finished work.

Coloured paper Available in handmade and machine-made qualities, the latter intended for use with pastels. Machine-made coloured paper has one textured and one smooth side, and comes in a range of both bright and subtle colours. It is ideal for greetings cards, bookmarks and other gifts.

Paper weight, size and grain

- **Weight** The weight of paper is measured in grams per square meter (gsm) or pounds per ream (500 sheets of any given size). It is most important to know the weight of paper when making manuscript books, because you need to consider the bulk of folded sheets.
- **Size** This refers to the glue incorporated with the paper fibres in manufacture rather than to the paper dimensions. Without size, the paper would absorb ink applied to the surface, as blotting paper does. Most handmade paper has glue added at the pulp stage (internally sized), but some is surface-sized, which can cause beading of ink or paint on the surface. Mix a drop of ox-gall liquid or gum arabic into the writing/painting medium to avoid this.
- **Grain** If machine-made paper is to be folded (or used to cover a support, *see pages 28–29*), you must establish the grain direction (the way the fibres lie) so that the paper does not curl at the edges. You can do this by folding without creasing, as shown.

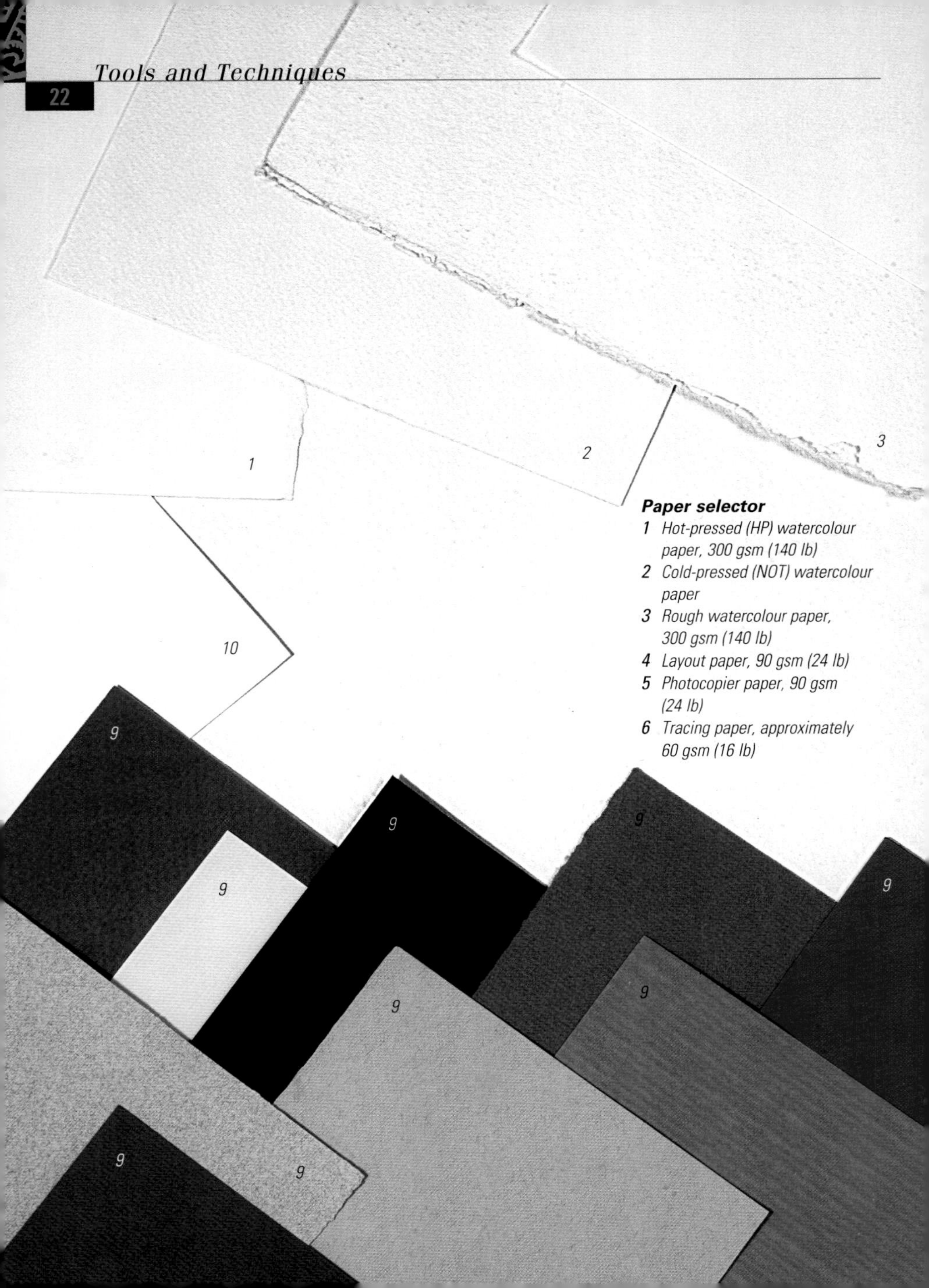

1

2

3

10

9

9

9

9

9

9

9

9

Paper selector

1 Hot-pressed (HP) watercolour paper, 300 gsm (140 lb)
2 Cold-pressed (NOT) watercolour paper
3 Rough watercolour paper, 300 gsm (140 lb)
4 Layout paper, 90 gsm (24 lb)
5 Photocopier paper, 90 gsm (24 lb)
6 Tracing paper, approximately 60 gsm (16 lb)

7 *Glassine*
8 *Handmade papers*
9 *Coloured papers*
10 *Sketching paper*

Basic paper selection for beginners

You will only need a few types of paper to start with. A good basic selection would be numbers 1, 4, 5, 6, 7 and 10. See page 21 for a description of each type and its uses in detail.

Vellum and Parchment

Traditionally, vellum was the writing surface used for early Western manuscripts. It is a very beautiful and very durable material, giving a subtle luminosity to painted colour that paper does not.

Vellum or parchment is made from animal skins, specially prepared in much the same labour-intensive way today as it was more than a millennium ago. Further preparation by the scribe (*see pages 26–27*) is needed before writing or painting can begin. Scholars sometimes differentiate between vellum (calfskin) and parchment (sheepskin). Calfskin is probably best for the illumination work described in this book and is also the most readily available. Sheep and goat skins have quite different surface characteristics and qualities; try experimenting with these at a later date.

Tips for choosing vellum

- Keep in mind the purpose of your piece. Thicker vellum is fine for a stretched panel but is not suitable for a manuscript book.
- The centre parts of the flanks are best, as the edges and the spine area of the skin can be too thick.
- Look for even colour and thickness for traditional illumination work, but skins with unusual markings or colour can be used on more modern pieces.
- Thinner areas will not show when the skin is stretched.

BUYING VELLUM

Vellum is sold as cut pieces in a variety of sizes (the best option for beginners), but it is more economical to buy a whole skin. The average skin size can be 0.55–0.75m^2 (6–8 sq ft), but it is possible to obtain larger skins up to 0.9m^2 (10 sq ft). If you buy a whole skin, the off-cuts are very useful for trying out paint colours, testing the quality of the prepared surface for writing or perfecting your gilding skills.

Vellum is only available from a few specialist makers and suppliers, and the handmade nature of the manufacturing process is reflected in the price. The extra time taken to prepare the skin is worth it, particularly for special pieces of work. It is the most beautiful and satisfying surface to work on. Mistakes can also be corrected, albeit slowly and carefully (*see page 33*).

STORING VELLUM

Vellum changes according to the atmosphere. An unstretched piece will move and curl as you work on it. A high level of humidity will also cause the skin to stretch and buckle. Cut off any sharp or inflexible bits at the edges before storing, because it makes the skin easier to roll.

Keep whole skins loosely rolled in a well-ventilated place, neither damp nor bone dry. When you are ready to use the vellum, first leave it in a cool, even slightly damp, room to help the fibres relax, then reverse-roll it over a wide, stout cardboard tube with a sheet of cartridge for support.

Leave it rolled in this way for an hour or so, in a cool place, then unroll it and place it between boards or weigh it down at the corners and edges to flatten it out.

Types of vellum

NB. Cut pieces of types 2 and 3 are a good starting point for beginners to work on.

1 ***Manuscript vellum (calfskin)*** *Usually white or off-white in colour, it can be prepared on both sides for writing. The lighter-weight skins are most suitable for books.*

2 ***Natural calfskin vellum*** *Creamier in colour and generally thicker than manuscript vellum, it is only suitable for writing on the hair side.*

3 ***Classic calfskin vellum*** *Similar to natural calfskin vellum but lighter in colour.*

4 ***Natural goatskin vellum*** *This has a characteristic dimpled texture. It is available in a variety of cream and light brown tones.*

5 ***White goatskin vellum*** *Similar to natural goatskin vellum but lighter in colour.*

6 ***Sheepskin parchment*** *The inner layer of a split sheepskin, this is white or greyish–white in colour. It is very thin, with a slightly greasy feel and is more suited to writing than gilding.*

7 ***Kelmscott vellum*** *Made from calfskin, but the surface is filled to make it smooth. It is more suitable for printing or miniature painting than illumination and writing.*

8 ***Vellum off-cuts*** *Useful for trying out paint colours and testing the quality of the surface for writing (*see Preparing Vellum, page 26*).*

9 ***Slunk vellum*** *Made from skins of very young calves. Very thin, it is finished for writing on both sides. Sometimes it has interesting patterns and colours.*

10 ***Whole skin*** *A whole calfskin, showing edges.*

Preparing Vellum

For single-sided pieces of illumination, the hair side (the animal's outer surface) is the most suitable; but before writing or painting, it needs extra preparation with abrasives to raise a suedelike nap on the surface. With cut pieces, use a magnifier to check which side is the shinier hair side before you begin. It is a good idea to practise preparing vellum on small off-cuts before you tackle a large skin – mistakes can be expensive.

The flesh side (the animal's inner surface) of the skin generally needs little more than a light dusting of sandarac. With classic calfskin vellum, only the hair side is usable.

Silicon carbide paper may not have been available to early artist–scribes, but it is an improvement on the traditional method, which used a mixture of powdered pumice and whiting (pounce) to remove the grease from the skin. Even though finely ground, it can scratch the surface and, if it is not carefully dusted off, it will clog the pen nib.

Preparing the hair side

Wear cotton gloves so that grease is not transferred from your fingers to the vellum and to remove some of the surplus dust from the surface. Work by an open window for good ventilation and wear a facemask as well as an apron or overall for added protection against the dust. For painting and gilding, no further preparation will be needed. Before writing, dust the area lightly with powdered gum sandarac tied in a small piece of cheesecloth, then brush off the gum particles thoroughly.

You will need

- *Vellum*
- *Facemask*
- *Cotton gloves*
- *Large, flat work surface, close to a window if possible, for light and ventilation*
- *Apron or overall*
- *Newspaper to pad the work surface*
- *Clean white sketching paper*
- *Cork sanding block*
- *Silicon carbide paper, 240-grit and 400-grit*
- *Large soft brush*
- *Powdered gum sandarac tied in a small piece of cheesecloth*

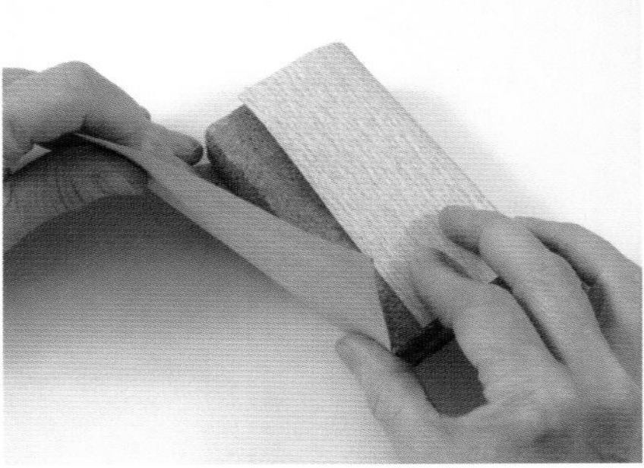

1 Pad the work surface with newspaper and cover this with sketching paper. Have the light at a low angle so that it rakes across the surface of the skin, which will help you see where you have worked. Cut and wrap a piece of 240-grit paper around the cork block to be ready to start sanding.

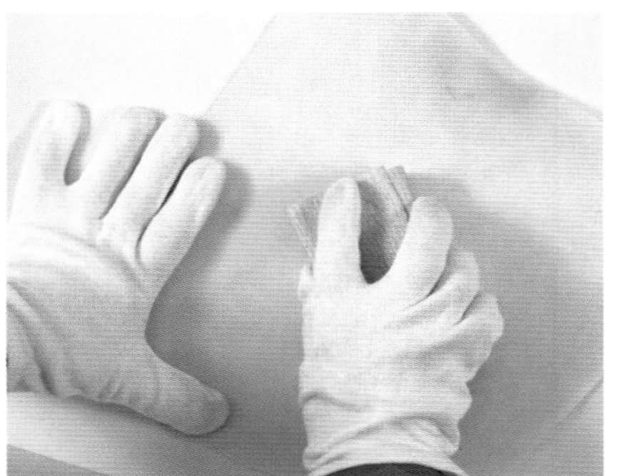

2 *Work steadily and evenly over the skin to begin raising the nap. Do not rush and do not press too hard. Hold the skin firmly in one hand and work away from that hand on one small area at a time, using a circular motion. Be sensitive to what is happening to the skin and keep testing the surface with your thumb as you work.*

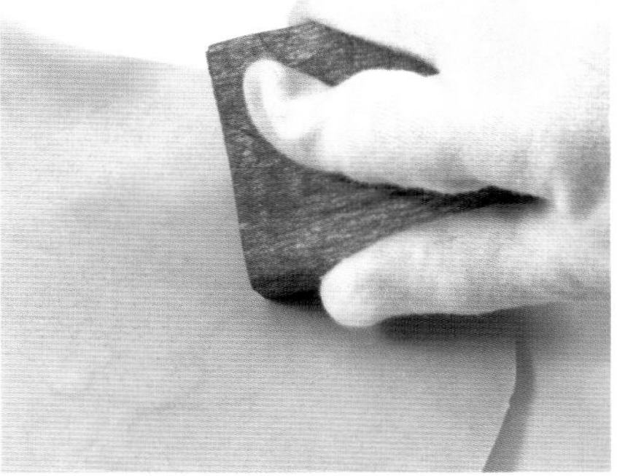

3 *Some of the marks and vein lines (dips in the surface) may need special treatment. When the surrounding areas have been flattened by sanding, use the corner of the block to work into the grooves to achieve a similar matt finish. Take care not to overabrade these parts.*

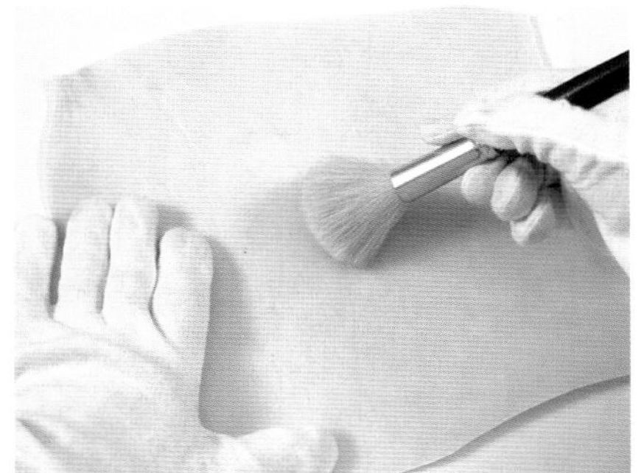

4 *When the skin has been uniformly sanded, repeat steps 2 and 3 using the 400-grit paper. Keep the sanding block flat and firmly in contact with the vellum, using the same circular motion. This removes any excess nap and refines the surface. Flick off the residual dust with a large soft brush or use a vacuum cleaner set on the lowest suction, with a (clean) brush attachment.*

Tips for preparing vellum

- Avoid having water anywhere near prepared skins, unless they are to be stretched.
- A soft, peachlike nap is what you need – do not be tempted to overprepare the surface. Some minor damage can be repaired by using a lift-and-twist movement with 400-grit paper to take off any excess nap.
- Creases or buckling (which can happen when unrolling the skin without a tube support) can be removed by using a bone folder to press the creases out gently over a cushion of mount board.
- With very bad creases, dampen the skin slightly with damp blotting paper first, then repeat the smoothing action described above. This will polish the surface a little, so you will have to go over the area again to restore the nap.

Stretching Vellum

Small, cut pieces of thicker vellum can be framed without much movement or buckling of the skin. Stitch the vellum to (or trap it between) a piece of acid-free card and a bevel-cut mount, which will keep the gilded surfaces away from the glass.

Thinner vellum or larger pieces are more stable and less susceptible to damp if they are first stretched over a support. Always prepare the vellum (*see pages 26–27*) before stretching. You can also transfer the drawing and ink it in at this stage to save time afterwards. The drawing is transferred as in the projects mentioned, then it is inked in with waterproof ink so that the image is not lost in the damping process. It just needs a little care to make sure the image is square to the edges of the support before you stick the flaps down (*see pages 93, 117, 169, 193, 217*).

Preparing the support

Before stretching the vellum, you will need to prepare the support by covering it with acid-free sketching paper as a buffer between the MDF and the vellum.

You will need

- *Support (piece of MDF or plywood 5 mm/⅛ in thick, 4–5 cm/1½–2 in smaller all around than your vellum)*
- *Sandpaper*
- *Damp cloth*
- *PVA glue (slightly diluted with distilled water)*
- *Glue brush*
- *White acid-free sketching paper*
- *Pencil*
- *Steel ruler*
- *Scalpel*
- *Cutting board*
- *Clean scrap paper (not newspaper, as the ink may transfer)*
- *Bone folder*
- *Weights (two or three heavy books)*

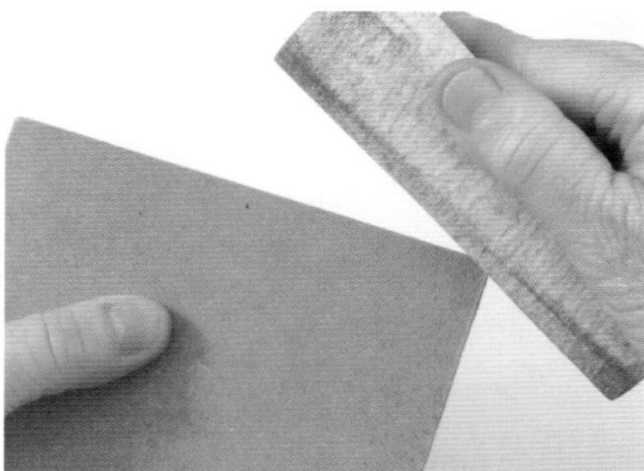

1 *Sand the surface of the support smooth, rounding the edges and corners. Wipe it with a damp cloth to remove dust, then apply a coat of dilute PVA glue to all surfaces and leave to dry.*

2 *Draw a rectangle on cartridge paper (*as Diagram A, page 32*), allowing 3 cm (1¼ in) plus extra for the board thickness all around. The grain direction in machine-made paper (*see page 20*) should run parallel to the board's short edge. Cut the rectangle out accurately (including mitres on long sides as shown) with a scalpel.*

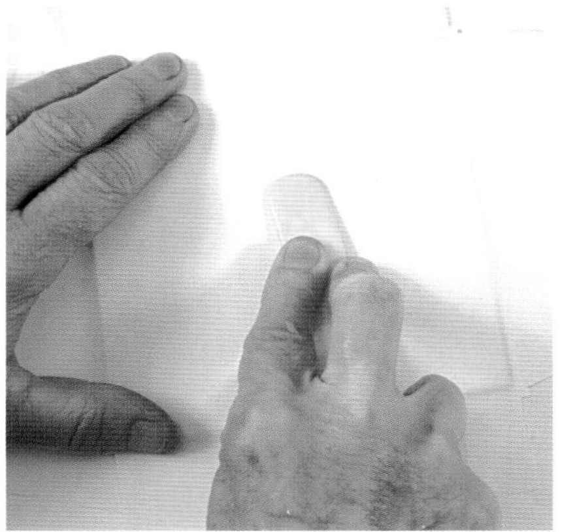

3 *Working on clean scrap paper, coat the central rectangle of paper with glue and lay the board onto this. Turn the board over and smooth the paper down with a bone folder.*

4 *Glue the long flaps first, with strips of clean paper underneath for each flap. Wrap flaps tightly over the edges, tucking in corners with the pointed end of the bone folder.*

5 *Glue the short flaps and wrap them around the board, as in step 4. Cut mitres to match those already cut on the long flaps. Leave to dry between clean sheets of paper under weights.*

6 *Mark and cut a piece of sketching paper slightly smaller than the board, then apply glue and smooth it down onto the back of the board. Put the board back under the weights with clean sheets of paper until dry.*

Stretching the vellum

Before stretching vellum for the first time, read the instructions carefully, so that you understand and are familiar with the procedure before you begin. After the damping stage, it is a very similar operation to preparing the support, described on page 28.

You will need
- *Prepared vellum (with or without design in place)*
- *Pencil*
- *Steel ruler*
- *Scalpel*
- *Cutting board*
- *4 sheets of white blotting paper*
- *Mist spray, filled with water*
- *Silicone release paper (if design in place on vellum)*
- *2 sheets of thick polythene*
- *2 heavy boards, larger than the work*
- *Weights (2 or 3 heavy books)*
- *Clean scrap paper (not newspaper, as the ink may transfer)*
- *PVA glue (slightly diluted with distilled water)*
- *Glue brush*
- *Bone folder*
- *White acid-free sketching paper*

Tips for stretching vellum
- Vellum can be difficult to handle. Read the instructions carefully, be patient and persistent, and stay calm.
- Always have clean paper under the flaps when gluing, then discard it afterwards, so the glue goes only where you want it to.
- If the flaps do not stick down the first time, lift them up one at a time, add more glue and then smooth flat again.
- Wipe off any excess glue with a clean, damp sponge.

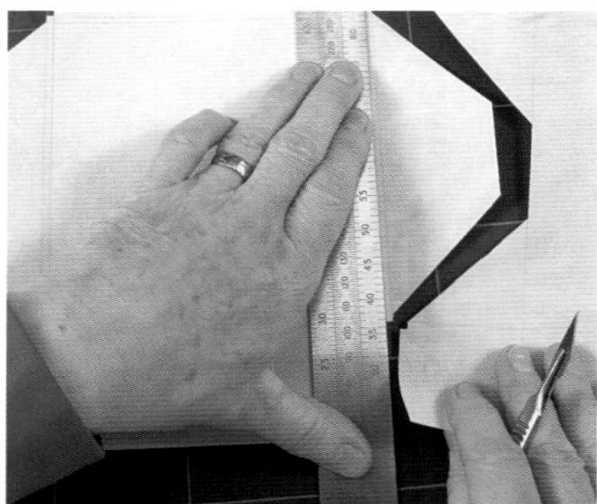

1 *Draw the required shape lightly onto the back of the vellum as Diagram A (*see page 32*), allowing 4–5cm (1½–2 in) plus the thickness of the board all around. Cut the corners and mitres as in step 2 of Preparing the Support (*see page 28*). Always do this before damping.*

2 *Damp the vellum. Spray one sheet of blotting paper with mist spray, and then sandwich the vellum face down between drawing boards and polythene as shown in Diagram B (*see page 32*), with damp blotting paper on the back of the skin. If design or writing has already been done, put the vellum face down onto a sheet of silicone release paper. Put a weight on top (*see Diagram C, page 32*) for 15–30 minutes, depending on the thickness of the vellum.*

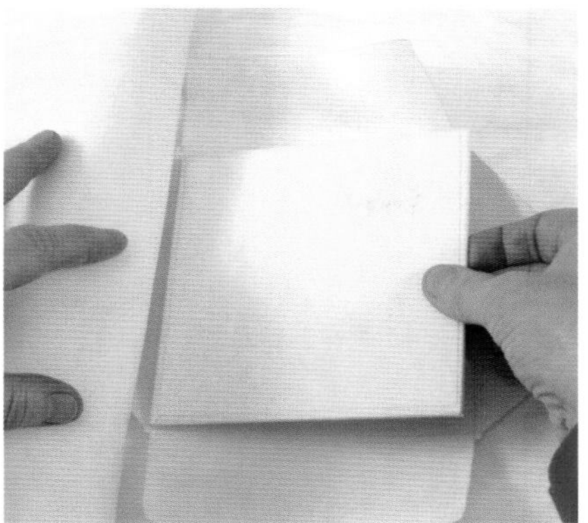

3 Check after 10–15 minutes to see if the vellum is damp enough – it should feel rubbery to the touch. Remove the weight and top board, and roll back the polythene and blotting paper carefully, as the damp skin may curl. Slip the prepared support into place between the ruled pencil lines, then lay it on a sheet of clean paper ready for gluing.

4 Slip a clean strip of paper under the first long flap and apply glue. Remove the paper strip, hold the board down firmly and work the flap of vellum down over the edge and onto the back of the board – a move outwards from the middle to each side. Glue and stick down the other long flap in the same way.

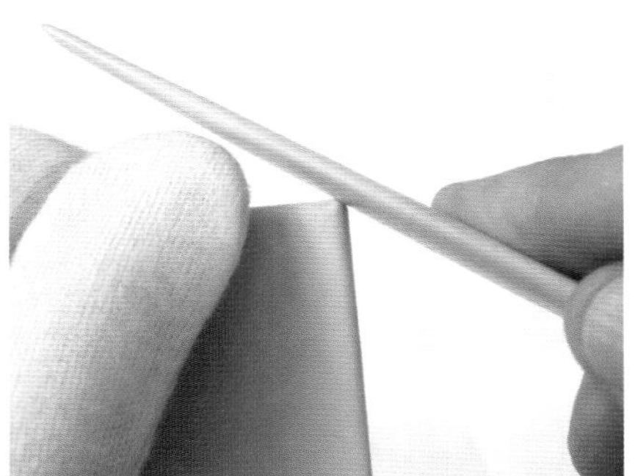

5 Repeat step 4 for the short flaps, tucking in the corners with a bone folder and moulding them into shape. Do this while the vellum is still damp, otherwise the corners will dry hard and pointed.

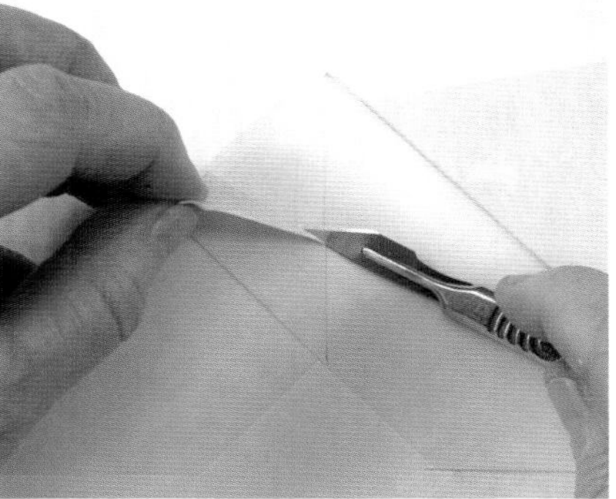

6 Cut the mitres neatly (as step 4 of Preparing the Support) and place the vellum under clean paper, a board and a weight as before. Leave overnight to dry out thoroughly, before covering the back with cartridge paper as described in step 6 of Preparing the Support. Put it back under a weight to dry for a minimum of three hours.

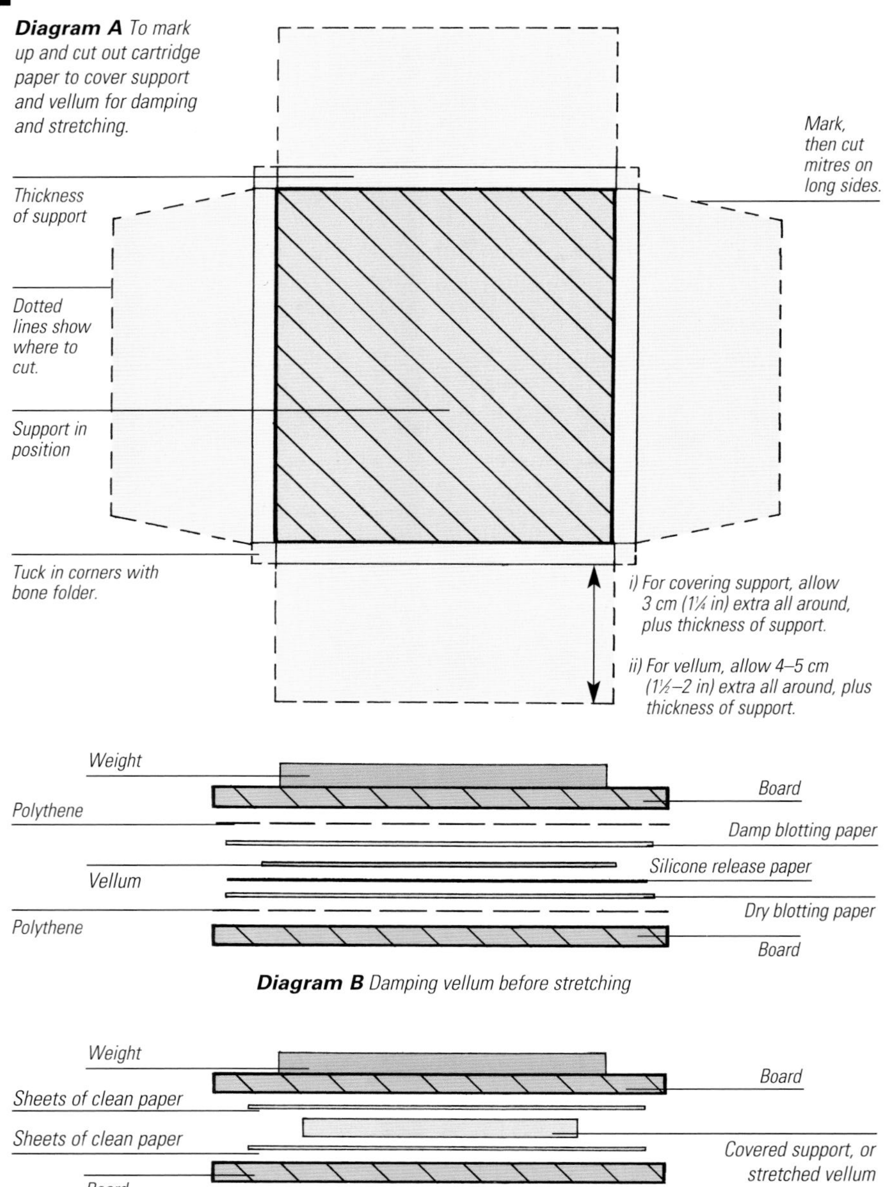

Diagram A *To mark up and cut out cartridge paper to cover support and vellum for damping and stretching.*

Diagram B *Damping vellum before stretching*

Diagram C *Leave to dry under weight*

Correcting mistakes on vellum

Corrections can be made with care. Where lines have overrun at the inking-in stage of transferring letter designs and they cannot be disguised with a painted outline, a pointed scalpel blade can be used carefully to scratch these off, without the need to use gum sandarac afterwards. It is possible to use the same technique to correct errors on heavier weight HP papers (*see pages 22–23*).

You will need

- *Cotton glove*
- *Round-bladed scalpel*
- *Dogtooth agate burnisher*
- *Glassine*
- *Gum sandarac*
- *Large soft brush*

1 *Use a round-bladed scalpel held at a slight angle to lift the ink or paint off the surface, moving the work around if necessary. Wear a cotton glove on the hand holding the work.*

2 *Burnish the erased area gently, through glassine.*

3 *Dust the erased area with powdered gum sandarac, then remove the dust carefully and thoroughly with a large, soft brush.*

4 *It should now be possible to write or draw over this area again.*

Brushes

The finest brushes for illumination work are made of Russian red sable. The bristles are springy, absorbent and hold a lot of colour. If you wash them out frequently to remove all traces of ink or paint and store them with the bristles uppermost, they will last a long time. Look for those with shorter hairs for detailed work. Save your best brushes for important work but do not discard old ones; they will come in handy for mixing and for applying gum ammoniac solution.

Synthetic bristles are not as flexible or sensitive in use as sable, and they tend not to hold as much colour, though the brushes are strong and inexpensive. They are very useful for mixing paint and applying gum and glue for gilding. Some paint colours will stain the bristles, but this does not cause a problem in use. Brushes made of a mix of sable and synthetic hair are a good compromise for beginners.

There are cheaper brushes available, made of squirrel or ox hair, which should be used only for mixing. The bristles are very soft and do not come to a proper point, as sable does, and they tend to wear out more quickly.

Basic brush collection
To begin with, you will only need a very small range of brushes for creating the letters in this book: sable brushes (artist's quality or similar), in sizes 000, 00, 0 and 1; synthetic brushes, sizes 00, 0 and 1, for mixing paint and applying gum ammoniac; and a large soft brush for removing excess gold.

Types of brushes

1 *Small sable brushes (000, 00, 0 and 1) for detailed miniature painting*
2 *Larger sizes (2, 3 and 4) can be used for painting larger areas of colour*
3 *Synthetic bristled brushes*
4 *Soft brush for removing surplus gold*
5 *Absorbent kitchen paper or clean rags for wiping or drying off brushes*

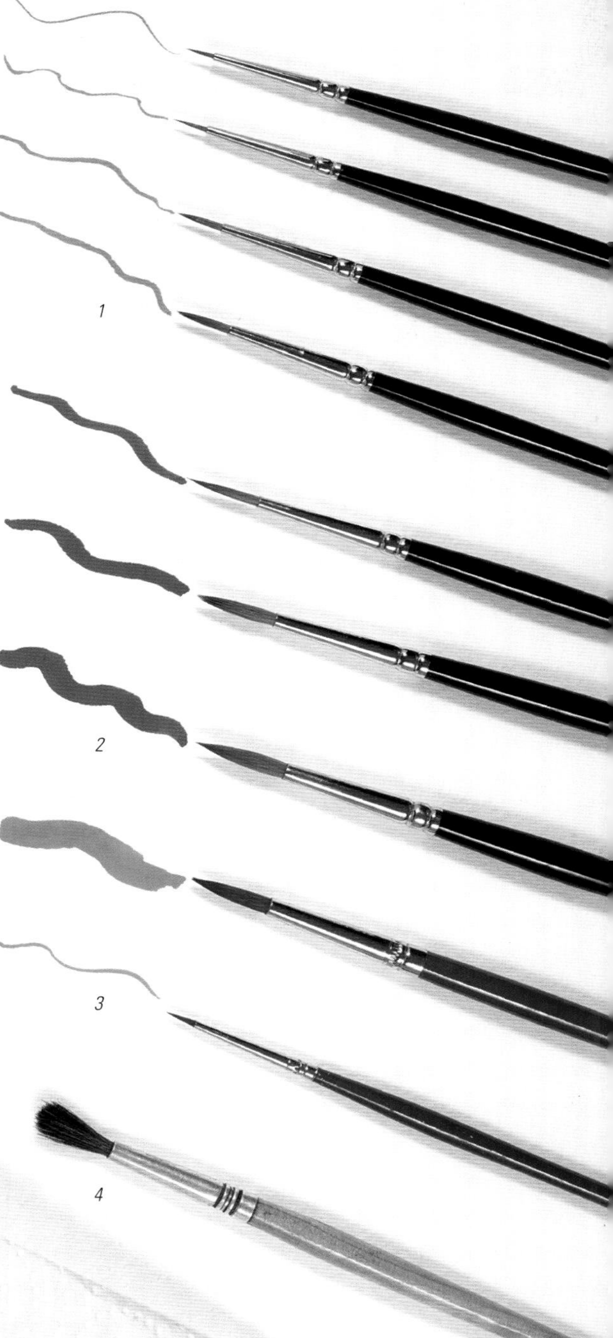

Pens

Penholders with fine-pointed flexible nibs are used for illumination work. They are dip pens, which must be recharged with ink as you work, used for drawing out final designs on layout or tracing paper, and also for inking letter shapes and decoration before gilding and painting. Mapping pens and crow-quill nibs are also used for this. Technical pens, which have a refillable ink cartridge, are a useful modern alternative, especially for working up final designs. However, they cannot be used with waterproof ink, which would clog the ink flow, or with paint, unlike the dip-in sort.

PENS FOR CALLIGRAPHY

The early scribe would prepare and cut his own quills or reed pens for writing, which requires both patience and skill, but the modern calligrapher can choose from a range of steel nibs with square-cut edges. These are also dip pens. Left-handers may find oblique-cut nibs more comfortable to use. Nibs are numbered from the smallest (size 6) to the largest (size 0), or are graded by actual nib width – for example, 0.5 mm or 1 mm. Larger sizes are available, but are not appropriate to the lettering and decoration in this book.

Pens and nibs
Illustrated here is a selection of the nibs and accessories needed for illumination and calligraphy.

1. *Drawing nibs: fine nibs with flexible points*
2. *Calligraphy nibs: straight-cut "round hand"*
3. *Calligraphy nibs: left-oblique nibs*
4. *Edged nibs with reservoirs attached above the nib*
5. *Reservoirs to hold ink underneath the nib*
6. *Penholders (various types)*
7. *Technical pens*

All new nibs are coated with a greasy lacquer that may cause problems with beading of ink and poor ink flow, so it is best to remove it before use. To do this, hold the nib in the flame of a match for two or three seconds, then plunge it into cold water. Test the nib by dipping it in some ink – if the ink appears as an even coating, the nib is ready to use.

RESERVOIRS

A small brass reservoir is slipped onto the underside of a nib to help it retain more ink and control the ink flow onto the paper. Ink is fed onto the back of the nib with a brush and the brass reservoir holds it in place, controlling the flow and preventing blobs.

Some nibs, often cut as right-obliques, which can be useful for writing the Insular half uncials (*see pages 104–107*), come with reservoirs already attached to the top. There is no danger of these coming off and they will certainly not pinch the nib, but they do not suit everyone.

PENHOLDERS

There are many different sizes and shapes of penholder to choose from, to suit the various types of nib and the sizes of people's hands. It is wise to try out penholders before you buy the first time and find one that suits you best. The round-barrelled sort is comfortable to use.

FOUNTAIN PENS AND FELT-TIPPED PENS

Because they are relatively cheap and easily available, fountain pens and felt-tipped pens are popular with beginners in calligraphy. There are no worries about ink running out at inopportune moments, and they are useful for drafting quick roughs. However, because they are only available in a limited range of sizes and cannot be used with paint, they are of little use as far as good finished work is concerned. The same applies to felt pens, especially as their colours are not light fast.

Fitting a reservoir

A reservoir needs careful adjustment so that the ink flows properly.

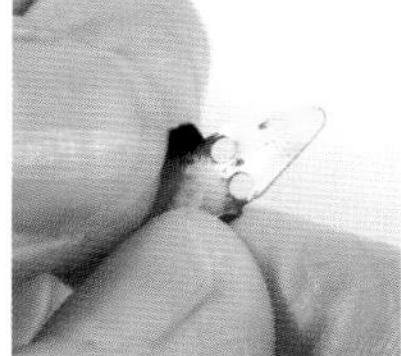

1 *If the reservoir is too tight, open the two wings slightly.*

2 *Hold the reservoir by the wings and slip it back onto the nib. It should slip on and off easily, but should not drop off.*

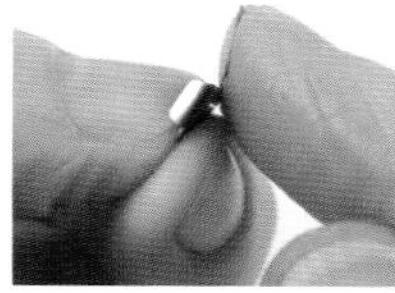

3 *Remove the reservoir and bend the point inwards a little.*

4 *As you replace the reservoir, the point should just touch the back of the nib, which allows the ink to flow into the slit between the tines. Adjust the reservoir if necessary.*

Pencils

Clay and graphite are combined to form the lead in drawing pencils. Lead is graded according to hardness from 9B to 9H. Hard pencils range from H to 9H, with the high numbers being the hardest, which make very light grey lines. Black, or soft, pencils are graded 9B to B, the higher numbers making rich black lines. HB is halfway between the two and is a good all-purpose lead for drawing, but try an F grade, which is the grade between HB and H. This is a little blacker than HB and smudges less easily.

PENCILS FOR ILLUMINATION

For illumination, you need only a small selection of pencils in the following grades: HB or F for initial drawings; 2H for transferring finished drawings to paper or vellum and for ruling up for writing (take care not to press too hard); and 2B or 4B for carbon transfer (*see page 78*). Buy good quality pencils, because the cheaper ones have very gritty leads that can be difficult to sharpen efficiently.

For best results keep your pencils sharp – it is very hard to draw fine, detailed work with a blunt lead. Softer pencils wear down more quickly and need sharpening frequently. A craft knife or scalpel will give a finer point than a pencil sharpener. The use of a glasspaper block between sharpenings to refine the pencil point saves time.

Clutch pencils, particularly those which take 0.5 mm or 0.3 mm lead refills (also available in grades, but with a reduced range), are very convenient to use. The leads require little sharpening, and if a breakage occurs a few "clicks" will advance enough lead to start work again.

COLOURED PENCILS

Use coloured pencils for colouring initial sketches of decorated letters and planning colour schemes for page layouts (*see pages 76–77*).

Look for artist's-quality coloured pencils or watercolour pencils – the latter can be blended with water to produce a wash effect. Pastel pencils or waxy oil-based crayons are not suited to this type of detailed work, as they are either too chalky or too sticky.

ERASERS

Soft, white plastic erasers are best for delicate illumination work, because they lift marks off, rather than abrading the paper surface or spoiling the nap on vellum. Pieces cut from eraser blocks to give sharp edges are handy for removing pencil marks with precision in tightly designed letters. Pencil-shaped erasers are also useful in this respect, and for removing masking fluid (*see pages 43 and 218*).

A kneadable putty eraser can be used as an alternative to a plastic eraser on paper or vellum. This kind of eraser can be cut, rolled or squeezed into suitable shapes.

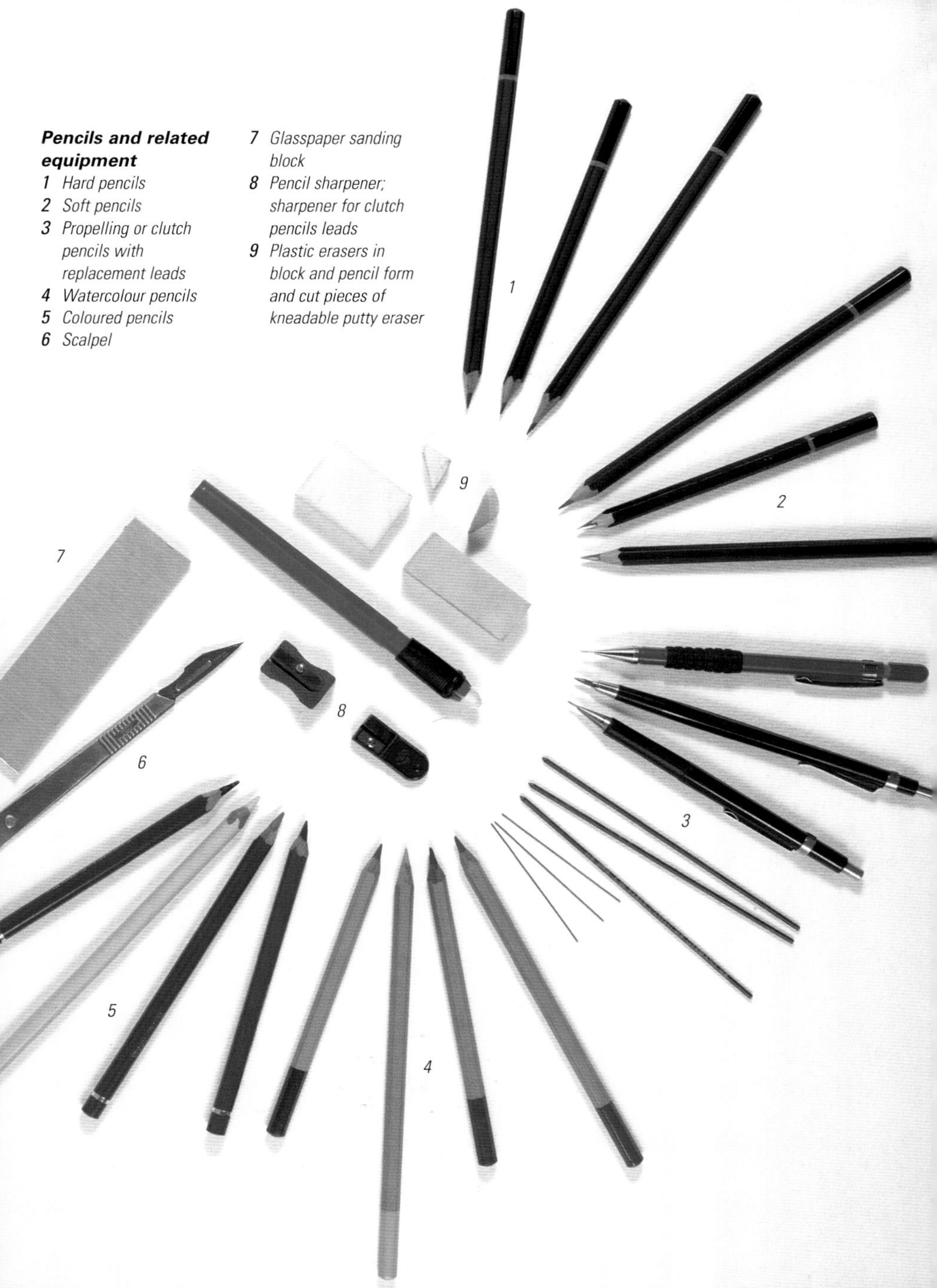

Pencils and related equipment
1 *Hard pencils*
2 *Soft pencils*
3 *Propelling or clutch pencils with replacement leads*
4 *Watercolour pencils*
5 *Coloured pencils*
6 *Scalpel*
7 *Glasspaper sanding block*
8 *Pencil sharpener; sharpener for clutch pencils leads*
9 *Plastic erasers in block and pencil form and cut pieces of kneadable putty eraser*

Paints

There are three different types of paint used for illumination, which are described here. Egg tempera was the only option for early illuminators and would have been used for all the alphabets included in this book. Gouache is generally the best all-round choice for beginners; it works equally well for both the painting and any accompanying calligraphy. Watercolour is used for transparent glazes, described in the Neo-Classical project on page 216.

Gouache

The paint that is commonly used for illumination is gouache, which is an opaque, water-based paint sold in tubes. It is the modern equivalent of the egg tempera paint used in medieval manuscripts (*see pages 44–46*). Carefully applied with a brush, gouache can be used for broad flat areas of matt colour as well as very fine detailed work. When mixed to the consistency of thin cream, it can be used in a pen for writing or drawing, producing consistently crisp marks.

Look for designer's gouache, which is the best quality. The wide range of colours is graded in series according to cost of pigments and coded for permanence.
All colours will fade eventually if exposed to light for any great length of time, so it is best to choose the most permanent shades where possible. In order to achieve the colour you want, you may have to settle for a lesser degree of permanence. Gouache made with extremely fine-ground pigments is available especially for lettering, but while excellent, the range of colours is restricted.

Always use clean, distilled water to mix gouache and all the other types of paint, to retain the clarity of the colours.

LAYING FLAT AREAS OF COLOUR

Use an old mixing brush to mix gouache with distilled water. The consistency should not be too thin or too thick and sticky. Test for consistency and opacity on scrap paper. Dip the point of a good sable brush into the paint and use the bristles' flexibility to work around pre-drawn shapes. Work steadily, wet into wet, for an even layer of colour.

It will take practice to mix and lay flat colour effectively. Too thin a mix, especially with semi-transparent pigments, will dry streaky. To cover streaks, adjust the paint consistency and re-do the whole affected area. For a more resilient finish, mix with gum water or egg yolk.

PALETTES

China palettes are more expensive than the plastic type, but they do not stain and will last for years. Multi-well palettes are particularly useful for mixing several tones of one colour, as used in the Gothic letter project (*see pages 168–171*). For mixing up larger quantities of paint, single-well dishes are ideal. They are stackable and have a lid for the top layer, so mixed paint can be kept moist and usable for several days.

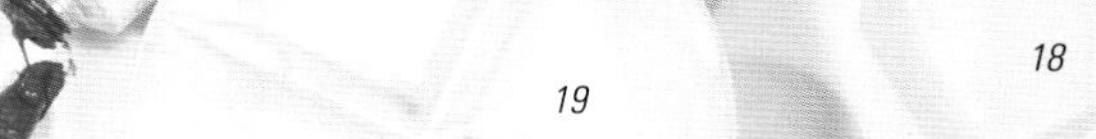

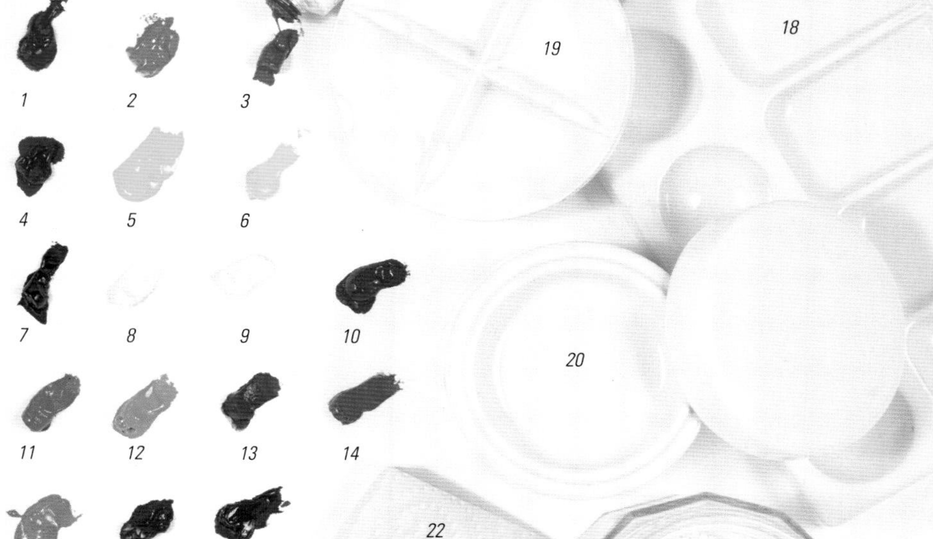

1 2 3 4 5 6 7 8 9 10 11 12 13 14 15 16 17 18 19 20 21 22

Gouache: basic colour selection

Paints numbered one to nine are a basic selection of colours that will be useful to begin with. Other colours are mentioned specifically within the project for each alphabet, so add these and others when you are ready. You will also need mixing palettes and water jars.

1 *Ultramarine blue*
2 *Cerulean blue*
3 *Scarlet lake*
4 *Alizarin crimson*
5 *Cadmium yellow pale*
6 *Lemon yellow*
7 *Ivory or lamp black*
8 *Zinc white (for mixing tints)*
9 *Opaque or permanent white (for highlights)*
10 *Permanent green deep*
11 *Oxide of chromium*
12 *Yellow ochre*
13 *Vandyke brown*
14 *Burnt sienna*
15 *Raw sienna*
16 *Purple lake*
17 *Spectrum violet*
18 *Multi-well china palette with mixing slopes and deep wells*
19 *Three/four-division round palette*
20 *Stacking palettes, large and small sizes with lid*
21 *Glass water jars*
22 *Absorbent kitchen paper or cotton rags for wiping brushes*

Tips for using gouache

- To avoid mixed colours drying up, either cover the palette with transparent food wrap or use a lidded palette.
- If colours dry up before you have finished painting, you can reconstitute them by adding a little more water – but check that the mix is of a similar strength before you resume work.
- If paint is a little dry from the tube and difficult to mix, use a flexible painting knife to work the water into the paint initially, and then use a brush.

Watercolours

Watercolours are graded, like gouache, for light fastness and for price according to cost of pigment. Artist's quality gives the best and most permanent colours. Unlike gouache, the colours are transparent, so the paper or vellum shows through, playing an important part in the colours' luminosity. White is not necessary, but when highlights are needed in illumination, use opaque white gouache.

Choose a similar basic range of colours to that mentioned for gouache, but you have the choice of buying tubes for mixing up large quantities of paint for background washes (really more suitable for landscape painting than decorated letters) or pans,

Basic range of colours

Colours 1 to 6 are ones you need as a basic range for illumination; 7 to 11 are useful extra colours to add later.

1 French ultramarine
2 Cerulean blue
3 Cadmium yellow pale
4 Lemon yellow
5 Scarlet lake or cadmium red
6 Alizarin crimson
7 Permanent rose
8 Burnt umber
9 Burnt sienna
10 Yellow ochre
11 Ivory or lamp black

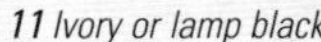

which last longer, are less wasteful and are perfect for mixing small quantities.

MEDIA FOR MIXING WATERCOLOURS
Distilled water is usually used on its own to mix watercolours, but they can also be mixed with gum water, egg yolk or glair (*see pages 46–47*). Using these alternative media in the mixture will give an extra sheen to the final surface and will help with waterproofing when overpainting several layers.

Tube or pan watercolours can also be used to modify ground pigments to achieve subtle shades if you do not have the full range of powdered colours.

Masking out tricky designs

Where you need to lay background colours, but the letter or number has complex decorative motifs around it, it is much simpler to cover the entire intricate design first with masking fluid.

You will need
- *Pre-drawn letter or number on watercolour paper*
- *Old small brush*
- *Masking fluid*
- *Paint for background*
- *Soft plastic eraser or pencil eraser*

Tips for using masking fluid
- Do not use your good brushes for applying masking fluid. It is very difficult to clean out of brushes.
- Rinse synthetic brushes in lighter fuel, and then wash in soapy water.
- Real bristles can first be coated with soap from a bar (not liquid soap), then washed out with more soap and rinsed after use.

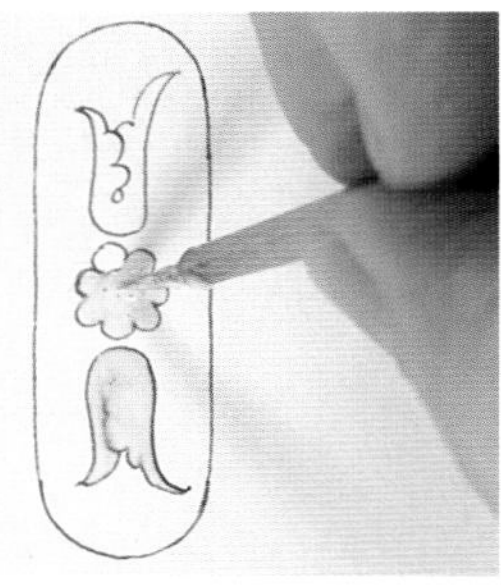

1 *On a pre-drawn letter or number, with an old brush or one with synthetic bristles, apply masking fluid to all areas that need to be kept white, then leave to dry thoroughly.*

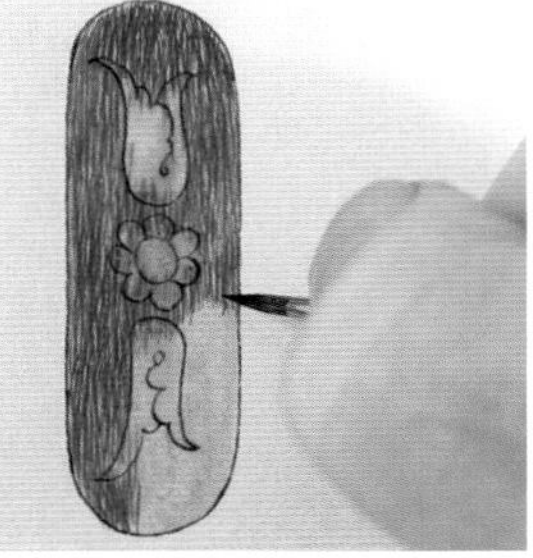

2 *Paint the background colours freely over the whole area.*

3 *When all the painting has been completed and is thoroughly dry, remove the masking fluid by easing it off with a cut piece of soft plastic eraser, a pencil-type eraser or a cotton bud. Take care not to spoil the colour area.*

Egg Tempera

The early scribe/illuminators mixed up their own paints, using pure pigments ground down to a fine powder, mixed with egg yolk or egg white (glair) as a binding medium to give the rich colours you can see in their magnificent manuscripts. Egg yolk gives the most permanent and durable finish, a waterproof surface with a slight sheen, which means layer on layer of semi-transparent glazes can be laid without the danger of the colours intermixing and turning muddy. On vellum especially, the colours seem to glow on the page with a deep radiance.

There are three stages to using egg tempera, as described here. First, you need to grind the pigments. Second, you need to prepare the egg yolk. Finally, mix the pigment and yolk together in order to be ready to paint.

Ground pigment colours

Pure ground pigments are used for egg tempera painting. Shown here is a basic range of useful colours as well as the tools that you will need for preparing the paint. There are many other colours in this form that you can add to your collection as you need them.

1. *Ultramarine blue dark*
2. *Alizarin crimson*
3. *Cadmium red (or scarlet lake)*
4. *Cadmium yellow light*
5. *Ivory black*
6. *Zinc white (for mixing tones)*
7. *Titanium white (for highlights)*
8. *Colours are mixed with egg yolk*
9. *Ground glass slab and muller (for grinding pigments)*
10. *China palette and glass stopper (for grinding small quantities of pigment)*
11. *Empty film canisters (for storing ground colours)*
12. *Eyedropper (for adding distilled water)*
13. *Flexible palette knife for mixing*

Grinding pigments

Some pigments are toxic and should be handled with care. As a precaution, wear a facemask while grinding pigments. Ground pigments should be kept in a drawer or cupboard or at least out of direct sunlight and also out of the reach of children. Stored in this way, it is possible to keep pigments almost indefinitely, just check from time to time to see if the water level needs topping up.

You can grind very small quantities of pigment in the way described below, but use a glass stopper with the pigment in a china palette with a deep circular well.

You will need

- *Pigment*
- *Ground glass slab*
- *Distilled water*
- *Eyedropper*
- *Palette knife*
- *Glass muller*
- *Plastic film canister or other airtight container*
- *Gum water* (see recipe, page 47)

1 Put a small spoonful of pigment onto the ground glass slab and add distilled water with the eyedropper.

2 Mix the water into the pigment using the palette knife. Add more water if necessary, to make a smooth consistency – the mixture will still be slightly gritty at this stage.

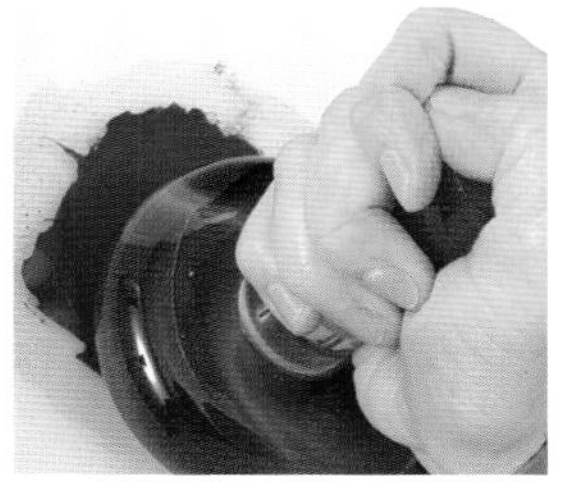

3 Grind the mixture with the glass muller using a figure-of-eight motion, until all the grittiness has been removed and the muller moves smoothly over the glass. Some colours will take longer to grind smooth than others, and you may need to add a little more water as you work. It is easier to get even pressure if you stand while grinding.

4 Use the palette knife to scrape up all the pigment off the muller and slab, and transfer it to a plastic film canister or other airtight container.

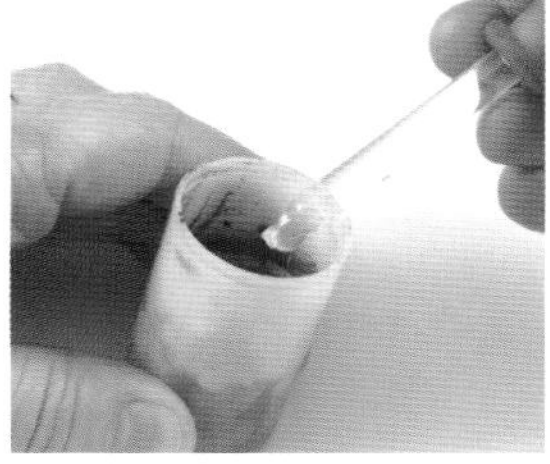

5 Add a little gum water to balance the mixture to a manageable consistency. Pour in distilled water carefully to cover the pigment completely and put the lid onto the container. Label with the date of grinding and a reminder of any toxicity.

Preparing the egg yolk

The egg yolk has to be separated carefully from the white and tipped into a clean jar before it can be mixed with the ground pigment.

You will need

- *One egg*
- *Kitchen paper*
- *Small glass jar with lid*

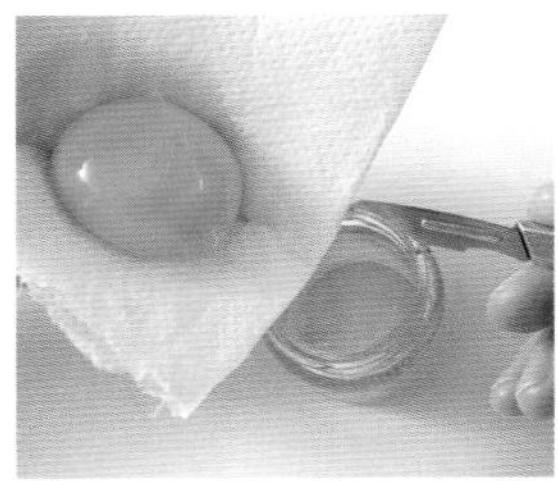

1 Crack open the egg and separate it carefully, retaining the white for making glair. Set the yolk onto kitchen paper to absorb any excess white.

2 Puncture the yolk sac and allow the yolk to drip into the glass jar, squeezing the paper gently to extract all the yolk. Put the lid on and keep in the refrigerator before and after use. Seven days is about the limit before it must be discarded.

Making the egg tempera paint

Only mix a small quantity of paint at a time, because it dries quickly on the palette and cannot be reconstituted. When powdered colour needs to be modified to make more subtle shades and you do not have the pigments at hand, you can use watercolour from either a tube or pan.

You will need

- *Ground pigment*
- *Palette*
- *Painting knife*
- *Egg yolk*
- *Distilled water*
- *Spare paper*

1 Remove lid and tip container, so the water drains away from the pigment. Scoop a small blob of pigment onto the palette using a painting knife. Add a dab of egg yolk and a similar amount of distilled water to mix.

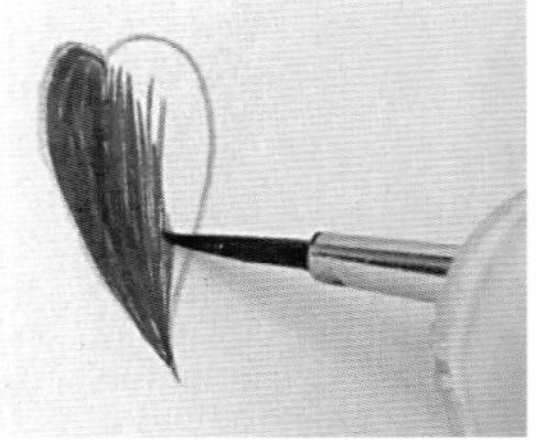

2 Check the mixture on spare paper first; it should look semi-transparent. If the mixture is greasy, you have used too much yolk – just add a little more water to balance it. When you feel the mixture is right, paint into a pre-drawn shape with fine, interlocking strokes. The colour should appear pure and brilliant.

Delicate detail
Very fine lines are possible using egg tempera, both for outlining parts of the decoration as well as for painting the larger areas of colour within the letter shapes.

Tips for using egg tempera

- Egg yolk will not affect the final colour of the paint. Any residual yellowness fades as the colour dries.
- Egg tempera dries very quickly, so colours need to be painted in fine strokes to build up an area of solid colour, unlike the method for using gouache.
- It is difficult to apply thin base-layer washes of colour in egg tempera because of its quick-drying nature, so the results can be patchy. This can be covered with subsequent stronger layers applied in interlocking strokes.

GUM WATER

As an alternative binding medium to egg yolk, you can use gum water, which can also be used in the preparation of ground colours. Mix one part liquid gum arabic (available from art stores) to two parts distilled water and store in a small glass jar with a tight-fitting lid.

Gum water is used in exactly the same way as egg yolk, mixing it with pigment to lay transparent glazes of colour. The finish can be slightly brittle, and it is not waterproof, so take care when overpainting to avoid any colour shift. Gum water is used in the project for the Neo-Classical alphabet (*see pages 212–215*).

GLAIR

Another alternative medium to egg yolk is glair, which uses the leftover egg white. Glair was used as the binder for the colours in the Lindisfarne Gospels and other similar manuscripts of the period.

Beat the white in a glass bowl until quite stiff (so that it will not fall out when the bowl is turned upside down), tilt the bowl on one side, and leave overnight. Strain off the liquid that settles out of the beaten froth into a glass jar and mix in a scant half teaspoonful each of liquid gum arabic (helps pigment adhesion) and white wine vinegar (a mild preservative). Dilute the mixture with a little distilled water when painting.

This mixture is more water-resistant than gum water and easier to reconstitute than the egg-yolk mixture. Store it in a refrigerator until ready to use.

Inks

There are many different brands of ink available and the composition varies from brand to brand, but the most important consideration is to choose the correct type of ink for the purpose. Fountain pen ink is not suitable either for illumination work or calligraphy; its free-flowing consistency is too thin for dip pens.

Filling a pen with ink
For crisp marks, load the pen by feeding ink between nib and reservoir with an old brush. Dipping the pen straight into the bottle is quicker, but is liable to overload the nib and result in a flood rather than sharp lines. If you do dip, shake or wipe off excess ink on absorbent paper; but it is worth taking the trouble to "feed" the nib with ink as shown, especially on your best, finished work.

INKS FOR ILLUMINATION

Waterproof drawing ink You will need this type of ink for the underdrawing of letters in most of the projects in this book. It is generally used very dilute. This enables erasure of inaccurate pencil lines from the initial drawing, without losing any of the design. You can also paint up to, or over, the ink lines without fear of the ink colour bleeding into the paint colours.

Acrylic inks Some colours of pigmented acrylic inks (black, sepia or scarlet) can be used in the same way as drawing ink. The fine pointed nibs used for underdrawing need to be rinsed off and dried frequently as you work, otherwise the ink will clog up.

INKS FOR CALLIGRAPHY

Nonwaterproof liquid ink This is used for the writing that accompanies decorated letters. Because there is no shellac in the mixture, it will not clog the nib. Bottled liquid ink (available from several different manufacturers) is a good starting point for beginners. More experienced calligraphers might like to try:

Inks for calligraphy
1 Nonwaterproof liquid inks
2 Chinese stick ink
3 Ink stone for grinding stick ink

Chinese stick inks Stick inks have been used in Eastern calligraphy for centuries, and they are often beautifully decorated. They are made from pine or oil soot mixed with resin. Too much resin will give a poorer quality ink, so it can be just as difficult to find a good, reliable source of stick ink as liquid ink.

It's worth taking the time to experiment with the different types, but whichever option you choose, the ink should flow well from the nib and give clear, crisp marks in a consistent black. It is not only the ink that can affect the quality of writing – the paper (or vellum), type of nib and even the slope of the drawing board all play their part.

Tips for grinding ink sticks

- It is better to grind a small quantity fresh each time you need it. It can be kept for a short while in a closed jar, but as there is no preservative it will eventually go slimy and mouldy.
- Use the ink stick from one end only.
- Don't leave the ink stick on the wet stone or the resin will set like glue and may damage the stone on separation.
- Cultivate the habit of drying the end of the ink stick on kitchen paper after use to stop it cracking.
- If you have an ink stone with a slope at one end, only use the flat surface for grinding.
- Ink stones are smooth to the touch, but if a stone becomes too smooth, the grinding surface can be revived by rubbing it gently with 400-grit wet-and-dry paper.
- Black gouache is an excellent alternative, mixed to the right consistency (*see page 77*).

Grinding Chinese stick ink

Choose stick ink with a slight sheen or matt finish (not glossy) and light in weight for its size. If there is a high carbon content, the ground ink should be a good, deep black, perfect for calligraphy. It is worth taking the extra time needed to make it.

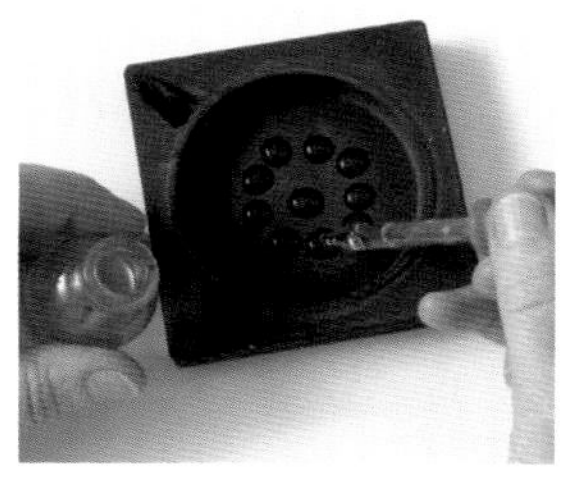

1 *Put 10 drops of distilled water onto the ink stone, using an eyedropper. Try to keep the drops a similar size.*

2 *Hold the ink stick vertically and grind in a circular motion for approximately 2½ minutes (about 200 revolutions). Feed some into a nib and test the ink's blackness. Grind for a little longer if necessary, to produce a deeper black.*

3 *If your ink stone does not have a lid, decant the ink into a small glass jar with a lid to keep it liquid.*

Gilding

Gilding has been used to enhance the pages of manuscripts for many centuries, either on large initials or as points of brilliance within decorative borders or line fillers. Gold can be beaten out into a very thin sheet, thinner than any other metal. It also has the property of sticking to itself, and every layer you put down increases the depth and brilliance of the shine.

The six historically-based alphabets in this book show how this very special material can be used to embellish your own work, using the techniques explained on the following pages.

GOLD LEAF

Gold leaf comes in books of 25 leaves and should be at least 23¾ carat. Patent gold (known as transfer gold in the U.K.) is attached to a backing sheet, which makes it easier to handle. Transfer gold (known as loose-leaf gold in the U.K.) is not attached, but is supplied between sheets of soft tissue paper coated with jeweller's rouge.

Both types of gold are available in single and double thickness. When applying gold to the gesso or other glues mentioned in this book, use a layer of single-thickness gold (of whatever type) first, followed by a double-thickness layer. After use, protect the books of gold by storing them between sheets of stout card.

Silver leaf is also made, but unless it is varnished after laying, exposure to the air will cause it to tarnish. Aluminium, platinum or palladium can be used as substitutes. However, the former is difficult to use and the others are very expensive.

Equipment for gilding

Most of the materials listed here are only available from specialist gilding suppliers. The gilder's cushion, knife and tip are expensive and are not essential for a beginner. They are usually used only for working with transfer gold.

1. *Loose-leaf gold (U.S.: transfer gold)*
2. *Transfer gold (U.S.: patent gold)*
3. *Agate dogtooth burnisher for polishing small flat areas and edges of gold*
4. *Agate pencil burnisher for fixing and polishing edges of gold, and for indenting patterns into gold*

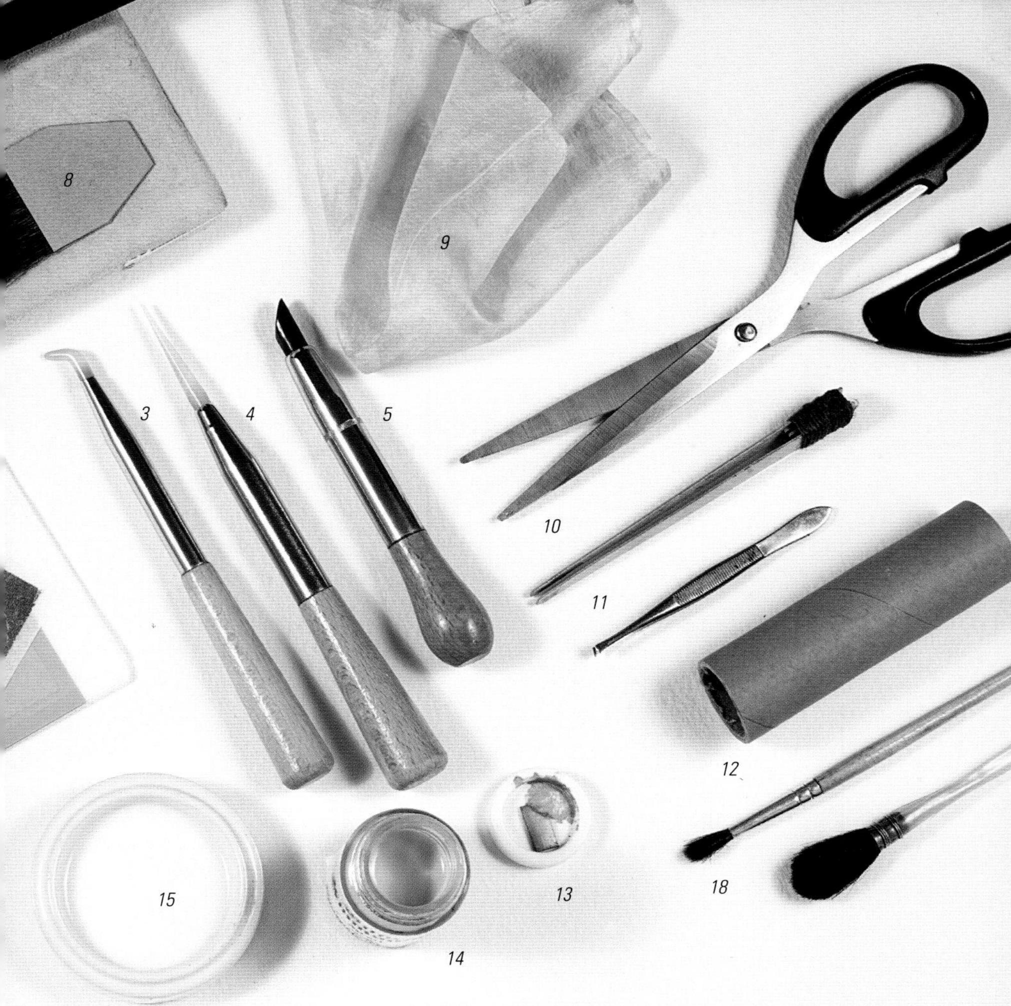

5 *Psilomelanite burnisher – the lipstick shape is good for polishing larger areas of gold*

6 *Gilder's cushion – loose-leaf gold is laid carefully onto the cushion, then cut into smaller pieces with the gilder's knife. Some experience is required.*

7 *Gilder's knife for cutting loose-leaf gold on the cushion*

8 *Gilder's tip for picking up cut pieces of gold*

9 *Soft, washed silk for polishing gold*

10 *Clean, sharp scissors kept only for cutting gold*

11 *Clean tweezers are an alternative to a gilder's tip for picking up loose gold. Wooden ones are better than metal, as gold does not stick to wood.*

12 *Breathing tube (1.5 cm/½ in diameter and approximately 8 cm/3¼ in long). Used to concentrate the breath onto gum or gesso.*

13 *Shell gold. Powder gold mixed with gum, pressed and dried into a tablet. Mix with distilled water to make real gold paint.*

14 *Gum ammoniac solution, used for flat gilding*

15 *PVA medium, used for flat gilding*

16 *Plaster gesso, used for raised gilding*

17 *Glassine*

18 *Soft brushes for removing surplus gold*

16

Flat Gilding

Gilding on paper or vellum requires some type of glue for the gold to adhere. Paper and vellum are pliable supports, so the glue used for gilding must be similarly flexible, so that the gold does not crack or flake off.

Gum ammoniac has been used as a gilding medium for centuries and remains a favourite with calligraphers as a simple, reliable method for flat gilding. It is made from the crystallized sap of an umbelliferous plant, has a rather acrid smell and can be bought ready-made in solution. The gold finish is brighter than shell gold (*see pages 61–62*), but not as brilliant as gold on plaster gesso (*see pages 54–60*).

Working on small shapes, familiarize yourself with using gum ammoniac and gold before you tackle any of the gilding projects in this book.

How to breathe on gum or gesso

- For gold to stick, the gum ammoniac (or gesso, *see pages 58–59*) must first be activated by breathing damp air onto the surface. Use deep, slow breaths from the bottom of the lungs.
- The number of breaths needed varies according to the relative humidity – low humidity needs more breaths; higher humidity needs fewer.
- For gum ammoniac or PVA glue, start with three or four breaths. Plaster gesso will need at least six breaths to begin with, as the relative "sticky" content is lower.
- Subsequent layers of gold will need fewer breaths because the gold sticks to itself.
- If you breathe on the gum or gesso too much, it can start to break down with the excess moisture, so practise on small areas first.

Tips for flat gilding

- On softer surfaced papers, you may need to apply more than two layers of gum. The first will seal the surface; the others will build up the adhesive sufficiently to enable the gold to stick.
- Rinse and dry the brush each time after laying the gum, then wash it out thoroughly in tepid soapy water when you have finished.
- You can use an agate burnisher very gently on the gold. However, the gum beneath is very soft and if you rub too hard it generates heat; the gum becomes tacky and the gold will be damaged. Stop if you feel the burnisher dragging.
- Use gum ammoniac or PVA in a chisel-edged nib for writing small letters or decorations. Gild as described opposite.

GILDING USING PVA

PVA glue or acrylic painting media can also be used (diluted 50/50 with distilled water) for flat gilding, like a modern version of gum ammoniac. The glue is colourless, so it helps to add a spot of red watercolour, so that it can easily be seen when dry.

The materials (substituting the PVA) and method are the same as for gum ammoniac gilding already described.

Using less water in the mix, applying two or three layers will give a slightly raised cushion of PVA to gild, similar to that achieved with plaster gesso (*see page 56*).

Gilding using gum ammoniac

Have all your materials at hand, as you will need to work quickly to lay the gold after you have breathed on the gum to activate it. Before you start, stir the solution slowly and thoroughly to incorporate all the gum from the bottom of the jar. This should avoid problems with bubbles, but allow it to settle for a while before use.

You will need

- *300 gsm (140 lb) HP watercolour paper with pre-drawn shape or letter*
- *Gum ammoniac solution*
- *Plastic or glass rod for stirring gum*
- *Old small brush for applying the gum*
- *Breathing tube*
- *Transfer gold (U.S.: patent gold)*
- *Glassine*
- *Dogtooth agate burnisher*
- *Large soft brush to remove excess gold*
- *Piece of soft washed silk*

1 Work on a flat surface so that the gum dries level. Using an old brush, lay a thin, even layer of the gum, working methodically across the area, wet into wet. Leave to dry for 30 minutes, then carefully add a second layer over the first and leave to dry completely for an hour or more.

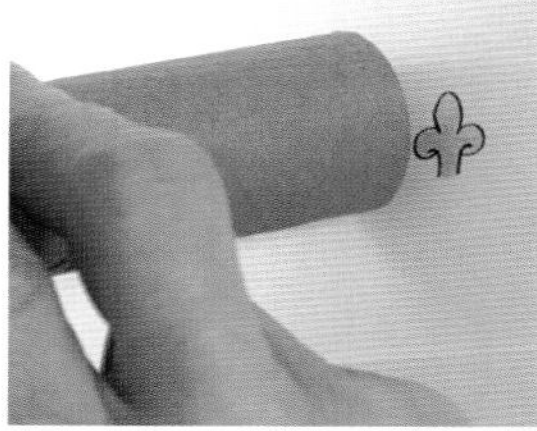

2 With the paper on a smooth, hard surface, use a breathing tube or small rolled piece of paper to direct your breath onto the gum and breathe three times (see Tips, on opposite page).

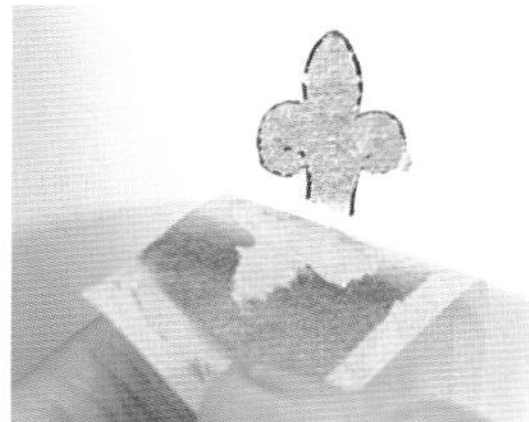

3 As soon as you have breathed on the gum, lay the transfer gold face down onto it, pressing down firmly (without twisting) with your fingers. If the gold does not stick, breathe on the gum again and re-apply the gold. Peel off the backing sheet to reveal the gold stuck onto the gum. Repeat this step to cover the whole area completely.

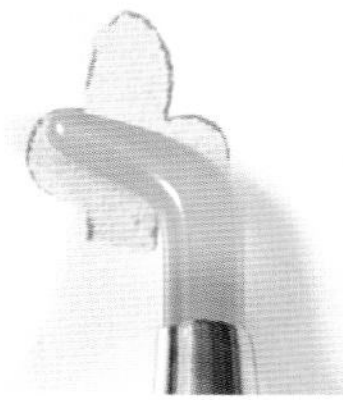

4 Burnish the gold gently through a sheet of glassine. Repeat step 3 to add a second layer of gold.

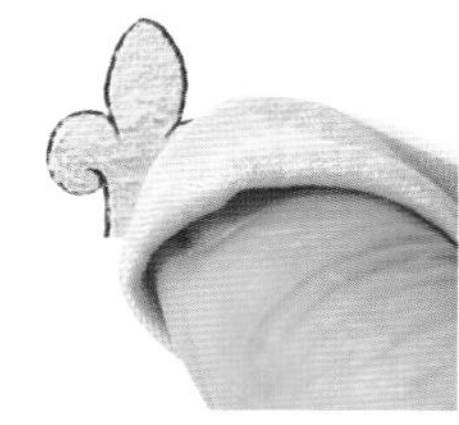

5 Leave to dry thoroughly for at least 30 minutes before removing surplus gold with a large soft brush, then give it another burnish through glassine before a final polish with soft silk.

Raised and Burnished Gold

Raised gilding, which has changed little since medieval times, uses layers of transfer gold and loose-leaf gold on a firm base of plaster gesso raised slightly from the writing surface (*see pages 168–171 and 192–195*). The gold can be burnished almost to a mirrorlike finish and its brilliance will light up your work, as it did the pages of early manuscripts. It is certainly not the easiest technique and is more time-consuming than flat gilding, but if it is done well it will give the best results.

There are several stages to raised gilding, including making plaster gesso, preparing it and laying it, before the actual gilding and burnishing begin. With any sort of gilding, it pays to make notes as you work – how many layers of medium or gum, how many layers of gold you use – but this is particularly important with raised and burnished gilding so you can repeat (as near as possible) the exact process and get good, consistent results every time. Don't trust your memory – you will forget!

Making plaster gesso

A calligraphic colleague (who used to be a science teacher) developed the recipe for the gesso given here after a great deal of research, trial and effort. I reproduce it here in preference to the traditional recipe, because although the ingredients still need careful handling due to their toxic nature, the method is very quick and easy, needs little special equipment and in my experience gives excellent results. Please read the safety notes below, before making the gesso.

Lorna Bambury's easy gesso

- *8 parts calcium sulphate dihydrate [$CaSO4.2H_2O$] (**toxic**)*
- *3 parts lead carbonate [white lead] (**toxic**)*
- *1 part sugar (granulated or castor, ground fine in pestle and mortar)*
- *1 part seccotine (fish glue)*
- *1 or 2 drops of concentrated liquid red watercolour*

You will need

- *Distilled water*
- *Dust mask*
- *Gloves if necessary (see safety notes, right)*
- *Measuring spoon: use for this purpose only*
- *Piece of plate glass*
- *Piece of acetate*
- *Flexible palette knife*
- *Plastic box for drying*

Safety Notes

- It is advisable to work in a well-ventilated room when making up this mixture.
- Avoid getting any of the powder in your eyes or mouth.
- If you have any cuts on your fingers or hands, wear rubber gloves.

1 Put on your dust mask (and gloves), and then measure out the first three ingredients onto the glass plate. Keep each ingredient in separate rows to check you have the right quantity.

2 Add the glue (scraping it off the spoon with the palette knife) and enough distilled water to give the consistency of glacé icing.

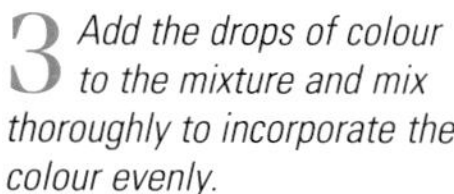

3 Add the drops of colour to the mixture and mix thoroughly to incorporate the colour evenly.

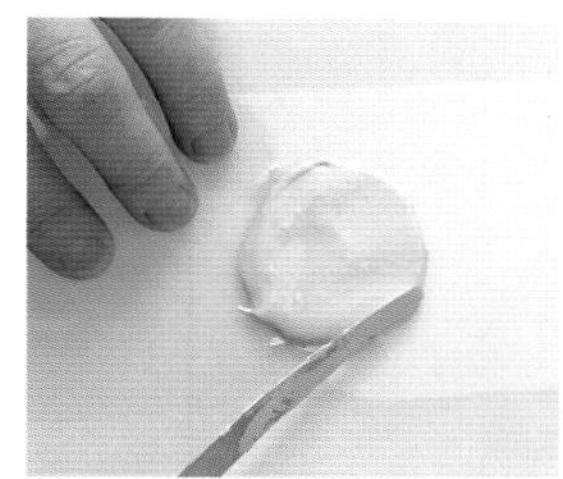

4 Spoon the mixture onto an acetate sheet, shaping it into small, flat cakes. Gesso takes about seven days to dry. Keep in a covered box for 24 hours to stop dust settling on the surface, then uncover and leave for three days. Use a palette knife to peel the cakes off the acetate, turn them over and leave for another three or four days before storing in an airtight container.

Reconstituting plaster gesso

Before gilding, you will need to reconstitute the plaster gesso

You will need

- *One cake or small piece of gesso (see recipe opposite)*
- *White china eggcup or glass jar with lid*
- *Distilled water*
- *Eyedropper*
- *Oil of cloves*
- *Needle or pin*
- *Cocktail stick for stirring – wash after use and keep* only *for this purpose*
- *Facemask and rubber gloves for protection against toxic powders*

1 *First, break up the gesso into small pieces in the eggcup or jar (wear gloves). Add two or three drops (depending on the amount of gesso you are using) of distilled water to surround the gesso, not submerge it. Cover and leave to soak for a minimum of three hours. If using a jar, tilt it to one side.*

2 *Press the damp crumbs gently with the cocktail stick to break them down completely, and then begin to stir slowly from the centre outwards to incorporate all the mixture. If the gesso hangs in a string from the stirrer, it is too thick to use, so add more water, a drop at a time. The mixture should look like thin cream.*

3 *However careful you are, bubbles will appear in the gesso. Dip a pin or needle into oil of cloves to get a tiny drop on the end. Dab it gently into the mixture and the bubbles will disperse.*

Laying gesso

Gesso is very sensitive to humidity so, if possible, work in a room without drafts and which is not too dry or too hot.

You will need

- *Small brush kept* only *for laying gesso*
- *One quantity of gesso, mixed, ready for use*

1 *Have an outline of a letter or shape ready drawn. Work on a flat surface so the gesso settles evenly. Dampen the brush, then dry it again to expel all the air. Thin a little of the gesso with distilled water and apply it as a sealer or undercoat.*

2 *While the undercoat is still damp, take up a large blob of gesso onto the brush and apply it to the letter or shape. Work from one corner, letting the gesso flow out to fill the area.*

3 *Tease the mix out into the corners with the brush tip. Flood in more gesso, wet into wet, until the whole shape is filled, making sure the surface is even and level (this applies particularly to larger areas). Leave it to dry out completely, at least overnight.*

Tips for laying gesso

- Do experiments on small, simple shapes first to get used to handling the gesso.
- For writing, dilute the gesso to give a consistent flow through the nib (use a slightly thicker mixture than for writing with gouache, *see page 77*). This works better without a reservoir.
- Try to avoid bubbles when laying gesso. They can be given the oil of clove treatment, but you will need to add a little more gesso while it is still wet, to fill the resulting hollow – experiment with this.
- Don't put any more gesso on top of the dried layer to fill in any dips or hollows (this may mean the mixture is too wet); it is better to scrape it even.

Gilding on plaster gesso

This method of gilding is used in the Gothic project (*see pages 168–171*) and White Vine project (*see pages 192–195*).

Work on a hard, flat surface – tack the paper or vellum to a piece of plate glass or Formica. The smooth surface gives a firm base when burnishing. Have all tools and materials laid out at hand on a flat surface, including ready-cut pieces of loose-leaf gold protected with glassine to stop them blowing away.

Stop burnishers from rolling onto the floor by putting them on corrugated paper, or something similar.

Cracking and crazing of gesso
Cracks in gesso may occur because of changes in the atmosphere, which can cause unstretched pieces of vellum to flex. Cracks can be repaired, but the surface polish will not be as good, so it is better to scrape off the gesso and start again.

Crazing (many fine cracks in the gold, like the surface of old oil paintings or glazed pottery) is the most frustrating problem, because it seems to happen for no apparent reason.

It may be that the gold is burnished too hard and too soon for the gesso to have settled after being breathed on, or possibly even from putting too many layers of gold down. If this happens, it is best to scrape off the gesso and start again.

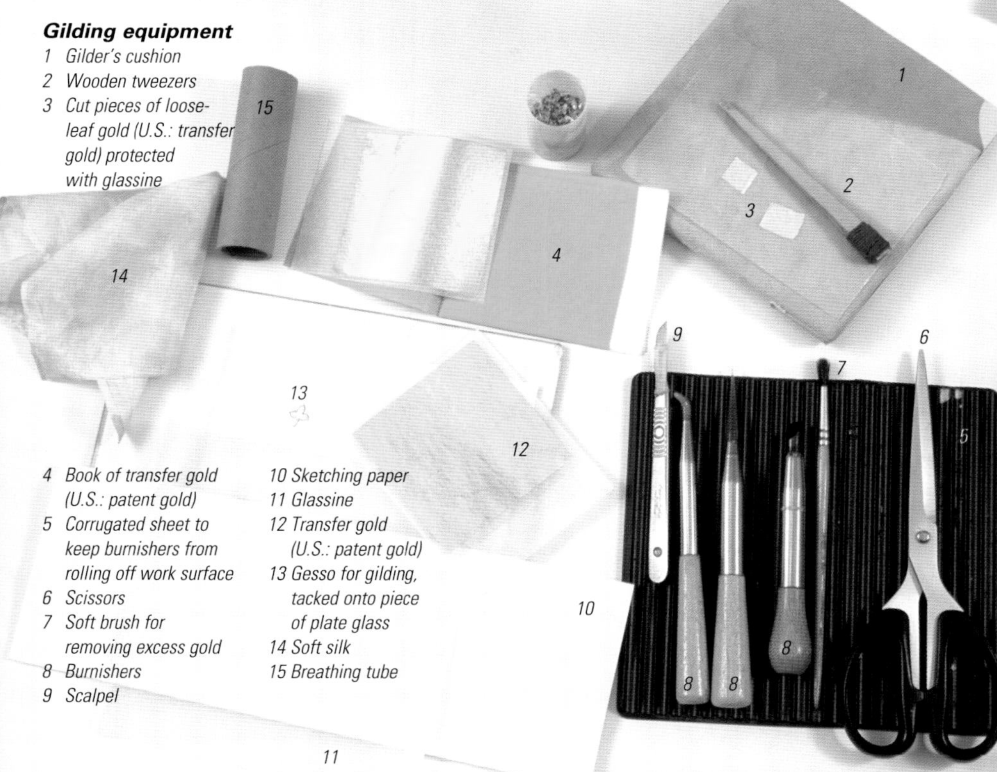

Gilding equipment

1 *Gilder's cushion*
2 *Wooden tweezers*
3 *Cut pieces of loose-leaf gold (U.S.: transfer gold) protected with glassine*
4 *Book of transfer gold (U.S.: patent gold)*
5 *Corrugated sheet to keep burnishers from rolling off work surface*
6 *Scissors*
7 *Soft brush for removing excess gold*
8 *Burnishers*
9 *Scalpel*
10 *Sketching paper*
11 *Glassine*
12 *Transfer gold (U.S.: patent gold)*
13 *Gesso for gilding, tacked onto piece of plate glass*
14 *Soft silk*
15 *Breathing tube*

You will need

- *Laid gesso (see page 56)*
- *Round-bladed scalpel*
- *Dust mask*
- *Kitchen paper*
- *Piece of soft washed silk*
- *Dogtooth agate or flat psilomelanite burnisher*
- *Transfer gold (U.S.: patent gold)*
- *Breathing tube*
- *Glassine*
- *Double thickness loose-leaf gold (U.S.: transfer gold)*
- *Scissors*
- *Tweezers*
- *Pencil burnisher*
- *Piece of plate glass (with edges sanded smooth)*
- *Gilder's cushion (optional)*

Safety Notes

- It is advisable to wear a dust mask when scraping gesso, to avoid inhaling any of the powder.

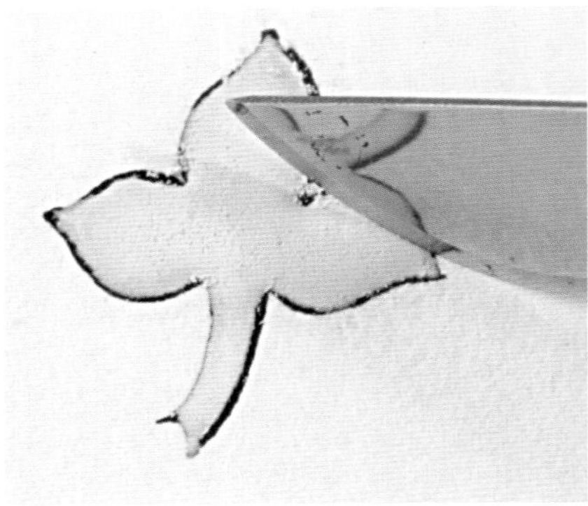

1 *Gently scrape the gesso level with the scalpel, to even out any bumps. You do not need to press hard – let the weight of the scalpel do the work. Tip the paper slightly and gently brush the scrapings onto kitchen paper, which can be carefully folded up and thrown away.*

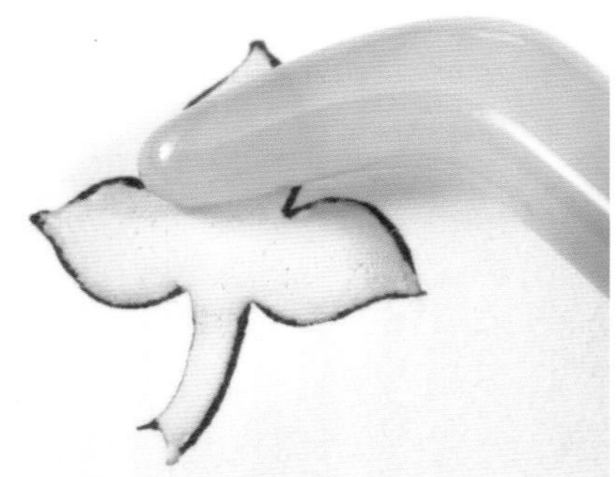

2 *Gently rub the surface with silk to reduce friction, and then burnish the gesso directly with either the agate or the psilomelanite burnisher. The shiny surface seems to take the gold more easily.*

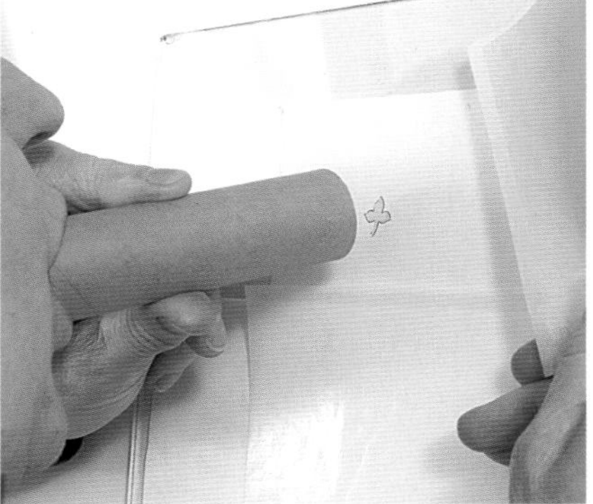

3 *Pick up the transfer gold in one hand, and then give six good breaths over the gesso using the breathing tube.*

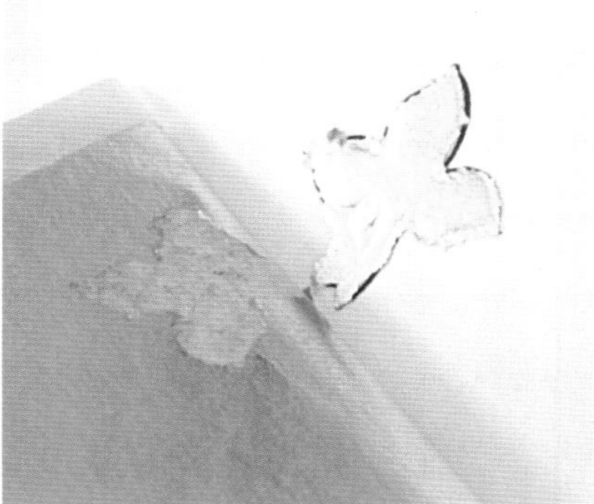

4 Press the gold gently onto the gesso surface, and then carefully peel off the backing sheet. Use the burnisher (without much pressure) through the glassine. Repeat until covered completely. Leave to settle for 30 minutes.

5 Burnish through glassine, using the point of the dogtooth burnisher to work around the edges.

6 Pick up a piece of loose-leaf gold using tweezers. In your other hand, hold the piece of silk. Because both hands are occupied, you cannot use the breathing tube. Breathe on the gesso, taking care not to let your mouth touch either gesso or paper. Lay the gold onto the gesso, pressing it into place with the silk. This will leave a slight impression of the weave on the surface.

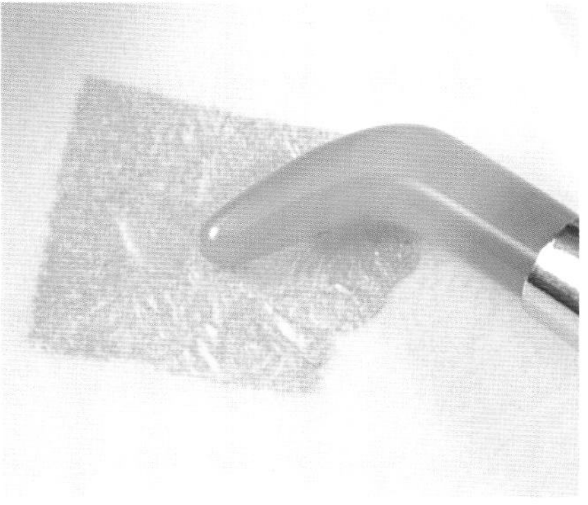

7 Burnish through glassine to smooth out the silk marks and tuck edges over.

8 *Repeat steps 6 and 7 for two complete layers (you will need fewer breaths for each subsequent layer). Allow the gesso to settle each time before burnishing. Burnish through glassine using a pencil burnisher carefully, to set the edges.*

Tips for gilding with gesso

- When cutting loose-leaf gold with scissors, it is easier to cut the last sheet of gold first. Hold the book by its spine and roll the other leaves back carefully, allowing the last page to fall open naturally. If done in this way, possible damage to the rest of the gold in the book is reduced.
- If the gold sticks to the scissors, use a soft brush to push it off onto a gilder's cushion or a sheet of glassine. Pick up with tweezers as described in step 6.

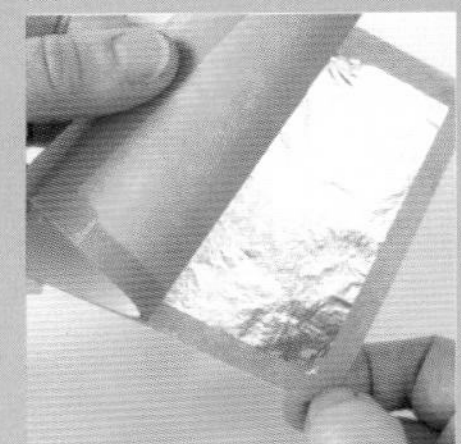

Carefully open the book of gold from the back, holding it by the spine.

9 *Remove any surplus gold with a soft brush and save the pieces in a film canister. They can be used for patching small areas of gesso. Leave to settle. (You can breathe onto the gesso and fold the surplus gold back over the raised shape and burnish as described.)*

10 *Burnish the gold directly with an agate or psilomelanite burnisher, using a circular motion and increasing pressure to produce a good shiny finish. Use the pencil burnisher carefully to polish the edges, taking care not to dent the gesso.*

Shell Gold

Shell gold is genuine powdered gold mixed with gum or glue as a binder and compressed into a small cake or tablet. It was originally supplied in half mussel shells, hence its picturesque name, but now comes in white plastic saucers.

Available in different "shades", yellow, red or green, it is mixed with distilled water to make a paint that can be applied with a lettering pen, ruling pen (for ruled lines) or brush (for small flat areas or filigree decoration), and overpainting on coloured letters.

When dry, the finish is matt. It can be burnished to a dull shine but its surface reflects less light than gold leaf. Indent dots and patterns with a pencil burnisher to catch the light and add brilliance.

Gilding with shell gold

The equipment you use for applying shell gold should be kept separately from your other equipment. Label both brush and water jars to remind you to use them for gold only.

You will need

- *Shell gold*
- *Eyedropper*
- *Distilled water for mixing, plus some in a separate small container to rinse brush*
- *Sable brush (size 0 or 00, depending on area to be covered)*

1 Use the dropper to add two or three drops of water to the edge of the tablet to moisten it.

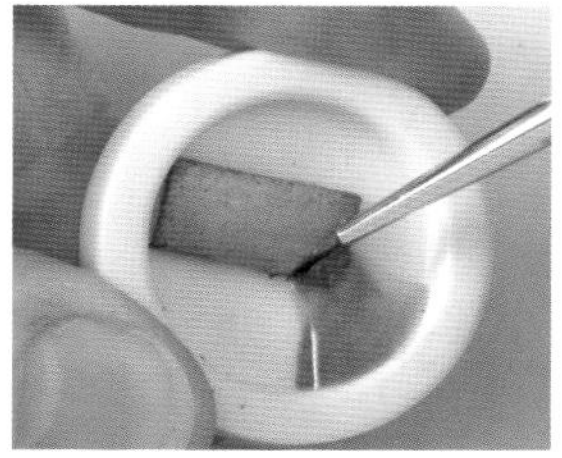

2 Mix the gold to the consistency of ink. Tilt the palette to one side, so that you can control the consistency.

3 When applying flat areas of gold, make the first layer quite watery and leave it to dry.

4 Mix the second layer thicker and lay it in flat or crosshatched strokes to build up as even a layer as possible. Leave it to dry for at least 30 minutes.

5 Burnish the gold through glassine first, to help adherence and smooth out any unevenness, then burnish the gold directly with a dogtooth agate.

6 *You can indent patterns with a pencil burnisher.*

Tips for using shell gold

- Stir gold frequently during use to mix the pigment evenly and reduce evaporation. Add more water a drop at a time as necessary.
- Experiment with the amount of water added, adjusting the flow as necessary. Too much water gives patchy results; but if the mixture is too thick, it will not flow from the pen. It needs to be more liquid to flow from a ruling pen.
- For writing small letters, feed the paint onto the back of the nib without a reservoir – progress is slow, only a letter or two at a time. Leave it to dry, then burnish as described above.
- Retain the sediment in the rinsing bottle and re-use. Drain off the water, add one to two drops of gum arabic solution and mix. Try it out on scrap paper. When it has dried, rub your finger over the gold to see if it has stuck. If not, add more gum, remix and try again.

Metallic Gouache and Bronze Powders

Metallic gouache and bronze powders are the least expensive options that produce a "gold" finish. While having little of the brilliance of the real thing, they are useful for beginners who are not yet confident enough to use real gold, and will give acceptable results. They can be very effective on some finished work, but are most useful in preparatory sketches.

METALLIC GOUACHE

Metallic flakes are combined with gum arabic to form gouache in rich shades of gold (and silver), which is supplied in tubes. Choose the gold shade that best complements the colours used in the decoration.

Metallic gouache mixes easily with distilled water to a good creamy consistency, ideal for laying flat areas and for writing with in exactly the same way as normal gouache. The paint must be stirred often as you work, so that the metal "pigment" is well distributed; otherwise, the results will be patchy. Some practice is needed to get the finish just right. It is easier to use than gold ink and, if mixed to the right consistency, can be painted to give good flat colour over large areas. It can also be used in a pen to write with, in a ruling pen to rule lines (*see page 73*) and with a fine brush for filigree decoration.

Tip for burnishing gouache

- Gold gouache can be burnished gently with a dogtooth agate burnisher, but the burnish is not retained. If you burnish the paint through glassine, you can smooth out any unevenness in the surface.

GOUACHE POWDER

To make gouache powder, metal flakes are mixed with dextrin, an adhesive derived from starch. It is supplied as dry powder in glass jars and needs to be reconstituted with distilled water. The powder can be gritty, hard to mix and less easy to handle than tube types, as the flakes tend to separate out. Adding two or three drops of acrylic medium to the mixture may improve coverage in flat areas and the crispness of writing, but frequent mixing is still necessary. Different shades of gold are available and, when mixed, the silver powder looks like molten metal.

BRONZING POWDERS

Available in different colours of gold, bronzing powders generally contain no adhesive, so some form of binding medium needs to be added. Try mixing with gum arabic solution, PVA or acrylic medium, plus distilled water to achieve a proper consistency. Some experimentation with quantities will be needed to get good adhesion. It will help to make notes of the relative proportions of powder and glue of each mix so you can repeat the best at will.

METALLIC WATERCOLOUR

Mixed and applied in the same way as ordinary watercolour, metallic watercolour will not give the same covering power as gouache, but it is fine for use in small spaces if applied in a similar way to shell gold. Apply a thin wash first, overlaid with a second coat of thicker paint using fine, crosshatched strokes to build up an even layer of metallic pigment.

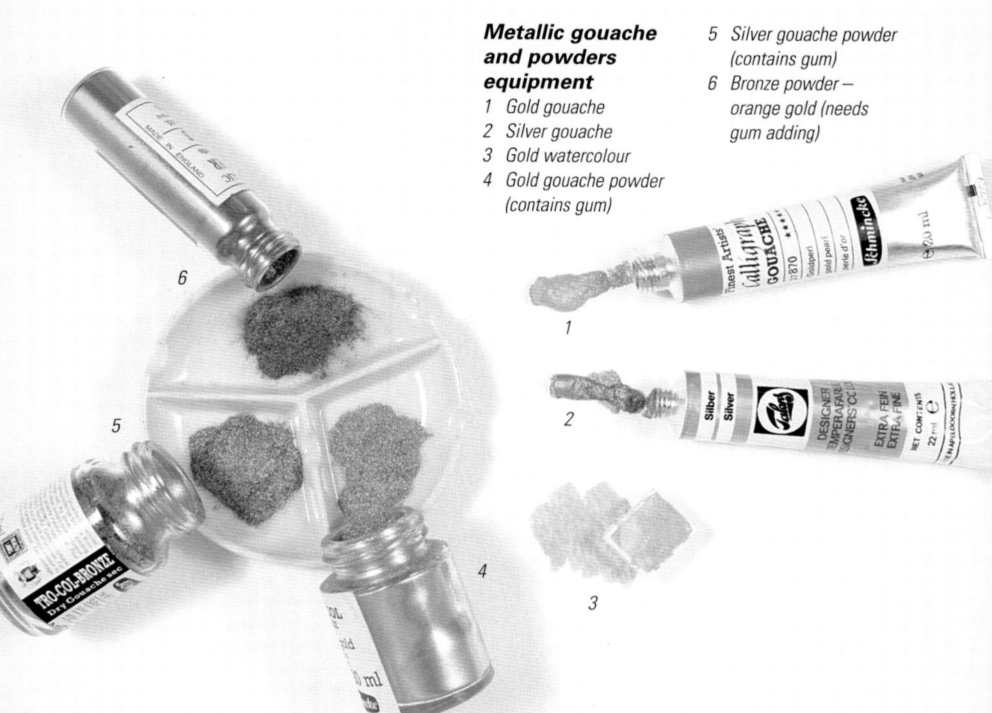

Metallic gouache and powders equipment

1. *Gold gouache*
2. *Silver gouache*
3. *Gold watercolour*
4. *Gold gouache powder (contains gum)*
5. *Silver gouache powder (contains gum)*
6. *Bronze powder – orange gold (needs gum adding)*

Chapter 2

Preparing to Work

The previous chapter described in detail the tools, materials and techniques you need for painting and gilding the decorated alphabets that appear in this book and for writing the text to accompany them.

This section outlines how to harness these skills to make well-crafted pieces of finished work, whether you wish to create facsimile pages or to use the same ancient techniques in more modern work (*see Gallery, pages 236–247*).

erat verbum et
verbum erat

Layout and Design

The main emphasis of this book is the making of decorated letters, following historically based models. Individual letters, in the form of cards or framed pieces, make beautiful gifts but their original purpose was to indicate new chapters and verses in both religious and secular manuscript books. You may wish to progress to creating more complex pieces like this for yourself (*see pages 81–83*). When used in this wider context, beautiful illumination and decoration deserve a sound basis of the best quality writing you can achieve. Decoration and writing should complement each other in colour, balance and design, and this chapter gives a summary of the techniques that will help you towards this goal.

Starting out: Ruling lines

Before you start writing, you need to rule up some lines at the appropriate letter height (*see also Nib widths, opposite*).

You will need

- *Padded drawing board (see page 19)*
- *Pencil*
- *Paper*
- *Ruler or T-square*
- *Edged pen and non-waterproof ink*
- *Dividers*

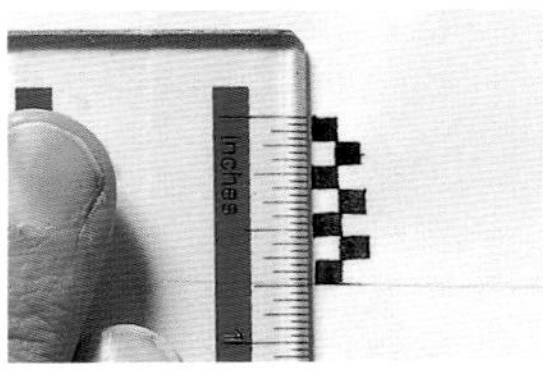

1 Measure accurately how wide apart your lines should be; generally, you are measuring "nib widths".

2 You may prefer to use a pair of dividers if all your lines are to be the same distance apart.

3 Walk the dividers down the side of the page, or mark the measurements with a ruler.

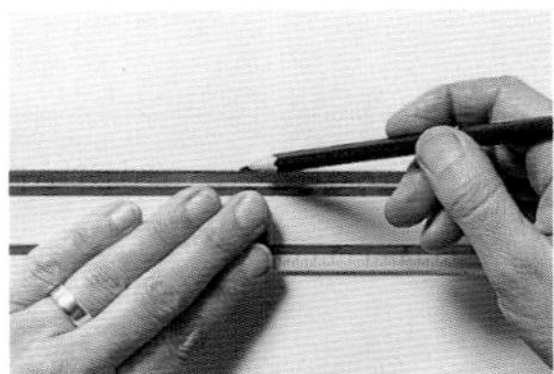

4 When you have marked the measurements on both sides, join the marks with clear, sharp lines across the ruler.

5 If you have a T-square, mark one side of the paper only, secure the paper to the board to prevent it moving, and use the T-square with its edge against the board as you rule lines across.

Nib widths: Making a ladder

Each script exemplar has a "ladder" of nib widths, which gives the correct height of the letter (capitals or lower case) (*see Ruling lines, opposite*).

You will need

- *Edged pen and non-waterproof ink*
- *Paper*
- *Ruler*
- *Dividers*

1 The full width of the nib must be used to mark accurately multiples of the nib's width. You may have to practise this several times to get precise marks. Do several ladders and measure them to get an average. Check that you have not overlapped, or left gaps.

2 Measure carefully with a ruler to the number of nib widths you know you need for the style you are writing (left), or use a pair of dividers (right).

LEARNING TO WRITE THE SCRIPTS

Following each of the decorated alphabets in this book are slightly modernized exemplars of text scripts used in the manuscripts of each period, which give a useful guide to choosing suitable lettering for your project. Time spent looking at and practising these hands will improve the quality of your finished work.

Be systematic with your study and work on one script at a time, so you understand the structure and characteristics of each before progressing to the next.

STARTING OUT – RULING LINES

First, you need to rule up some lines for writing, at the appropriate letter height.

NIB WIDTHS – MAKING A LADDER

Each exemplar has a "ladder" of nib widths, which shows the number of full widths of the broad-edged nib measured to get the height of each letter style.

PEN ANGLE

A broad-edged pen naturally makes thick and thin strokes. Where these occur in any script is governed by the angle at which the pen is held relative to the writing line. A pen angle guide is given for each script – look carefully to see how this affects the letterforms.

Writing at a consistent angle is not as easy as it sounds and requires some practice. It is easy to alter the angle inadvertently as you write, especially if you only move your fingers rather than the whole arm when making the strokes. When you have ruled up a series of lines (at the appropriate height) on layout paper, practise writing the individual letters at first, but progress to writing words and sentences as soon as you are reasonably confident of the letter shapes and can write them rhythmically.

SPACING

The spacing between letters should be done visually, not mechanically, to look even and equal to the space contained within the letters (counters). Word spacing should be neither too tight nor too open – approximately the width of a lower case o.

Line spacing depends on the script. Those with long ascenders and descenders that might clash need more space than those with relatively short ones. For example, Carolingian or Italics need 2–2½ times the body height (x-height) of lower case letters; Insular half uncial script needs 2 times the x-height; Foundational needs 1½ times the x-height; and Gothic needs 1 times the x-height. Careful study and measurements taken from examples of original manuscripts are very helpful.

Letter and word spacing

IH

Two straight letters (verticals) are furthest apart.

IC

Straight and curved letters have less space between them.

OC

Two curved letters are closest.

DOMINE

Letters spaced to appear correct visually.

FILIO

Letter spacing too close, text looks uneven.

et in

Word space is equal to approximately one lower case o.

Line spacing

Italics need more space between lines than Gothic.

qui cum patre
et filio simul

Gothic

qui cum patre
et filio simul

Italics

Planning Your Work

Beautiful illumination deserves good quality lettering, but it also needs a considered design planned in advance of the finished work. This planning stage is crucial – not only does it sort out which size and style of decorated letter, script and border to use, as well as the choice and balance of colour, but also where to place these elements in a given space and how to decide the margins around the writing. It will increase your confidence in the outcome of the finished piece, if you know that all the tricky decisions have been made at the rough stage – don't be tempted to skip it!

THUMBNAIL SKETCHES

Thumbnails are a good way of visualizing your layout ideas quickly at a small size. Glean initial ideas on layout from books on illumination, but experiment with your own. As you work, think about alignment, format and balance of white space to text, as well as size and weight of writing.

Here are some permutations to try:

Alignment and margins

The examples shown here all have equal, quite generous margins at top and sides, with more space at the bottom.

Ranged left: *The simplest arrangement and easiest to control. This is the most common arrangement in books.*
Centred: *Symmetrical, formal style that is mainly used for title pages and colophons in books, and for posters and formal documents.*
Centred visually*: Longer lines are counterbalanced with shorter ones.*

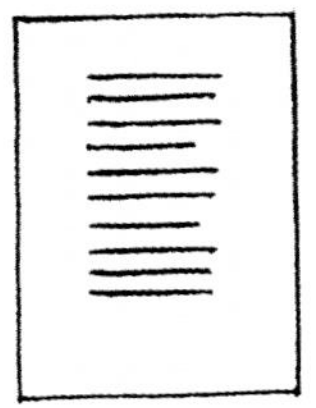

Ranged left.

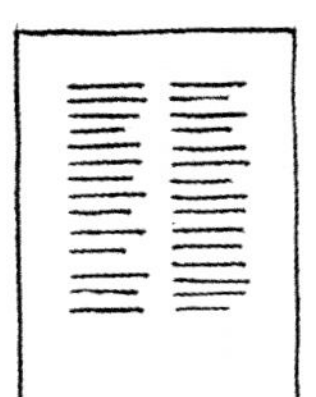

Ranged left, two columns.

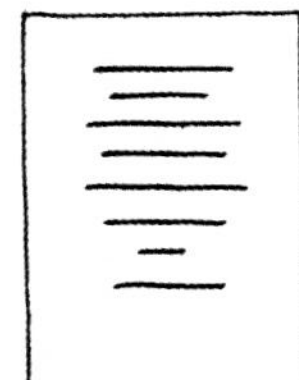

Centred.

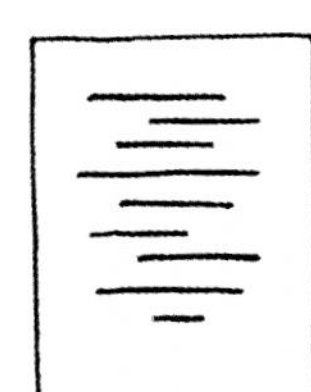

Centred visually.

Format

Note how extra white space draws the eye into and around the design.

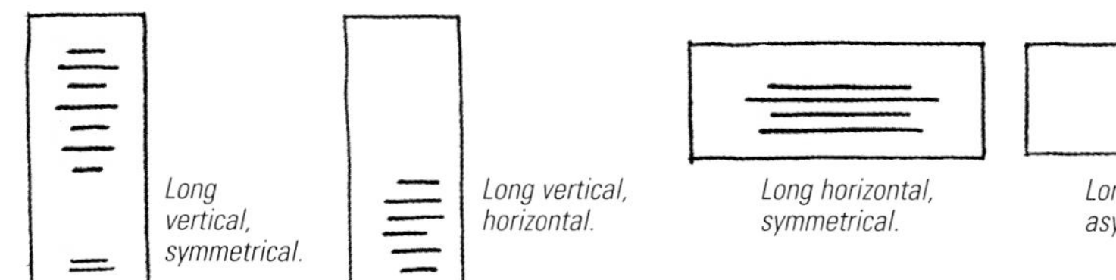

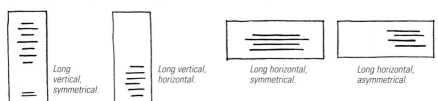

Long vertical, symmetrical.

Long vertical, horizontal.

Long horizontal, symmetrical.

Long horizontal, asymmetrical.

Contrast and emphasis

*Change of weight and/or size of lettering (shown by heavier lines) can add contrast or emphasis – and interest – to the layout (*see below and opposite*).*

Large, bold heading.

Large, bold heading and bold subheadings at text size.

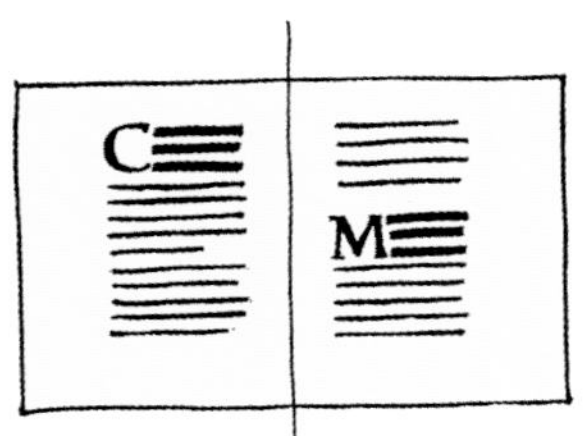

Large capital and first three lines in bold.

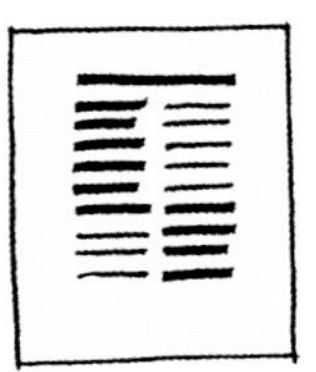

Bold heading and counterbalanced paragraphs in text size bold.

Bold weight for short sentence or paragraph.

Preparing a paste-up layout

Before embarking on any project, you should prepare a paste-up layout. When you are entirely satisfied that the design, balance of weight, size and colour of lettering and decorated letter all work well together, go ahead and rule up to write out the finished piece on your choice of paper. Instructions for transferring decorated letters are given on pages 78–80.

You will need

- *Pencil*
- *Sheets of layout paper*
- *Ruler*
- *Pens and ink*
- *Scissors*
- *Sheet of tracing paper*
- *Black or dark-coloured paper strips (approx. 7.5 cm/3 in wide), longer than the longest edge of the layout paper*
- *Repositionable glue or masking tape*

1 *Make thumbnail sketches of your ideas for text, featured letter(s), and any decoration in pencil on layout paper (*see also page 69 and above*). Try both portrait (vertical) and landscape (horizontal) formats.*

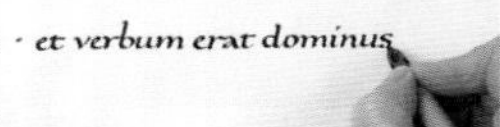

2 *Rule up (*as shown on page 66*), write out text and draw the main letter on layout paper. At this stage, there is no need to follow the layout, except to consider the relative sizes and weights of the lettering. Allow enough room around everything for cutting out. Check spelling and the quality of letterforms and spacing.*

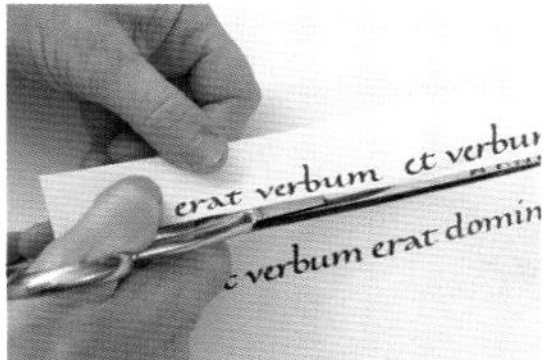

3 *Cut everything out carefully with scissors, trimming off any excess paper that might confuse the line spacing.*

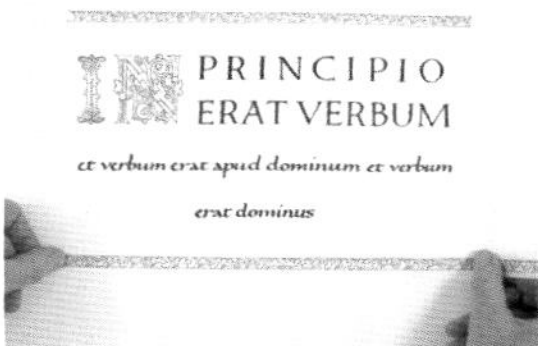

4 *Assemble all the elements on a large sheet of paper to follow one of the thumbnail designs. You may need to modify your ideas when working at full size, possibly changing size or weight of letters.*

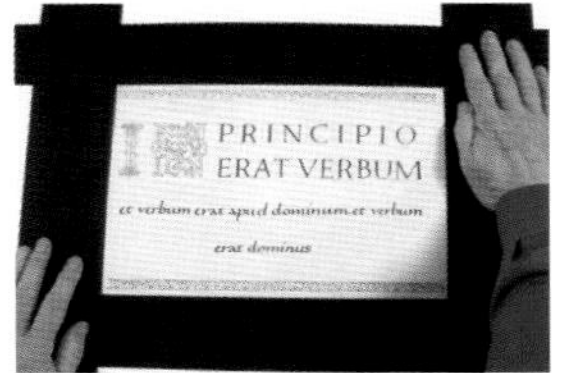

5 *Assess the overall effect. Cover the pieces with a sheet of tracing paper to keep them roughly in place. Use the black paper strips to decide the size of the margins, starting with them laid quite close to the text.*

6 *Move the strips out to allow more breathing space all round and a bit extra at the bottom. Focus on the overall shape of the design – white space is as important as the text itself, because it draws the eye into the design.*

7 *Rewrite or photocopy the elements (you need to keep the original version so the two can be compared) and rearrange them in an alternate format. Repeat steps 5 and 6 to assess the margins, then decide which version works best.*

8 *Remove the tracing paper, mark the correct line spacing, then stick the pieces down with repositionable glue or masking tape. Make sure that the corners work into the border pattern. Mark important measurements and pen sizes used on the layout.*

9 *Make a colour rough with coloured pencils or paint. Lay another sheet of layout paper over the original (you will be able to see through it) and draft in the colours to assess the effect.*

Order of work from sketch to finished piece

1 Thumbnail sketches to plan the design.
2 Write out text and draft out decorative elements.
3 Cut out elements and make paste-up layout.
4 Decide margins with coloured paper strips.
5 Do colour rough and trials on paper samples.
6 Rule up on good paper, following paste-up layout and transfer letter outlines.
7 Write out all text in ink or paint.
8 Cover up writing to protect from smudges before gilding and burnishing.
9 Do all painting, including highlights and outlines.

Enlarging Letters and Details

You may want to enlarge or reduce the size of the decorated letters shown on the alphabet pages to suit your design better. You can do this in various different ways, as described below. With all these methods, transfer the resulting scaled-up letters to paper or vellum for gilding and painting as described on pages 78–80.

Using a scanner If you have access to a computer, flatbed scanner and printer, you have the means to adjust the letter size up or down accurately to the exact size you want.

1 Place the original face down onto the scanner glass, aligned square to the edge of the frame.

2 Open the scanner software programme. If it has the image type option "text/line" in the subject type box, select this, otherwise click on "b + w illustration".

3 For accurate resizing, once the quick preview scan has been done, crop the image as tight as possible without cutting off any parts of the drawing. (N.B. Remember that the new size is measured across the cropped area, not the actual drawn image.)

4 Once cropped in the image window, select the new size for the image either by using the dimensions boxes under "target", or by entering a percentage enlargement (or reduction).

5 Click "scan" and save the resulting image, which can then be printed out as your reference.

Using a photocopier Photocopying does not offer such a wide range of size options as a scanner, but it is a quick and cost-effective way of resizing the decorated letters you want to use.

Using a grid to enlarge details

This method requires no special equipment, but it is much more labour- and time-intensive. For example, each of the decorated alphabet project letters is shown in outline on a grid.

You will need

- *Ruler*
- *Pencil*

1 Draw a diagonal line through the grid from bottom left to the top right corner. Mark out the intended new width and draw a vertical from this to the diagonal. Where the two coincide, draw in the horizontal for the top.

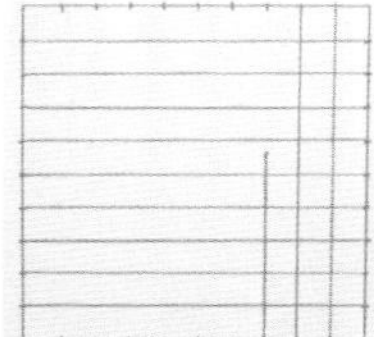

2 Recalibrate the grid by marking out accurately and drawing in exactly the same number of vertical and horizontal lines to fit the new rectangle.

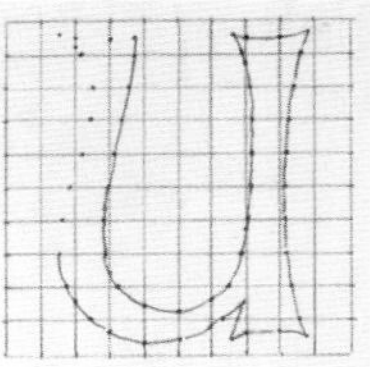

3 Redraw the image by marking dots on the grid to correspond with where the lines of the shapes crossed the original. Join the dots to create the resized letter.

Ruling Lines With Ink or Paint

If your design includes straight lines to be drawn in either ink or paint and your hand is not steady enough to do them freehand, there are two easy ways, with a little practice, to get it right.

Tip for moving work around
Don't attempt to keep the piece straight in front of you all the time. It is a lot easier to work with the piece at different angles and the paper or vellum taped onto a piece of glass.

Using a brush to rule lines

It will take a little practice to get the pressure right even when using a brush, but it is an ideal method to use for outlining both the straight parts of decorated letters as well as the surrounding coloured or gilded backgrounds (*see Alphabet Directory*). The angle of the brush can be adjusted easily to follow the contours. Where slight variations of line thickness do occur, it adds to, rather than detracts from, the liveliness of the letter, because it looks less mechanical.

You will need
- *Fine sable brush (size 0 or 00)*
- *Paint mixed ready to use, or ink*
- *Ruler*

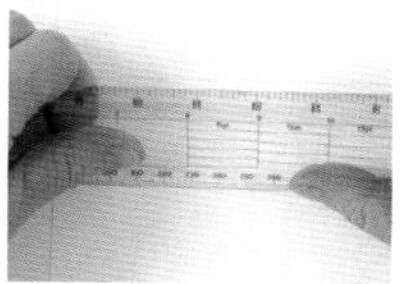

1 With the paper on a flat surface, align the ruler with a pre-drawn pencil line. Hold the ruler up at an angle, using your fingers as a rest.

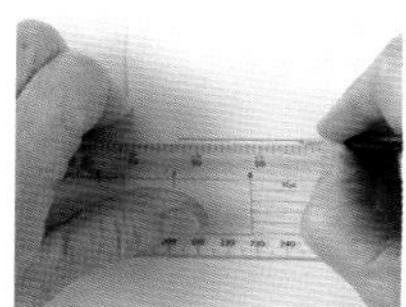

2 Load the bristles with either ink or paint, and then rest the brush's metal ferrule on the ruler. Lower the bristle onto the paper, and then move the brush along the ruler, keeping the pressure as even as you can to keep the same width of line throughout.

Using a ruling pen to rule lines

Ruling pens are draftsmen's tools that can be adjusted to produce reliable, if mechanical-looking, straight lines of different widths. As they can hold more ink or paint than brushes, they are perfect for ruling longer lines. Some have numbered dials to simplify selection and reselection of line width, rather than relying on guesswork.

You will need
- *Ruling pen*
- *Old brush, for loading the ruling pen*
- *Paint mixed ready to use, or ink*
- *Ruler*

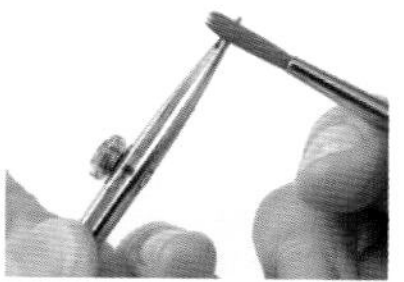

1 Adjust the turn screw on the ruling pen to the desired width and load with ink or paint. Wipe off any excess on absorbent paper or a rag.

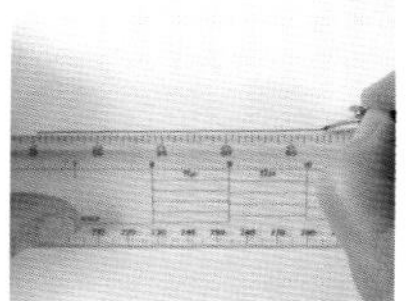

2 Rest the ruling pen on the angled ruler (as described for brush rules) and draw in the line.

Colour

We take for granted the bewilderingly wide range of colours available to us in easy-to-use tubes and pans. The palette of the early illuminators was much more restricted; they also had to make up the paints themselves. The raw materials were sourced either from animals and plants or from earth or semi-precious stones. Brown-black sepia came from the ink sacs of squids; blue was extracted from the wild plant woad; ochres and siennas are earth-based, and the highly prized pigment ultramarine was made by grinding lapis lazuli to a powder.

Many of the colours were poisonous and corrosive, to both the writing surface and the scribe. Some pigments were not permanent and would fade if exposed to light. Modern paints are mostly of synthetic origin, particularly where natural resources are dwindling. They are safer to use and more reliable in terms of permanence.

To use colour well and confidently, you need to know about the materials and how to use them. You will also need to do your own mixing experiments, so that you can see how the theory works in practice.

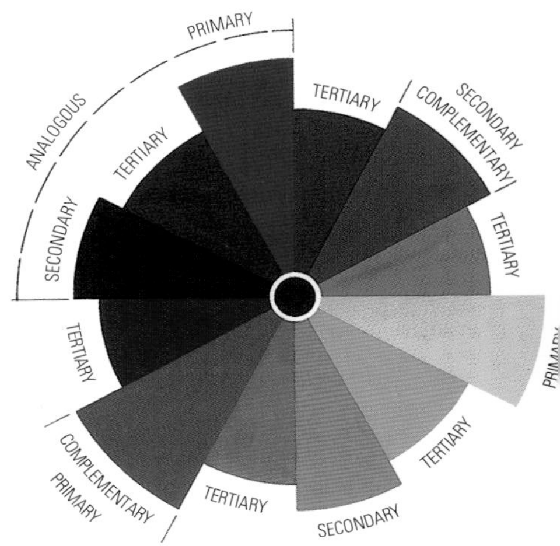

The colour wheel
Shows how primaries, mixed secondary and tertiary colours, and complementary and analogous colours relate to each other.

THE COLOUR WHEEL

Primary colours The basic colours, red, blue and yellow, which cannot be made by mixing.

Secondary colours Equal amounts of two primaries mixed together (for example, red + yellow = orange).

Tertiary colours Equal amounts of a primary and a secondary colour mixed together (for example, blue + green = deeper green).

Try mixing these colours yourself and see how many more subtle tones can be achieved by adjusting the balance of the two constituents.

Complementary colours These are directly opposite each other on the colour wheel (for example, blue and orange). You can mix any two primaries to get the complementary colour of the third (for example, red + yellow = orange, complementary of blue). Placed next to each other, complementary colours cause a visual disturbance, appearing to "vibrate" as the equal tones try to neutralize each other. Used in small amounts and strategically placed within a design, they can give vibrancy to the work.

Analogous colours These colours are next to each other on the colour wheel (blue, blue–purple and purple). Used together they give a feeling of unity and harmony.

MIXING COLOURS ACCURATELY

The theory of mixing all colours from three primaries is somewhat simplified. It is better to start with six basic colours, two reds, two blues and two yellows (*see below*) and understand how the colour bias of these can affect accurate mixes.

OTHER COLOUR MIXES

Grays can be made by mixing cerulean + scarlet lake or burnt sienna.

Shades Mix black with colours to make different shades. Use lamp black for cool shades and ivory black for warm shades. Adding colour to black gives the most reliable results (*see Tints, right*).

Tints (tones) Mix zinc white with colours for lightfast tints. To mix a related series of tones effectively (*as used in the Gothic alphabet, pages 168–179*), add the colour to white rather than vice versa, as the effect is easier to see. Use a multi-well palette and mix the tones side by side, so the relationship between light, medium and dark tones can be assessed easily.

Try them out on a scrap of the paper or vellum you intend to use, to make sure that the differences are correct when the colours have dried.

Primary colours

Look at the colours carefully and you can see the relative bias of each quite clearly. Mix with bias and the richest, most intense secondaries are formed. Mix against bias and the secondaries are duller, more subtle.

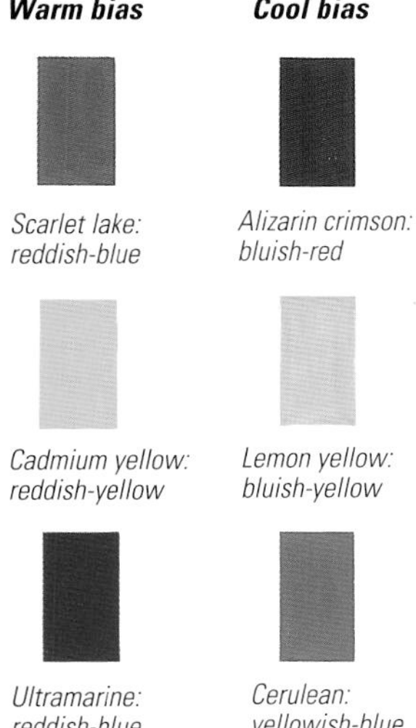

Mixing colours: How the bias of primaries affects secondaries

These mixes are all based on equal amounts of each colour. They show just a few possibilities; more subtle variations can be made either by mixing different primaries or by adjusting the proportions of each colour.

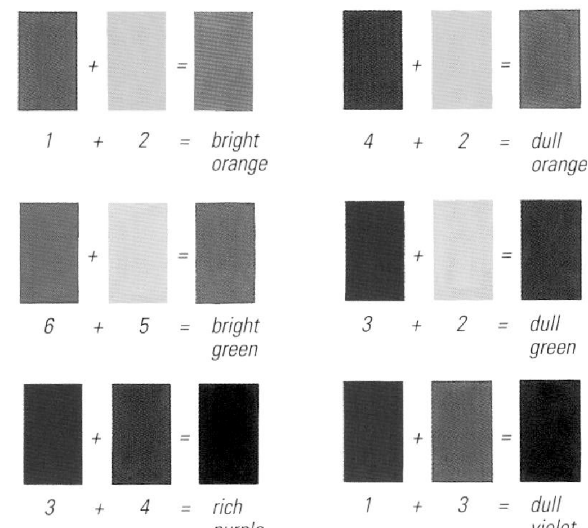

Planning Colour Schemes

Each decorated letter style included in this book has its own colour scheme, which is fairly limited and seldom varied. The predominant colours were most often rich reds and blues which, combined with gold, gave a very luxurious appearance. The Neo-Classical letters are the exception (*see pages 216–227*), employing some fairly striking and unexpected colour combinations, although they do relate to the colour wheel principles already mentioned.

When planning your own work, borders and other decorative elements need to be considered carefully so they complement, rather than compete with, the featured letter. Look at examples of whole pages from early illuminated manuscripts to get a feel for the style and colour content for each period. Rough out your designs (*see pages 58–59*) with coloured pencils to get the balance right, using the simple guidelines below, which hold good for both traditional and more modern ideas.

Colour schemes

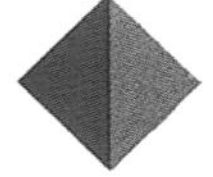

Add a touch of drama or contrast *Use a strong primary colour or gold sparingly to catch the eye. Two strongly contrasting colours will achieve the same effect.*

Don't overcrowd the colour scheme *Too many colours compete for attention and are distracting. If in doubt, keep it simple.*

Create harmony *Use a close tonal range of colours to create a feeling of unity or serenity. The analogous colours on the colour wheel can be used in this way.*

COLOUR ON COLOUR

This chart of coloured paint on coloured paper (*right*) shows clearly how they affect each other, so you can exploit the effects successfully in your work. Adjustments can be made in terms of paper or colour of paint (consider the Ottonian-style manuscript with gold letters on purple vellum, *see pages 113–114*), but the general principle still holds good.

- **Warm colours** come forward and are more dominant.
- **Cool colours recede** and are less dominant.
- **Dark on light dominates**; dark on dark recedes or even disappears.
- **Light on dark dominates**; light on light recedes or even disappears.
- **Colours close in tone** "vibrate" (*see complementary colours, page 74*).

COLOUR ROUGHS

Within each alphabet section, there are line drawings of each letter alongside some coloured examples to give you inspiration. Whether you wish to follow the set colour scheme or devise your own, use tracings or photocopies of the letter(s) on which to work out a pleasing balance of colour across the letter(s) using coloured pencils.

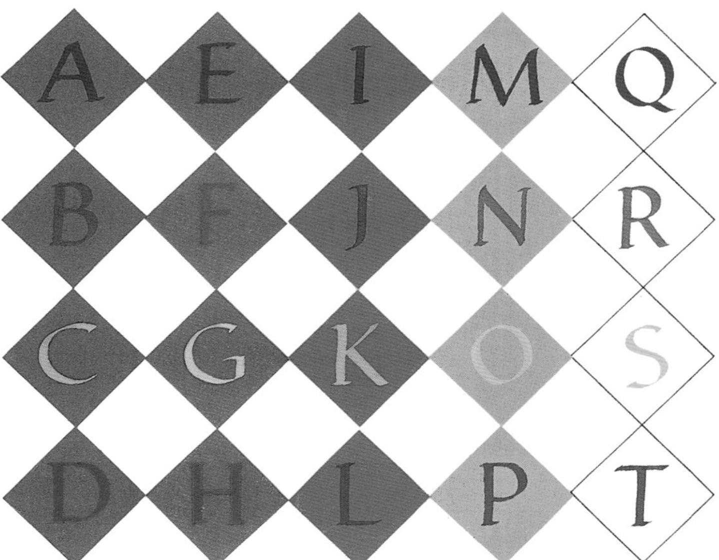

WRITING WITH COLOUR

The use of colour for main headings or text is sometimes beneficial within a design, so that attention is drawn to them. Either gouache or watercolour can be used for this. The paint needs to be mixed to the consistency of thin cream, slightly thinner than for painting flat areas of colour (*see page 40*), so that it flows smoothly from the nib.

Colour on colour

In this example, paint is used straight from the tube to write letters on mid-toned paper.

Tips for writing with colour

- Stir the paint frequently to stop pigments separating out.
- Clean the nib often, as with ink, to prevent the nib clogging up.
- Set the drawing board at a slightly shallower angle, which will stop the colour settling towards the bottom of the letters.
- Load the pen by feeding the paint between the nib and the reservoir with the mixing brush.
- Uneven paint flow can be improved by adding either a drop of ox-gall liquid or liquid gum arabic to the mix. Ox-gall helps adhesion as well as flow; gum arabic acts in a similar way, but adds an extra gloss to the colour when dry.
- If the paint is inclined to be sticky, put the gum arabic in the mixing water rather than the paint.
- Always use clean, distilled water for mixing colours and keep a large, separate jar of water to rinse out brushes thoroughly.

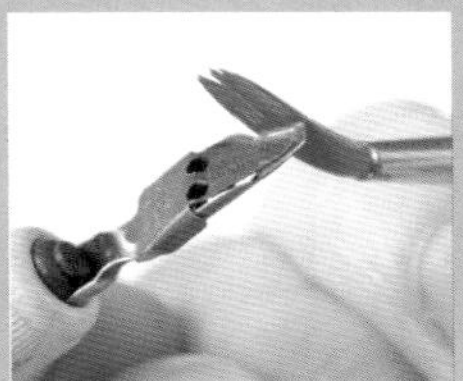

Loading nib with colour from brush.

Transferring Designs to Paper

When you have done all the hard work of refining the design and colour balance of the decorated letter you have chosen to use, you need to transfer the drawing to the vellum or paper before you can start your finished piece.

Old-fashioned carbon paper is not suitable because the ink is greasy and the marks made cannot easily be erased, but there are three simple alternative methods of achieving the design transfer, and each is described in the letter projects that follow.

Carbon transfer

Using the carbon transfer method is the easiest and quickest way to transfer your design to paper, and it uses the minimum of materials. This technique is used in the Romanesque and White Vine projects (*see pages 142–145 and 192–195*).

You will need

- *Sheet of tracing paper*
- *2B or 4B pencil*
- *Cotton wool*
- *2H pencil for tracing off*
- *Good paper or vellum*

1 Complete the final drawing in ink on tracing paper. Turn the drawing over and using either a 2B or a 4B pencil, go over the back of the drawing, just covering the lines.

2 Remove excess graphite by smoothing over the pencil marks with your finger or a small piece of cotton wool.

3 Place the drawing right side up in the correct position on paper or vellum, and then tape it down lightly into place with masking tape. Use a sharp 2H pencil to transfer the drawing by tracing the lines.

4 Remove the tracing paper to reveal the drawing. If some parts are a little pale, where your carbon transfer was too thin, go over these lines lightly with an HB pencil to fill in the gaps prior to the inking-in stage.

Graphite transfer paper

Making your own re-usable graphite transfer paper is easy.

You will need

- *A5 piece of tracing paper (approximately 60 gsm/16 lb)*
- *2B or 4B pencil or graphite stick*
- *Cotton wool*
- *Finished drawing on tracing paper*
- *Good paper or vellum*

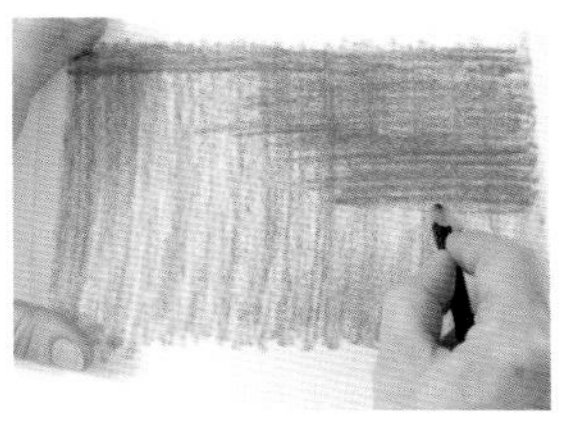

*1 You can cover a whole piece of tracing paper (A5 size) to make a re-usable sheet. Scribble down a good layer of carbon with vertical and horizontal strokes. Smooth down as step 2 (*opposite*).*

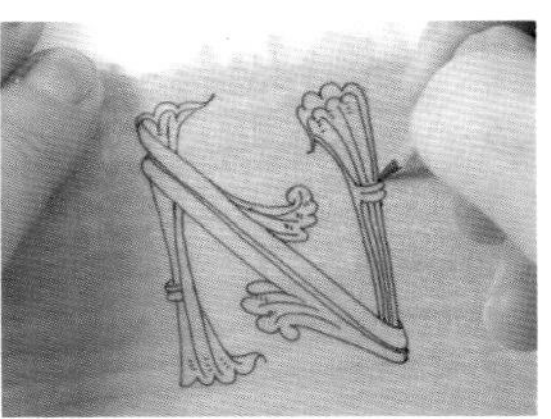

*2 Mask any writing already done to protect it from the carbon. Tape the good paper down onto the drawing board, having first ruled a base line. Line up the base of the letter with this line and tape down. Slip the carbon sheet between the good paper and tracing paper, and start drawing in, as step 3 (*opposite*).*

Red ochre carbon paper

This type of carbon paper was used for transferring designs to lithographic plates and was once available through art suppliers, but it is no longer made. It is simple, if a little messy, to make your own.

Because the "carbon" is red ochre, not graphite, it is easier to erase and to paint over. It is also more visible than graphite if you are working on darker coloured papers. It does tend to transfer pigment where you don't want it, so you will need to mask off any writing first. Red ochre carbon paper is used in the Ottonian project on page 116.

You will need

- *Newspaper or other scrap paper*
- *A4 sheet white acid-free tissue paper (cut down to size required)*
- *Red ochre powder (ground artist's pigment)*
- *China palette*
- *Cotton wool*
- *Rubber gloves (to stop your fingers getting stained)*
- *2H pencil for tracing off*
- *Finished drawing on tracing paper*
- *Good paper or vellum*

1 Cover the work surface with newspaper and spread the tissue on top of this. Tip out some pigment into a china palette.

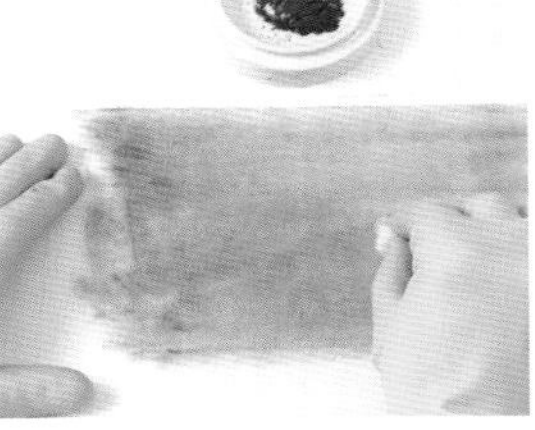

2 Dip the cotton wool into the red ochre powder and rub it into the tissue paper, working out from the centre of the sheet to the edges. Keep adding more pigment and rubbing it in until the sheet is well covered.

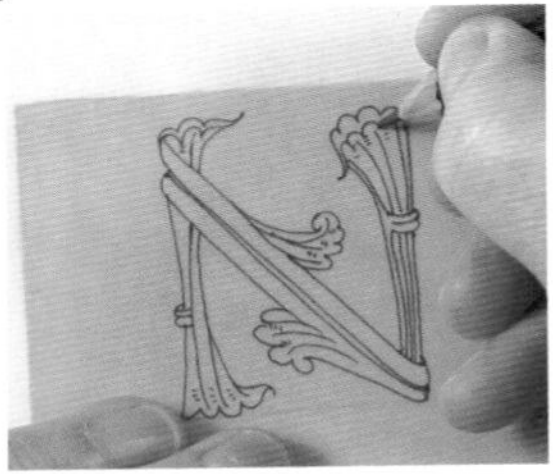

3 Shake off any excess pigment (best done outside), then use the paper in exactly the same way as a carbon transfer sheet (see page 78).

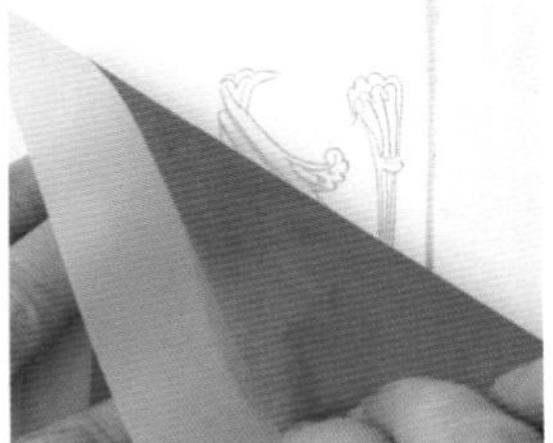

4 Peel back tracing and carbon sheet to check that the drawing has been transferred.

Transferring designs onto black or other very dark-coloured papers
Use the method described for carbon transfer on page 78, substituting a white watercolour pencil for the 2B or 4B pencil to go over the back of the drawing. However, note that some coloured pencil leads can be rather greasy, making errors difficult to erase and less easy to paint over.

Light box

If you have access to a light box (lit by fluorescent tubes below an opaque Perspex sheet to give good, even lighting), it is a very effective tool for transferring designs. If you don't have a light box, you can tape the drawing and good paper to a convenient window (so the daylight will reveal the design) and draw in the design as step 2, below. It is not quite so comfortable, as you have to work vertically.

The light box method is used for the Celtic and Neo-Classical projects (*see pages 92 and 217*).

You will need

- *Light box*
- *Masking tape*
- *HB or F pencil*
- *Good paper or vellum*
- *Spare sheet of paper for protecting the work from grease*

1 Tape the finished design to the light box surface with masking tape. Switch on the light box and tape the vellum or paper in position over the design. (Rule a baseline on the vellum or paper first, and then line this up with the base of the traced letter.)

2 With a guard sheet under your hand to protect the work from any transfer of grease, draw in the image very lightly using an HB or F pencil. Take care not to press too hard or the vellum (or paper) surface will be indented, which will be difficult to disguise.

Using Illumination and Decoration

Creating facsimiles of whole manuscript pages or even single letters in the different historical decorative styles is useful for familiarizing yourself with the traditional tools, techniques and materials already described, but sooner or later you will want to incorporate their decorative themes into your own work.

Traditional decoration can be quite readily adapted for more modern applications – study good historical examples (as shown in the history pages for each alphabet and in the books listed in Further Reading on page 252) and extract the essence of each style to suit your purpose, whether it be books, broadsheets, special occasion presentations, greetings cards, bookmarks or even personal stationery.

Use thumbnail sketches and the paste-up layout technique (*see pages 69–71*) to explore the possibilities.

Traditional ideas

Learn about traditional techniques by copying historic manuscripts, either single letters or whole pages. The layouts here and on page 82 were sketched from original sources. Look at the history pages and the books in Further Reading on page 252 for good photographic reference to decorative details and colours.

Celtic

Celtic

Ottonian

Romanesque

Gothic

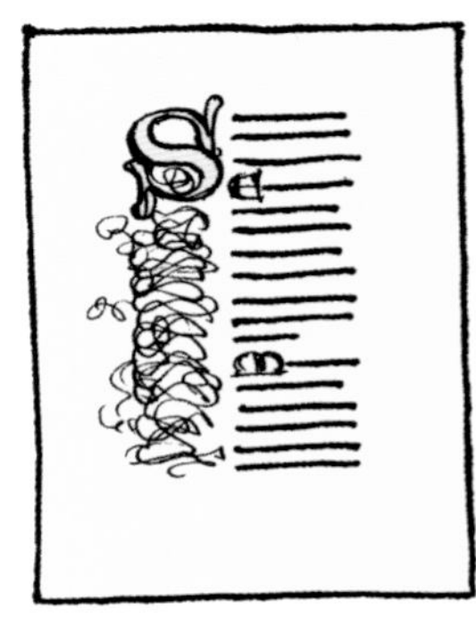

Gothic

White Vine

White Vine

Neo-Classical

Neo-Classical

Modern uses

Extract ideas and elements from original manuscripts and adapt them for your own use. Decorative borders can enliven large broadsheets as well as small calligraphic panels, greetings cards, bookmarks or even personalized stationery. Decorated letters can be incorporated in a similar way. Use thumbnail sketches like these to start with, followed by a paste-up layout (see pages 70–71) *to firm up your ideas.*

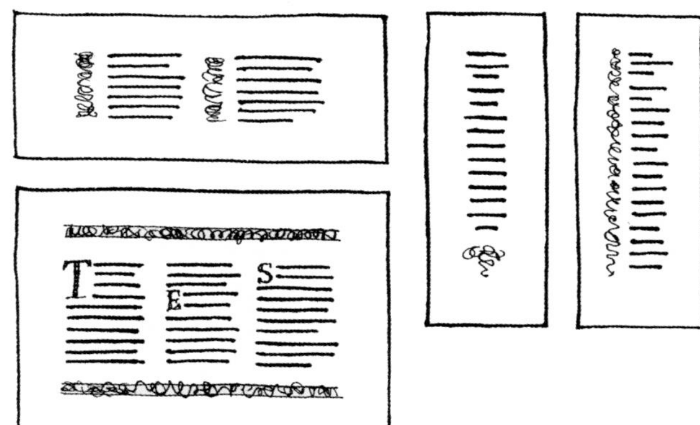

Borders on broadsheets and small calligraphic panels.

Incorporating decorated letters.

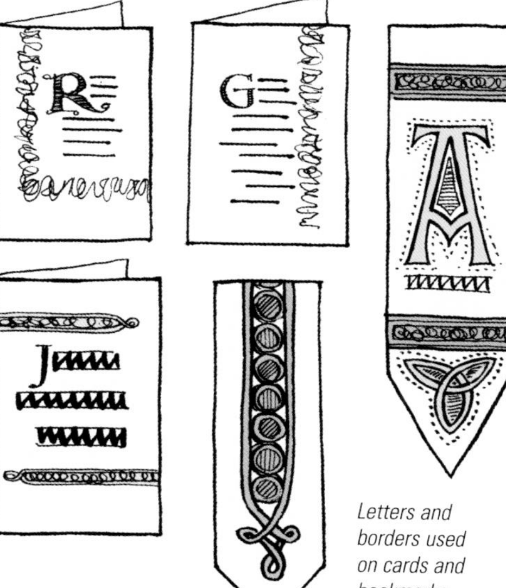

Letters and borders used on cards and bookmarks.

Chapter 3

Alphabet Directory

This chapter contains complete decorated alphabets and numbers based on six different historic styles, ranging from 7th-century Celtic to 15th-century Renaissance. All the various techniques described in the two previous chapters are employed in the creation of these beautiful letters, with step-by-step projects to guide you. The special alphabet sections are each followed by a selection of scripts suitable for writing out accompanying text.

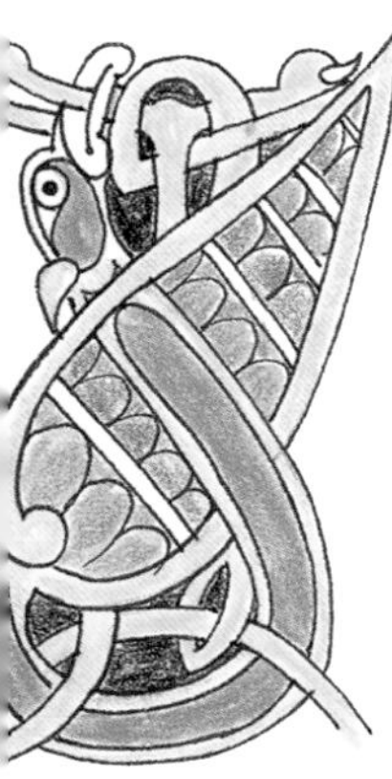

Celtic

The talent of the monastic artist–scribes responsible for creating these early decorated manuscripts was prodigious. In spite of having only a limited palette of colours, which they made themselves from local materials, the complex patterns of spirals, knots, animals and birds glow richly on the page, enhanced by the surrounding characteristic rows of red dots.

Celtic

The earliest flowering of illuminated manuscripts in the West began in Ireland in the 7th century, when the monks of St. Columba wrote out and decorated service books for their own use.

As missionaries, they also used these books on their travels to spread the word of God to the pagan areas of Britain and Europe, where they founded monastic settlements. The decorative style they developed incorporated elements of Celtic, Germanic, Antique and early Christian art. It is known as Insular, which reflects the close cultural relationship of Ireland and Britain at that time.

The *Book of Kells* and the *Lindisfarne Gospels* are the most outstanding examples of this period, although the styles of illumination in the two books have distinct differences. The decoration has many similarities with stone carving, jewellery and other metalwork of the period, using richly stylized patterns that incorporate animals and birds.

The *Lindisfarne Gospels* (which have been used as the basis of the alphabet that follows on pages 92–103) are thought to have been made around 715–720 by one artist–scribe working in the island monastery of Lindisfarne in the northeast of England. The opening pages of each gospel are a well-ordered mixture of colour and

▶ ***The Lindisfarne Gospels***
Cotton MS Nero D.iv fol. 211r
England, Northumberland, c.698
The initial page of St. John's Gospel: Interlacing, knots, spirals and zoomorphic forms in a rich palette of colours combine to form these wonderfully complex patterns. Following the spectacular opening INP, the rest of the text on this page is written in the angular, spiky capitals that have their counter spaces filled with colour. Red dots not only outline the letters, but are also used to make intricate infill decorations.

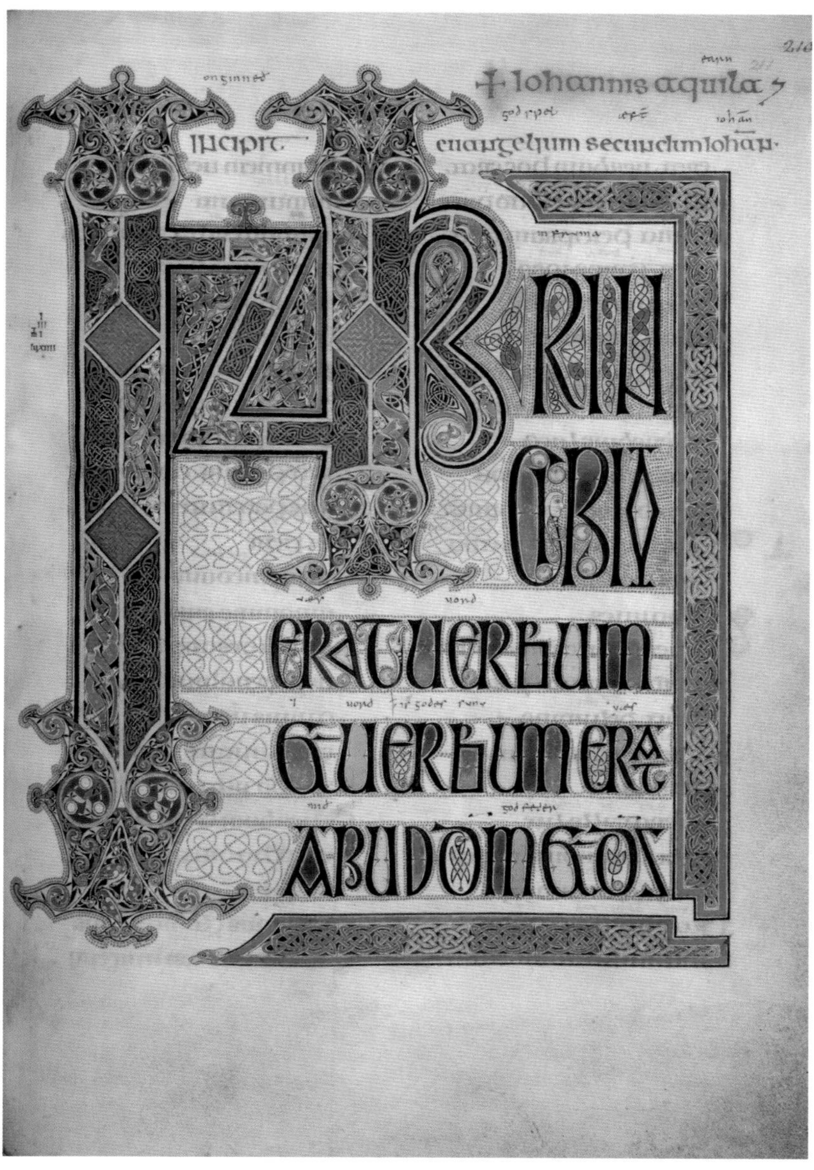

complex pattern, both within and around the letters. The letterforms fall into two categories: one is a form of the Insular half uncial hand (*see page 104*) used to write the text, the second is composed of angular capitals. Both types have been compressed into tall, narrow shapes to suit the design of the page. The changes of size and the degree of decoration of letters down the page are reminiscent of banner headlines and subheadings in a newspaper.

The use of both letterforms in the same line of text provides visual interest. They are unified by the colour scheme and the outline of red dots. These red dots were also used to create whole areas of infill patterns. The pigments used were varied and brilliant. Gold was available but was not part of the illuminator's repertoire, so a rich yellow pigment called orpiment was often used instead.

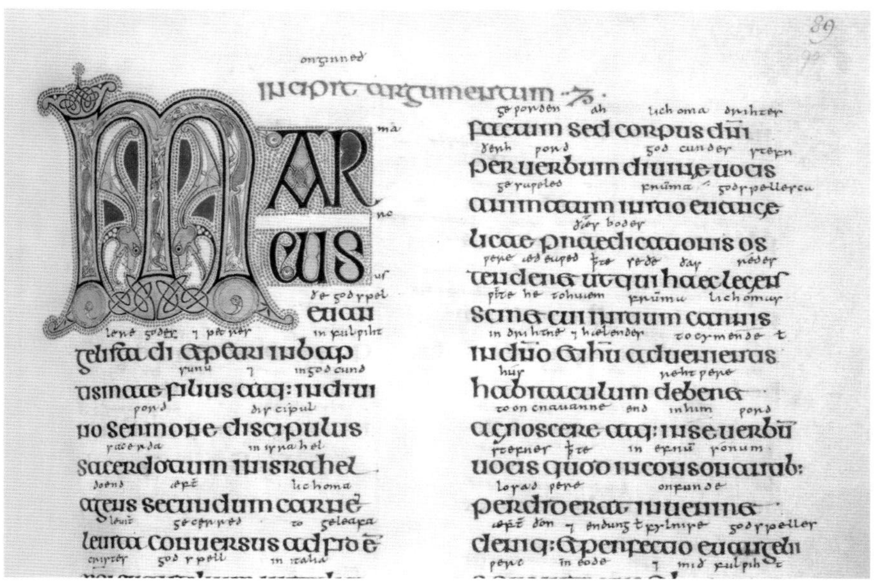

◄ ***The Book of St. Chad***
MS 1 p.220
England, second quarter of 8th century

The carpet page preceding the opening of the Gospel of St. Luke: This is a page of pure, exuberant decoration, with intricately intertwined strapwork and animal forms filling the central cruciform shape, as well as the outer borders. Colours are rather more subtle than those on the Lindisfarne Gospels.

▲ ***The Lindisfarne Gospels***
Cotton MS Nero D.iv, fol. 90 (detail)
England, Northumberland, c.698

Decorated initials from the preliminaries of St. Mark's Gospel: The apostle's name appears with an initial decorated with knots, spirals and stylized animal heads. The text follows in the characteristic Insular half uncial. The tiny writing between the lines of uncials is a translation of the Latin into Anglo–Saxon.

Celtic Initial "U"

The bright yellow pigment, orpiment (yellow arsenic sulfide), was most often used in Insular-style manuscripts of the period. It gave off a gold-like glow due to the proximity of other rich colours used around it. Here, an imitation gold gouache is used, which can be polished to a soft sheen. Note that the colours are thin washes, rather than thick and flat.

Tools and materials

- *HB pencil*
- *Tracing paper*
- *300gsm (140 lb) hot-pressed watercolour paper*
- *4B pencil for carbon transfer* or *a light box* (see pages 78–80)
- *Dilute waterproof black ink*
- *Fine pointed nib (Gillott 659 or mapping pen)*
- *Kneaded rubber eraser*
- *Sable brushes, sizes 0, 00, 000*
- *Glassine*
- *Dogtooth agate burnisher*
- *Synthetic fibre brush, size 000, for dots*

Gouache paints

- *Vandyke brown*
- *Lamp black*
- *Imitation gold*
- *Lemon yellow*
- *Permanent green deep*
- *Zinc white*
- *Alizarin crimson*
- *Scarlet lake*
- *Permanent white*
- *Distilled water for mixing*

1 Trace the outline of the letter onto the tracing paper using an HB pencil.

2 Transfer the design to the watercolour paper, using either a 4B pencil over the back of the drawing or the light box method (see pages 78–80).

3 Use a fine nib and dilute waterproof ink to outline the knotwork areas in the central space and in the letter itself.

4 Carefully remove any visible pencil marks in the knotwork areas with a piece of kneaded eraser.

5 Mix Vandyke brown and lamp black gouache (approximately 1:3) and fill in the spaces of the interlaced pattern in the body of the letter using a size 00 sable brush.

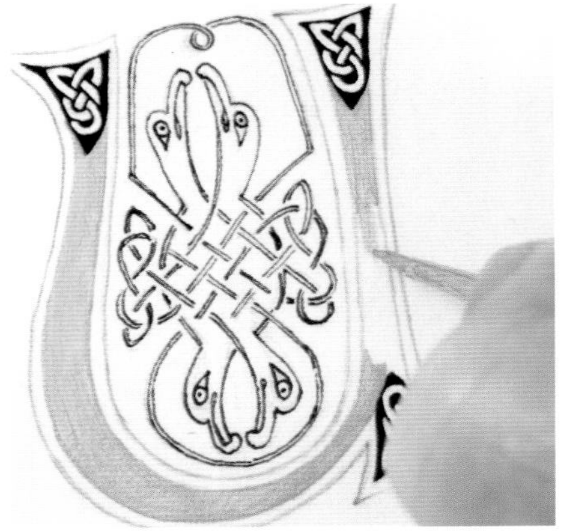

6 Use the same size brush to paint in the letter shape and the centre of the knot with a reasonably thick mixture of gold gouache to give an even coverage. Start with small blobs of paint and tease out to the edges and corners.

7 When the paint is quite dry, burnish it gently through glassine to smooth any unevenness.

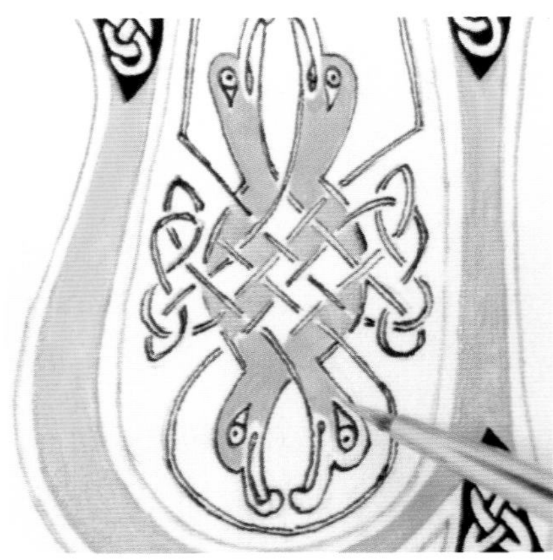

8 Mix lemon yellow + permanent green deep + a little zinc white to give a soft green wash. Use this to fill in the birds' heads.

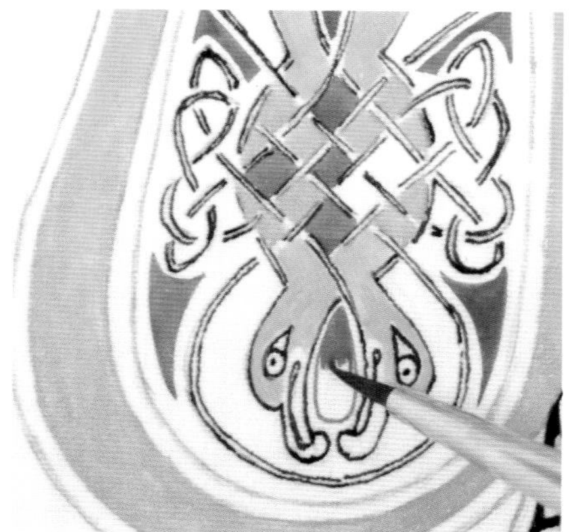

9 Next, add the remaining details of the knotwork in a dark red wash (alizarin crimson + a little scarlet lake).

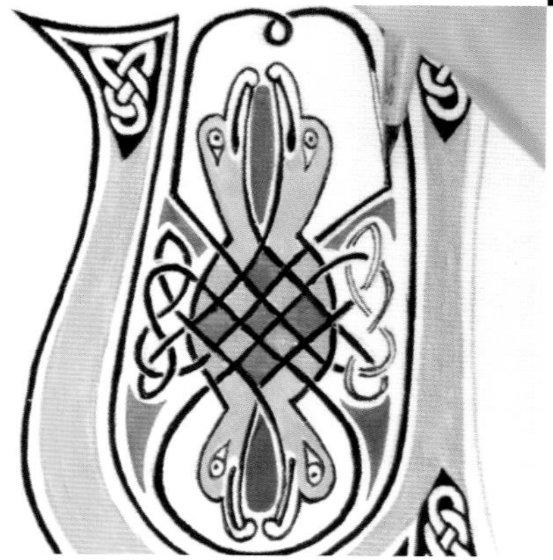

10 With the brown/black paint mixture used in step 5, use a size 00 or 000 sable brush to paint the outline of the letter, the interlacing and the birds' heads in the central space.

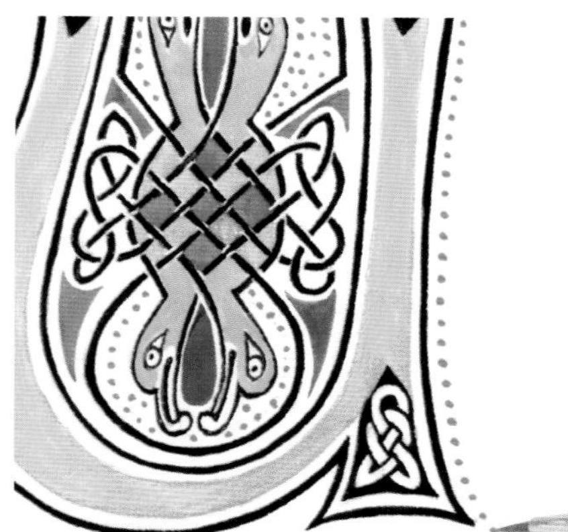

11 Finally, add red (scarlet lake) dots with the fine synthetic brush, keeping the pressure even. Fill in the dots in the centre first, and then add two rows all around the outside of the letter. Try to keep the dots small. You can tidy up mistakes with permanent white gouache.

12 The finished letter. Outlining the interlacing with dilute waterproof ink at step 3 should have enabled you to lay the coloured washes and still see the pattern clearly enough to paint the knotwork in brown/black gouache at step 10.

Celtic Oval letters

*The letters on pages 96 and 97 are adapted forms of the Insular uncial text hand of Celtic manuscripts (*see page 104*). Compressing the shape while retaining the relative proportions means that more and larger letters could be included on each line. The body of the letter can be varied in several ways, such as a black outline around colour (*see left, and page 95*), solid black or black with an inset line of colour and some knotwork (*see opposite*).*

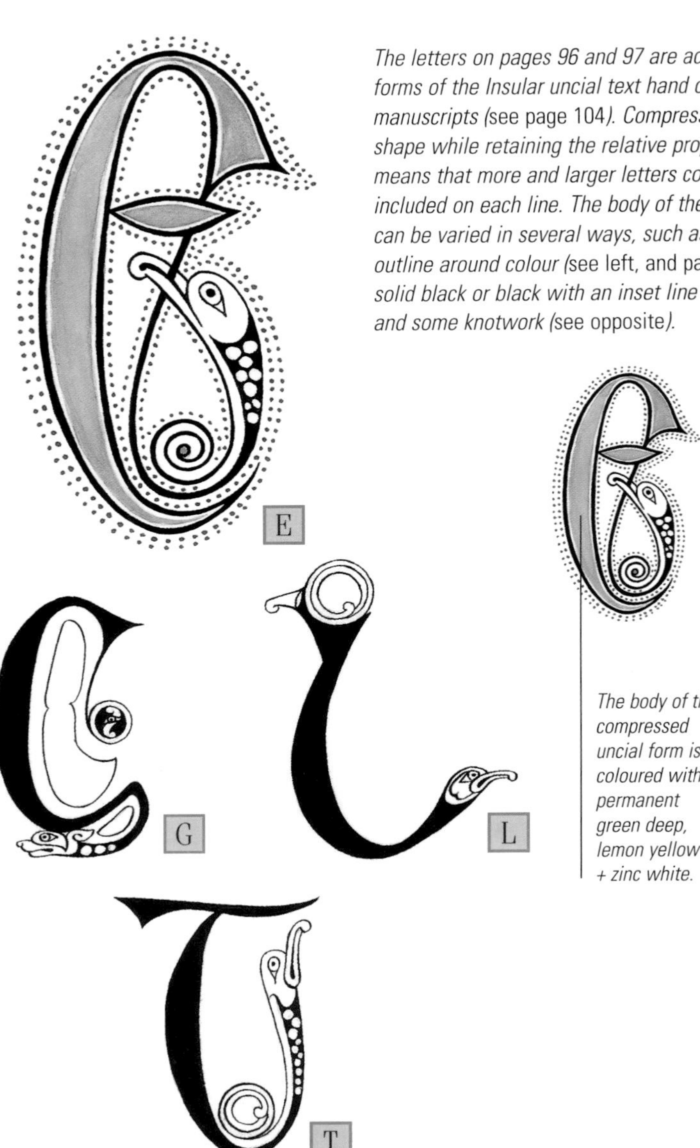

The body of this compressed uncial form is coloured with permanent green deep, lemon yellow + zinc white.

All the large letters used like headlines on title pages, or for marking important divisions in the text of chapter or verse, have two and sometimes three layers of red dots around them. Sometimes the dots were used to enclose the negative shapes of letters or to make decorative patterns as line fillers.

B

A fine line of yellow (cadmium yellow pale + raw sienna) lights up both the body and the centre of the knotwork in this compressed uncial B. Scarlet lake + purple lake are used for the dark red areas.

C

D

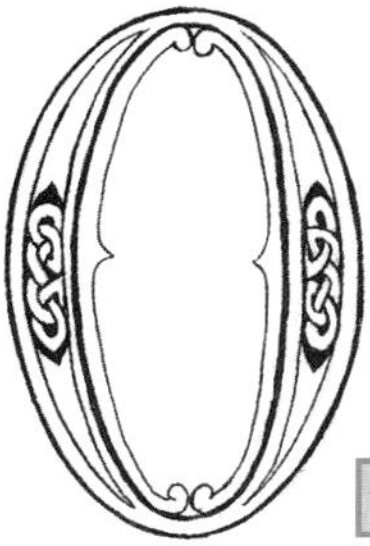

O

Celtic Arched letters

*Colours are the same as those used for F and A. The design could be varied by inserting a human or animal head (*see the C, page 97, or the M on this page*); the knotwork is similar to that on page 97. The letter U, which is the project on pages 92–95, is also part of this group.*

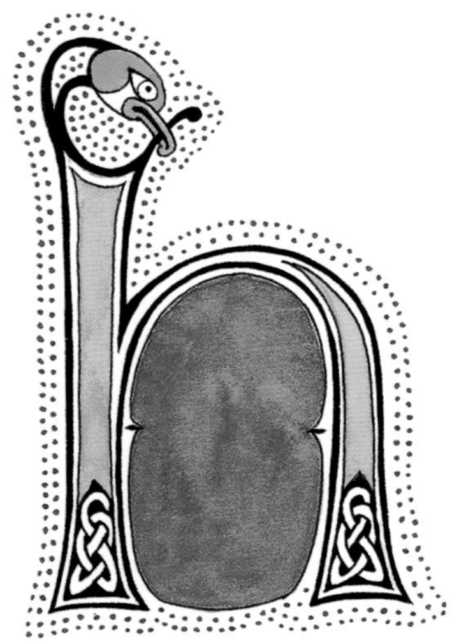

H

There are many different variations in the type of heads used to decorate Celtic letters; several are shown below and opposite, as well as on pages 96 and 97.

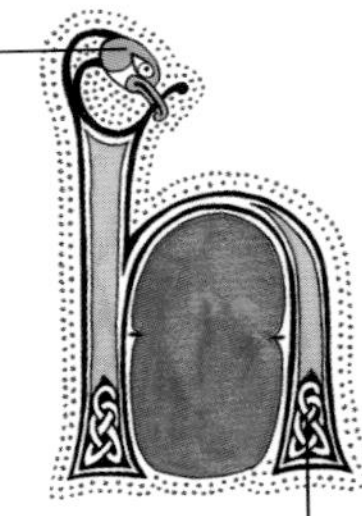

Knotwork or interlaced patterns of varying degrees of complexity are often used within the letter shape as well as in the internal spaces like W and N below.

K

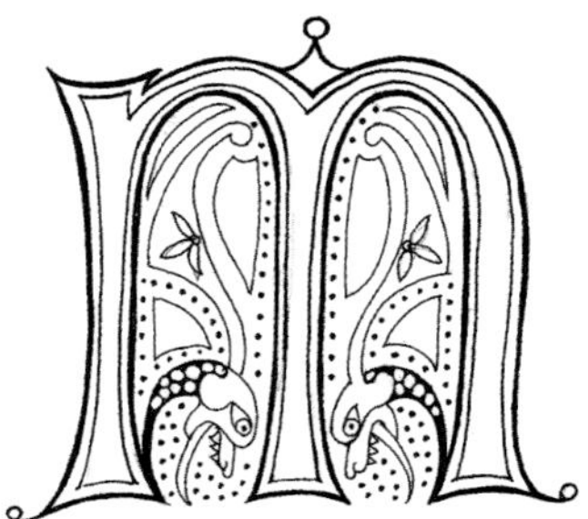

N

W

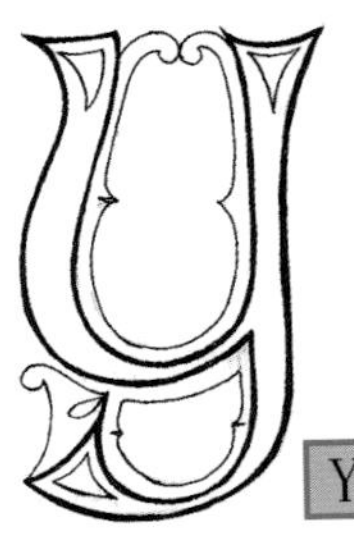

Y

Celtic Curved letters

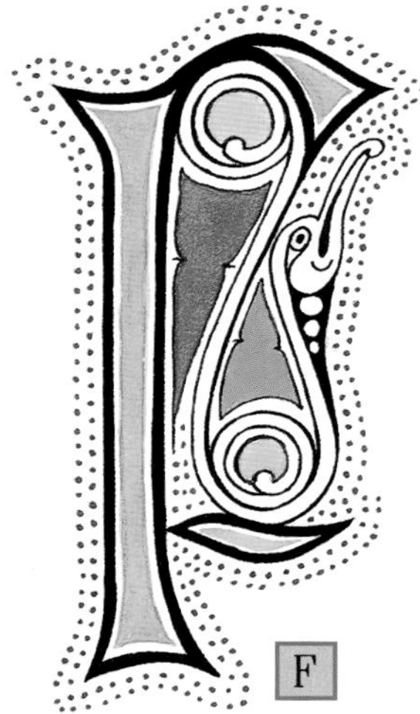

F

Letter outline as on page 95. Other colours are the same as for A. The letter outline here (and on several of the letters opposite) is painted in the same way as described in step 10 of the project on page 95, in a mixture of brown and black gouache. The colour infill is cadmium yellow + raw sienna, although you could use gold gouache as in the project.

Spirals are commonly occurring motifs in Celtic manuscripts. A few of the possible variations are shown on page 109.

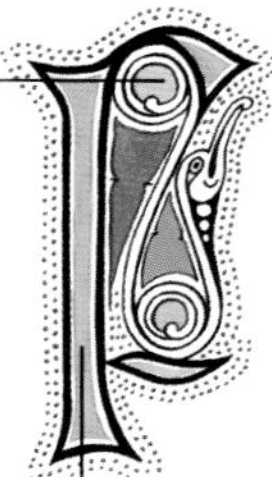

The colour mixes used in the painting of F are the same for A on page 100, using a paler red wash within the letter and a stronger red in the top enclosed space.

B

P

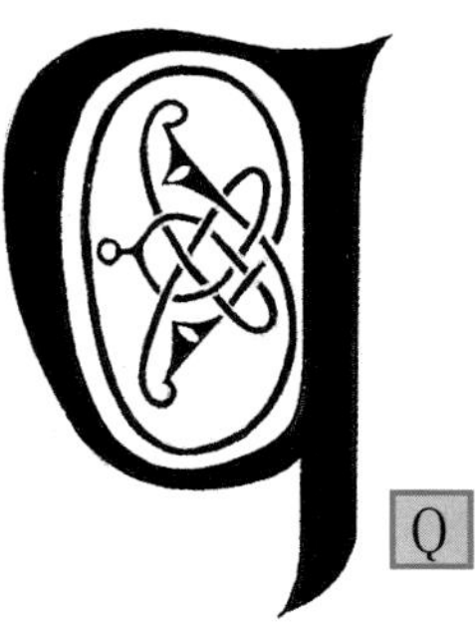

Q

R

S

Celtic Diagonal letters

This letter shows the angular, spiky capital form in contrast to the uncial-related shape of A below.

The small areas of yellow enclosed in these interlaced patterns could be painted either in gold gouache or with real gold leaf on gum ammoniac (see page 53).

This letter is painted in permanent green deep + lemon yellow + zinc white. The red wash is scarlet + a little purple lake. Details in the interlacing are cadmium yellow + raw sienna. Z and V were not originally found in alphabets of this period, but have been designed here in the spiky capital form.

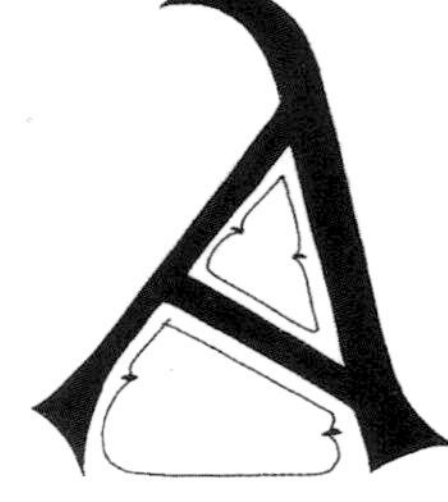

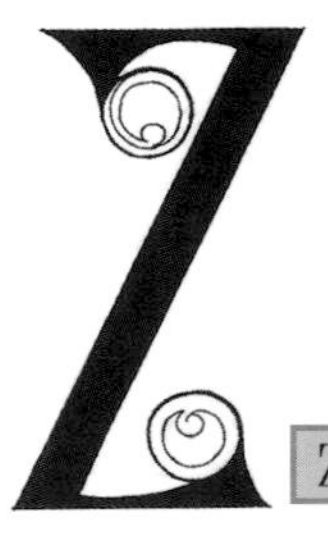

Celtic Narrow letters

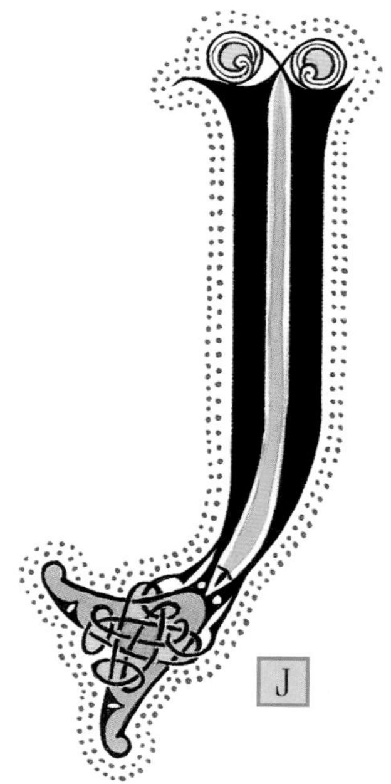

The spirals at the head of the letter are formed by extending the inner corners of the serifs of the two downstrokes. Look at other spiral designs on page 109.

The downstrokes are extended into this complex interlaced toe, using the same green, red and yellow mixes as in A (opposite).

The colour mixes used are the same as for A (opposite). The letterforms below are all spiky capitals, although I as a single stroke is the same in the uncial style. Spiky and uncial letters have the same characteristic wide serifs at head and foot.

Celtic Numbers

Numbers used in these early manuscripts, particularly in the canon tables, were plain Roman numerals, so these decorative numbers have been devised specially for this alphabet, incorporating the most common motifs and interlaced patterns. The stylized bird is compressed and folded into the bowl of the number. The blue is a wash made from ultramarine + cerulean blue + some zinc white. A deeper shade of blue is found in borders and in the complex designs on carpet pages.

The pigments used by the monks for painting these intricate designs were ground to a fine powder (similar to the technique shown on pages 44–45) and mixed with beaten egg white (glair) as a binding medium.

*The body of the number could be changed to an outline containing a colour infill (*see 1 (opposite) and letters on pages 92–101 for ideas*)*.

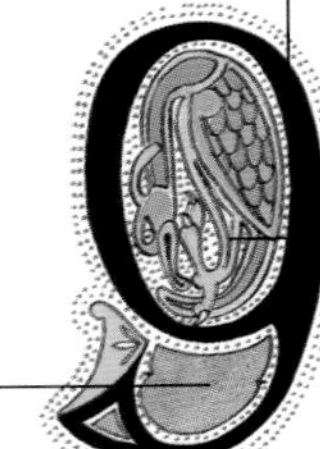

The bright red/orange pigment was made of toasted lead.

The purples, crimsons and blues used in the original manuscripts of this time were made by adding acid or alkali to plant extracts like woad (blue) and lichen (purple).

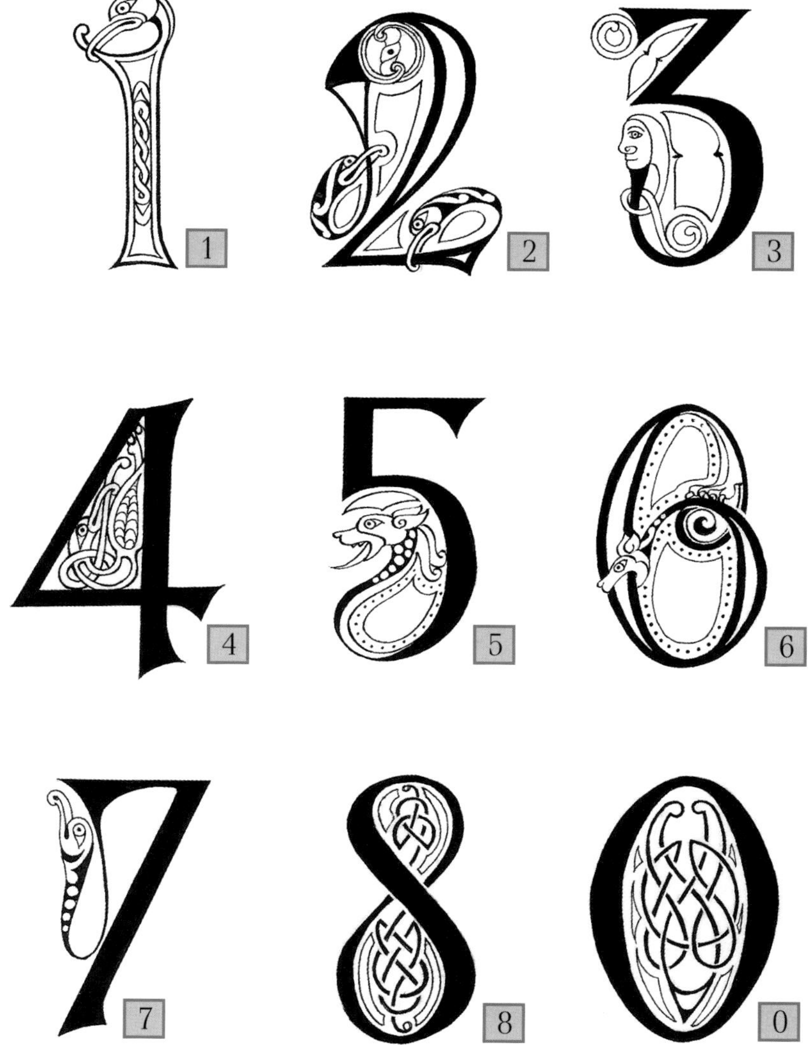
1
2
3
4
5
6
7
8
0

Insular Half Uncials

These pages show a basic half uncial hand and numerals, as well as some suggested variations, which are suitable for text incorporated into more complex projects (*see pages 69–71 and 81–83*). Study the letters carefully to observe their shapes and how they are formed, using the numbered strokes. Letter height is given in the nib width "ladders" and this remains constant whichever size nib you choose.

The pen angle diagrams indicate the angle at which the nib is held to the horizontal writing line, in order to achieve the naturally occurring thicks and thins typical of the letter style. Look to see where these are. Practice is needed to keep this angle consistent as you write. Try this exercise to help you: Use either the diagram or a protractor to check the angle and "set" your pen nib against it in relation to the writing line, then make a letter shape using your whole arm to move the pen, rather than just your fingers. Check the thicks and thins, and adjust your pen angle as needed. Note that significant pen manipulation is required in some of the letters; this is indicated by red asterisks as appropriate and approximate pen angles are given in the list below.

This is a very rounded, curvy Celtic hand (including the original form of "g"), which stands on its own as a complete alphabet without accompanying capital letters. This style evolved alongside uncials between the 7th and 11th centuries; it is especially suited to early Christian texts (*see page 91*).

Hold the pen very flat (only 5–15°) to make thick verticals with thin tops and bottoms of curved letters. The wedge-shaped serifs add weight to compensate for that thinness; make them by adding a separate curved stroke, which is blended carefully into the main stem. If you look at the relevant letters opposite, the directional arrows will help you work this out. Keep the ascenders and descenders short. Alter pen angles for certain strokes on the following letters (angles are approximate and will take some practice to get right):

"d," stroke 3: 40°
"g" (archaic form), stroke 1: 30°
"t," stroke 1: 45°
"z," stroke 3: towards the end of the stroke, turn the pen to about 35°, using the left-hand side of the nib to make the curve.

Calligraphy by Mary Noble

5° 15°

a b c d

e f g h i j

k l m n o p

q r s t u v

w x y z ß

& ! ? ; è û é

Insular Half Uncials Numbers

Insular Half Uncials Anglo-Saxon

This is another form, with soft wedges on some serifs. Two "r"s are shown. The third letter that appears to be an "r" is actually an ancient form of "s"! This style was used to write the translation between the lines of Latin in the Lindisfarne Gospels (see page 89).

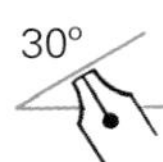

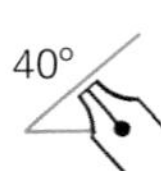

Insular Half Uncials No wedges

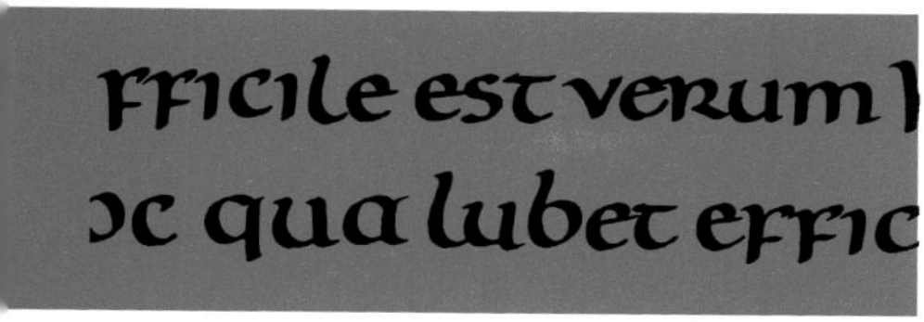

fficile est verum h
oc qua lubet effic

A freer version with a more comfortable pen angle and curved serifs. Notice how the curve on "h", "m", "r" and "p" branches from the main stem.

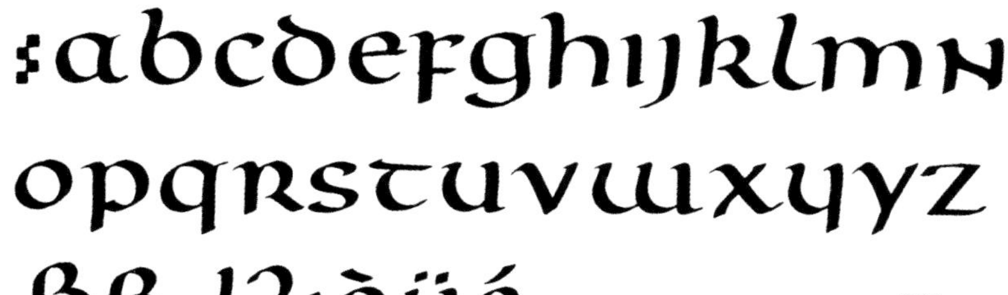

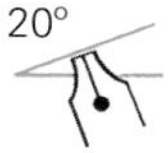

abcdefghijklmn
opqrstuvwxyz
ß&!?;èüé

20°

Insular Half Uncials Lightweight

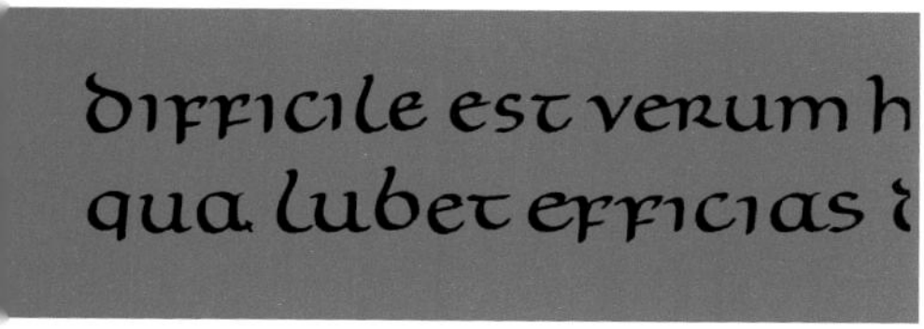

difficile est verum h
qua lubet efficias

The body height of the letter is 6 nib widths, with curved serifs and branched arches. Keep the letters open and matching in width.

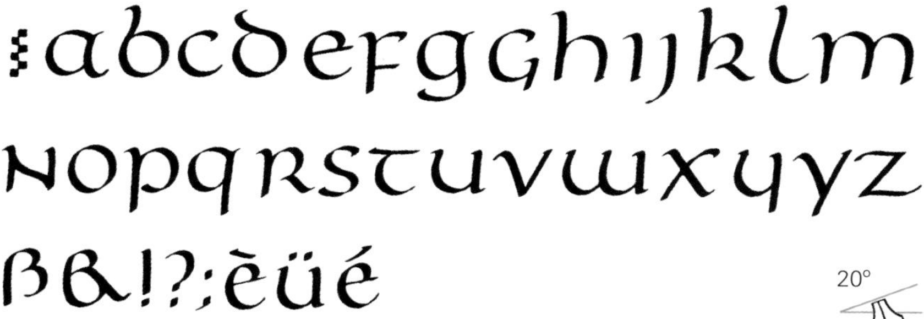

abcdefgGhijklm
nopqrstuvwxyz
ß&!?;èüé

20°

Borders and Motifs

Celtic illumination shows infinite variety and great imagination. Although the scribes worked with a limited palette of colours, they made up for this "lack" with an awe-inspiring ability to use basic motifs in incredibly complex patterns. Although carpet and incipit pages incorporate spirals, knots, dots and zoomorphic forms, they are all quite different from one another. These coloured sketches show just a few possibilities.

Borders, letter shapes and terminal decorations utilize stylized zoomorphic forms such as these.

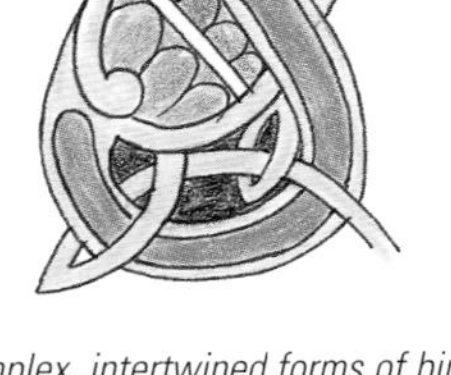

"Biting" forms are commonly used.

*Complex, intertwined forms of birds and beasts are used in borders and letters (*see also pages 92–103*).*

Human forms are less common, but are drawn in a similar, simplified way.

Geometric patterns.

Spirals are often used.

Interlacing in knots and braids.

Knots and braids are used in alternating colours.

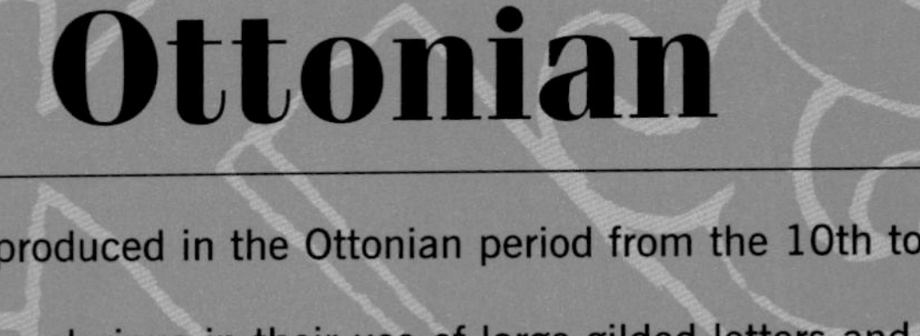

Ottonian

The manuscripts produced in the Ottonian period from the 10th to the early 11th century were glorious in their use of large gilded letters and coloured vellum pages. A simple colour scheme of purple-blue, light green and outlines in red enhances the richness of the effect.

Ottonian

The Ottonian dynasty ruled the eastern part of the Carolingian Empire, in modern-day Germany, from 919 to 1024. Its extensive patronage, as well as that of its clerics and courtiers, encouraged the art of illumination to flourish and develop.

The Ottonian court travelled from place to place and had no court scribes. The making of books was not something that could be done while constantly on the move, so manuscript production was encouraged around the realm to satisfy the Ottonians' desire for luxurious volumes. The most important illuminated books of this period were made in the monastic scriptoria at Echternach, Reichenau and Regensburg, and the luxurious nature of the manuscripts commissioned by the Ottonian emperors demonstrated their huge wealth.

The style of the illumination is recognizably a continuation of Carolingian art, but enriched by influences from Anglo–Saxon England in the Celtic feel of the interlaced patterns, and by Italy and Byzantium in the painting of figures, which is most reminiscent of icons. Otto II married Theophano, a Byzantine princess, and her influence played a significant role in the transmission of Byzantine style to the West.

Many of the books of this period were sumptuously decorated manuscripts for use in church services. They are characterized by a lavish use of gold, as well as purple

▶ ***Trier Gospels***
Latin MS 98, fol. 1v
Germany, Trier, late 10th century
The opening of St. Jerome's letter to Pope Damasus, which precedes the Gospels. Flat gilding, which is used lavishly on this page, shines out of the deep purple and green background colours and surrounds the acanthus leaf borders. Note the decoration on the central letter B, which clearly derives from the Celtic knotwork from three centuries earlier.

SIMO PA PAEDA
MASO HERONIMUS

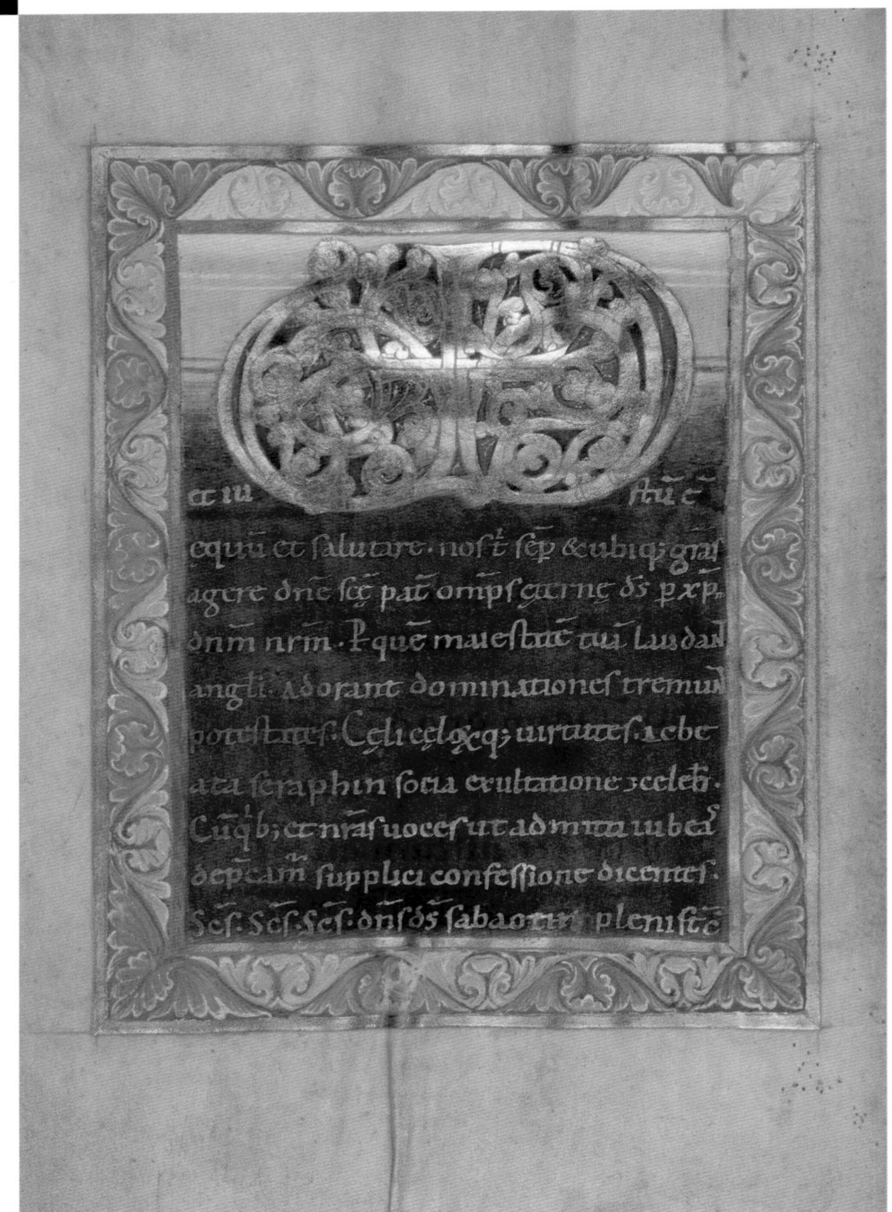

◀ ***Sacramentary***
MS Ludwig V2 (83.MF.77) fol. 21v
Germany, Mainz, mid-11th century

Incipit (initial) page: The acanthus leaf and gilded border contains an area of text written in a fine Carolingian hand, in shell gold on a dyed purple background. The whole page, particularly the splendid gold initial, is a prime example of the style of illuminating and lettering which influenced the Renaissance scribes.

▲ ***Gregori Moralium, Libri XI–XVI***
Latin MS 118, fol. 2r
German, 10th–11th century

Decorated letters such as this provided inspiration for the White Vine style letters of the Italian Renaissance scribes. The complexity of the design is complemented by the simple clarity of the script. The bright orange-red used both for outline and infill is characteristic.

pages that indicated imperial connotations. Sheets of vellum were dyed or painted purple with a dye derived from murex, a tropical marine mollusc.

The illuminated letters are often quite large and, characteristic of the period, decorated with interlinked foliated branches with patches of intense flat colour in the spaces they create. Red, rather than black, outlines complement the richness of both gold and colour. The text of such decorated pages fitted around the dominant letter.

Ottonian Initial "K"

On this initial, two layers of transfer gold are laid on a base of gum ammoniac, a technique known as flat gilding (*see page 53*). Patches of light blue and green and the red outline lend a glow to the gold, enhanced in original manuscripts by the dyed purple vellum on which the letters were drawn. Note that the branched stems grow directly out of the letters.

Tools and materials

- *HB pencil*
- *Tracing paper*
- *300 gsm (140 lb) hot-pressed watercolour paper*
- *Red ochre carbon paper (*see page 79*)*
- *Dilute waterproof black ink*
- *Fine pointed nib (Gillott 659 or mapping pen)*
- *Soft plastic eraser*
- *Gum ammoniac solution*
- *Old brush (size 0) for applying size*
- *Transfer gold*
- *Glassine*
- *Dogtooth agate burnisher*
- *Large soft brush*
- *Piece of soft washed silk*
- *Sable brushes, sizes 0, 00*
- *Ox-gall liquid*

Gouache paints

- *Ultramarine*
- *Spectrum violet*
- *Zinc white*
- *Permanent green deep*
- *Cadmium yellow pale*
- *Scarlet lake*
- *Distilled water for mixing*

1 Stir the gum ammoniac solution thoroughly and leave for the bubbles to disperse (see page 53). Trace off the design using the outline above.

2 Transfer the design to watercolour paper using a sheet of red ochre carbon paper (see page 79). Go over the drawing using a pointed nib and very dilute waterproof ink. Erase any pencil marks carefully.

3 Using an old size 0 brush lay a thin layer of gum ammoniac size with flowing strokes. Leave to dry for about 30 minutes and apply a second coat. The first coat seals the paper surface; the second should ensure that the gold sticks well. Wash the brush with warm water after use.

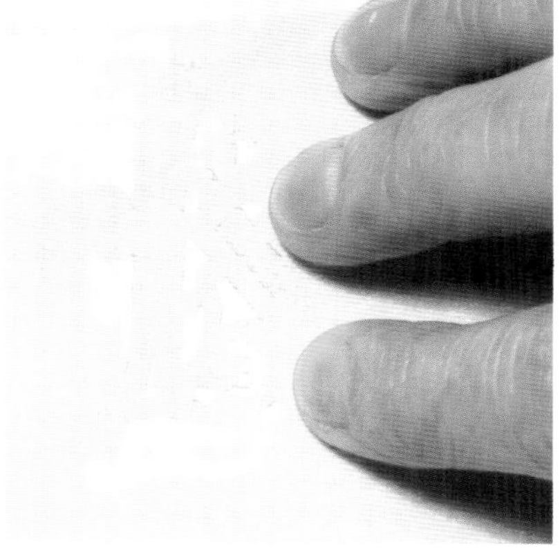

4 Breathe on the gum to activate it, and apply the transfer gold immediately, pressing down firmly but not too hard with your fingers.

5 Carefully remove the backing paper from the transfer gold. Repeat the process if necessary to cover the letter completely – two layers of gold give greater brilliance.

6 Lay a sheet of glassine over the gold and work evenly and lightly across the whole area with the dogtooth burnisher.

7 Remove any surplus gold with a large soft brush, easing it gently away from the edges of the gum.

8 Wrap a piece of washed silk around your finger and gently polish the gold.

9 Mix up blue (zinc white + ultramarine + a little spectrum violet) to the consistency of thin cream. Apply with a size 0 brush, working to the edges of the gold. If the paint runs onto the gold, wipe it off with a clean damp brush.

10 Mix and paint in the green (zinc white + permanent green deep + cadmium yellow) as for step 9, using a size 00 brush for these smaller areas.

11 Mix up the red paint (scarlet lake + a little cadmium yellow) and use a size 00 brush to outline the gold and fill the spaces within the letter. The outline can tidy any ragged edges. If the paint does not adhere over gold, add a tiny drop of ox-gall to the mixture.

12 The finished letter. Try experimenting with these letters on purple paper or dyed scraps of vellum for a luxurious effect.

Ottonian Round letters

In this alphabet, the round letter group includes E, which harks back to the uncial hand of the 8th century. The top and bottom "arms" of C, E and G are flattened slightly.

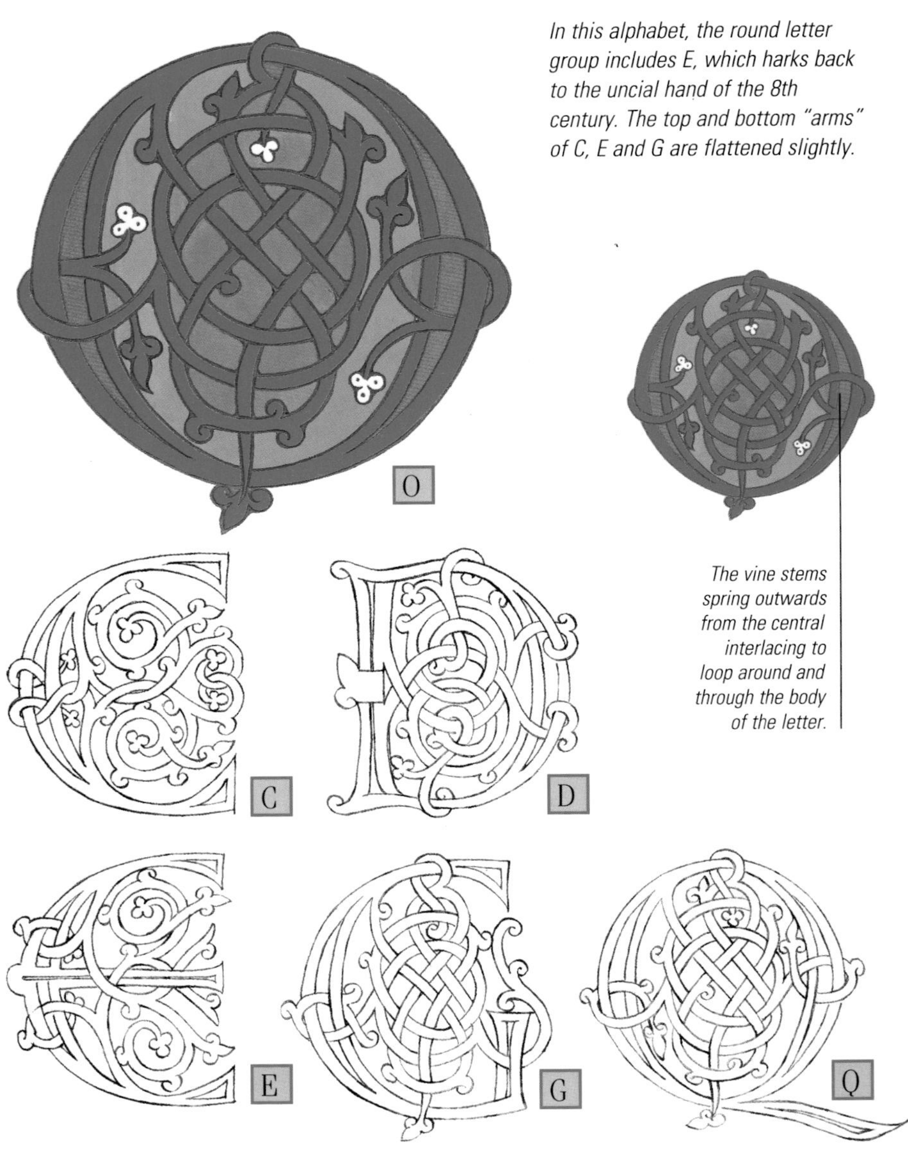

The vine stems spring outwards from the central interlacing to loop around and through the body of the letter.

Ottonian Wide letters

Note that small details can be left unpainted, with red dots added (see also pages 120, 122, 125*)*.

The wide letters have strong diagonals like the rectangular/diagonal letters (see page 123*). W was not part of the Latin alphabet. This version has been designed following the classic proportions of the versal letters on page 131. The W is as wide as two Vs side by side. The central section of the M is similar to that of a V.*

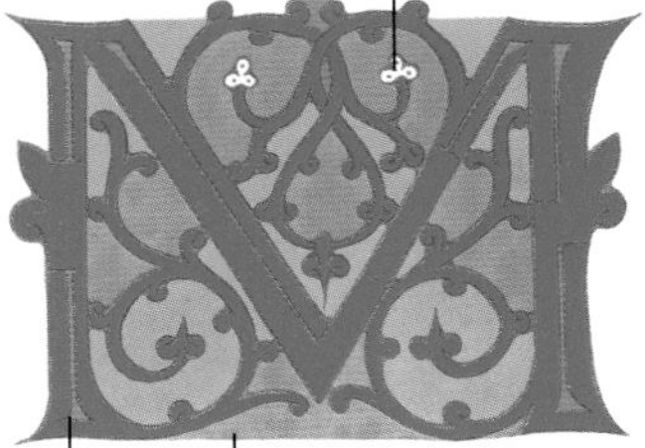

If the letters are not completely enclosed (see the O and D opposite*), use the patches of colour to create "edges".*

The red areas within the gold add greatly to the luxurious appearance of the letters.

Ottonian Rectangular/straight letters

T

*Where the branched stems are not entirely within the letter itself, the colour patches can be used to enclose them (*see also pages 123, 124*). Experiment with this on your colour rough.*

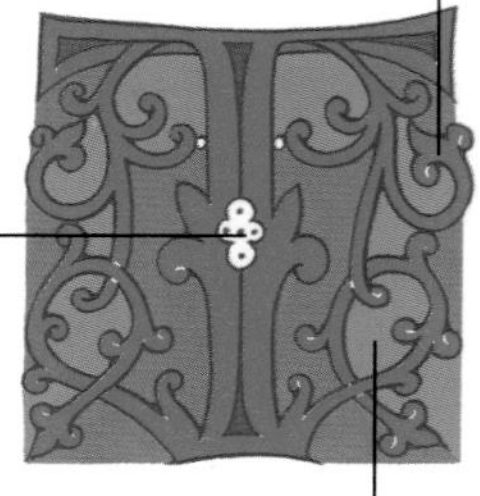

*Rectangular letters occupy the same visual area as the circle that contains O. H, T and U are all the same width. Note that the crossbar of the H is slightly above centre. This form of U is related to early uncial letter forms. In the Latin alphabet, U was actually represented by V (*see opposite*).*

The flower shape on the stem is left unpainted with red dots inserted – this also occurs on page 125.

Small, enclosed areas like this could also be painted in red to vary the colouring.

H

U

Ottonian Rectangular/diagonal letters

*This group of letters also occupies the same visual area as an O, and all are approximately the same width. The V is slightly more generous to accommodate the elaborate twined vines. The form of A shown here is 8th century uncial in its derivation. K (*see pages 116–119*) is also part of this group.*

The branches both grow from the diagonal crossbar to fill the V-shaped spaces.

A

V

X

Y

Z

Ottonian Narrow/straight letters

F, J and L are approximately half the width of the rectangular letters on pages 122 and 123. I and J have no counter spaces and are quite simply decorated. I has a heart-shaped interlace at the head and foot, recalling Celtic designs from two centuries earlier.

The extended stem links the top half of the letter to the bottom half.

Compare this complex linked-stem decoration with the simpler form on J (see also pages 120, 121).

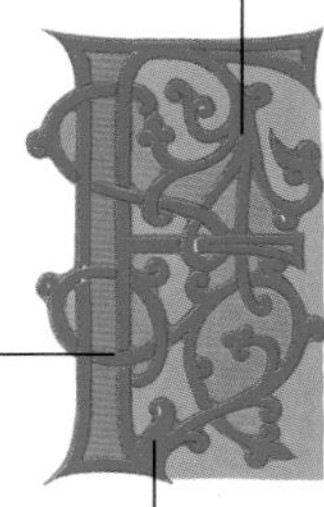

This stem grows directly out of the base of the letter. Also see the letter T (see page 122).

Ottonian Narrow/curved letters

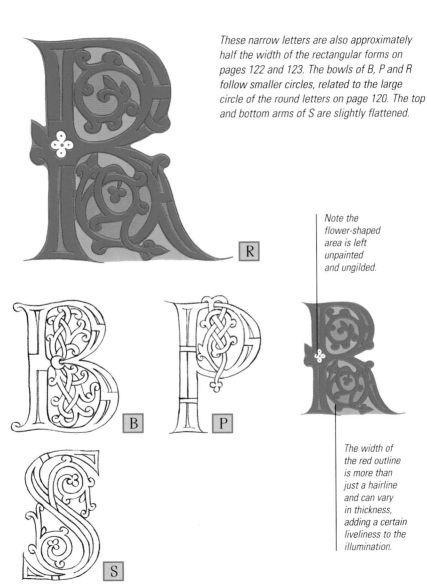

These narrow letters are also approximately half the width of the rectangular forms on pages 122 and 123. The bowls of B, P and R follow smaller circles, related to the large circle of the round letters on page 120. The top and bottom arms of S are slightly flattened.

R

Note the flower-shaped area is left unpainted and ungilded.

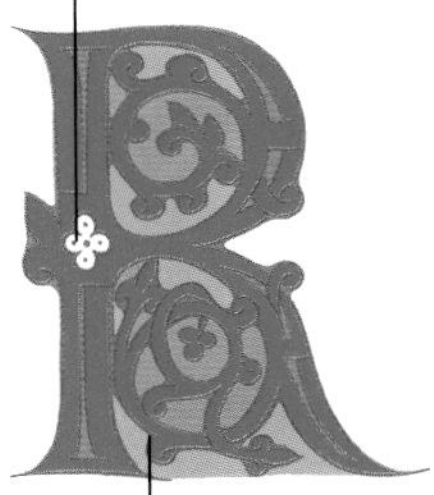

The width of the red outline is more than just a hairline and can vary in thickness, adding a certain liveliness to the illumination.

B

P

S

Ottonian Numbers

These numbers have been specially designed for this book, following the designs of the richly decorated letters of the period. When numerals occurred in original manuscripts, they were usually written in Roman form (X, XV, III, etc.) and were not illuminated.

To avoid blobs when outlining letters and numbers, don't overload the brush with paint.

For a really opulent appearance, try experimenting with the letters and numbers from these pages on purple paper or dyed scraps of vellum. See the historical examples on pages 113 and 114.

*Tiny patches of red can be used in small awkward spaces and add to the overall richness (*see also pages 120–125*).*

As with the letters, try to balance the green and blue areas in the design.

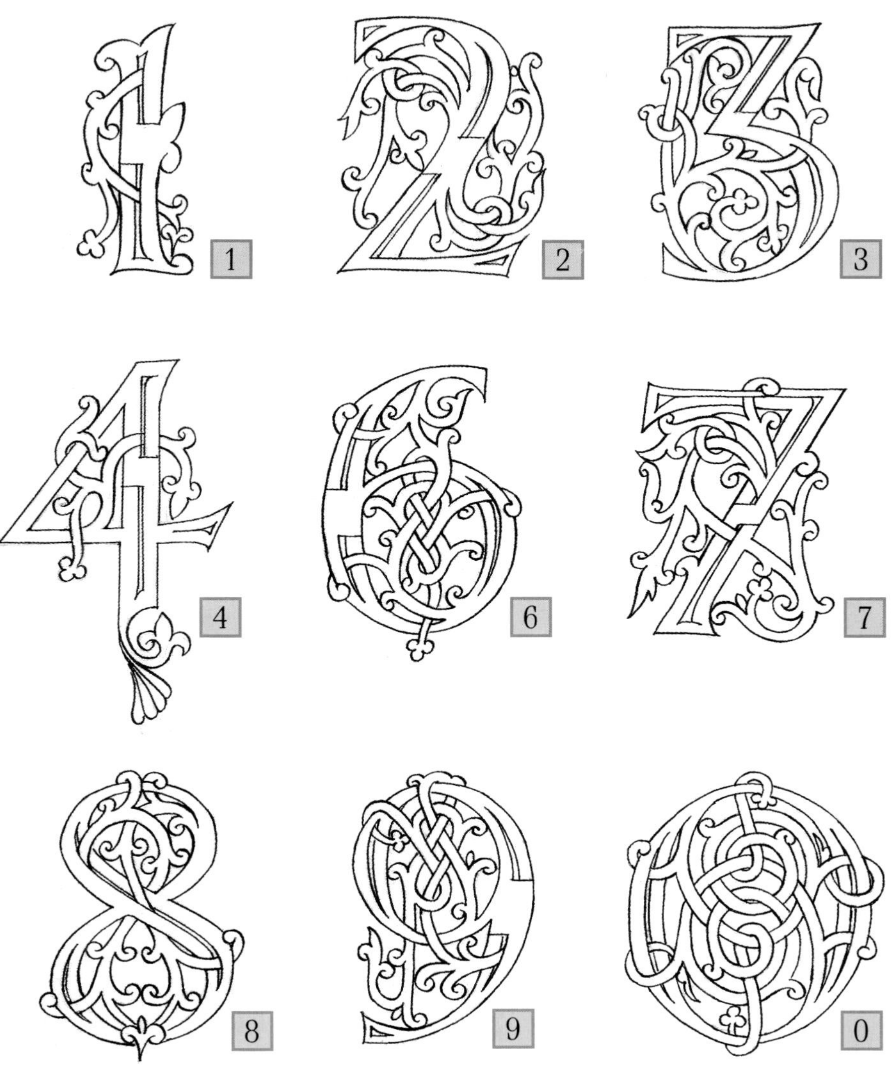
1
2
3
4
6
7
8
9
0

Carolingian Capital and lower-case letters

These pages show a basic Carolingian hand and numerals, as well as some suggested variations, which are suitable for text incorporated into more complex projects (*see pages 69–71 and 81–83*). Study the letters carefully to observe their shapes and how they are formed, using the numbered strokes. Letter height is given in the nib width "ladders", and this remains constant whichever size nib you choose.

The pen angle diagrams indicate the angle at which the nib is held to the horizontal writing line, in order to achieve the naturally occurring thicks and thins typical of the letter style. Look to see where these are. Practice is needed to keep this angle consistent as you write. Try this exercise to help you: Use either the diagram or a protractor to check the angle and "set" your pen nib against it in relation to the writing line, then make a letter shape using your

whole arm to move the pen, rather than just your fingers. Check the thicks and thins, and adjust your pen angle as needed.

This is a rounded letter based on an extended "o" shape, written at a constant 30° pen angle. The interlinear space is large (almost three times the x-height of the letter), giving an open, flowing letterform. Original manuscripts were written with uncial and/or versals (*see pages 113 and 114*). These modern capitals are sloped Roman capitals written at 6 nib widths height.

Note the springing arches at the top of "B", "D", "P" and "R" in relation to the minuscule arches. Carolingian was a 9th–10th century standard bookhand, pleasant to read, that evolved in the court of King Charlemagne. It is used as a bookhand today.

Calligraphy by Janet Mehigan

Lower-case letters are written at an x-height of 3 nib widths. Ascenders and descenders are both 4 nib widths.

Carolingian Extra characters and numbers

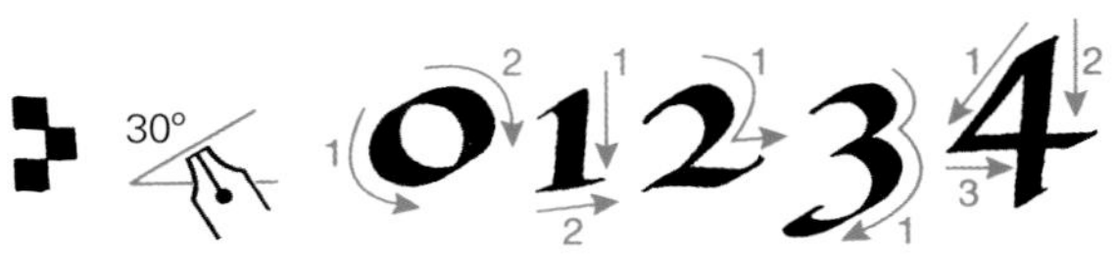

Numerals are based on the lower-case x-height, but the old style figures extend 1½ nib widths above the x-height (even numbers) or 1½ nib widths below the base line (odd numbers).

Carolingian Lightweight with "club" serif

anbncndnenfngnhninjnkn
nonpnqnrnsntnunvnwnxn

Write with a small nib. Based on an extended "o". The "clubbed" serifs (heavy top on the ascenders) were a feature of the original archaic script. They can be made in one movement, added when the letter is complete, beginning part way up the main stem – upwards, turn slightly and then down, partly covering the first stroke.

abcdefg
hijklmnopqrstuvw
xyzB&!?; èüé

30°

Versals and numbers

Versals are an important letterform in manuscripts from the 9th century onwards. The structure closely follows classical Roman capitals, but versals are made with compound pen strokes, with "waisted" stems for elegance. Three strokes are needed for stems and curves, with a change of pen angle (see diagram); serifs are horizontal hairlines. Heavier forms are usually outlined with a pen and painted with colour.

Borders and Motifs

Ottonian borders and motifs, as with the decorated letters, make much use of gold. In these sketches, yellow generally represents areas of flat gilding. The most frequently used motif is the acanthus leaf, which was drawn in many different ways and colours, and, combined with geometric patterns, offers tremendous variety. Borders are often multilayered, with one or more strips of painted decoration being enclosed within gilded bands, adding to the luxurious appearance.

Interlacing on letter forms and borders.

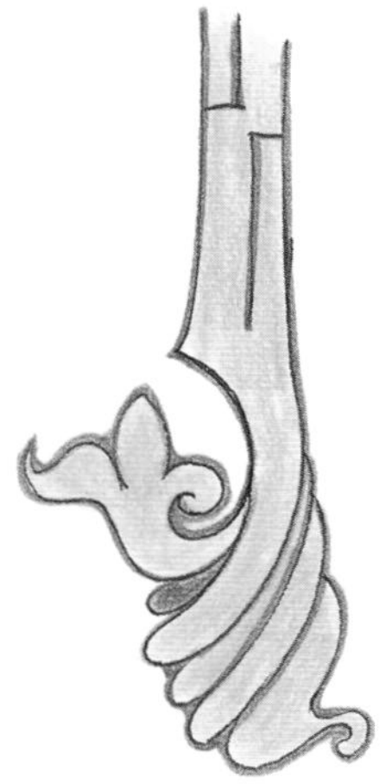

Interlacing within borders, letters and as terminal decorations can be traced back to Celtic illumination. Simplified, but recognizable, flower and leaf forms are also used.

*While the colours used within the decorated letters (*see pages 116–127*) are formulaic, painted borders are much more adventurous and varied in their use of colour. Naïve architectural forms with their flattened perspective (the principles of which were not discovered until the Renaissance) are drawn as borders for areas of text and also to contain illustrations.*

Architectural details.

Geometric patterns.

Geometric patterns occur in decorative corners as well as borders (see opposite). The acanthus leaf is used in many different forms and colours in page borders.

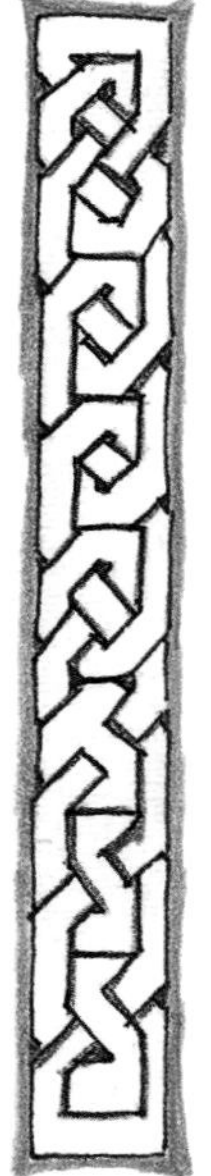

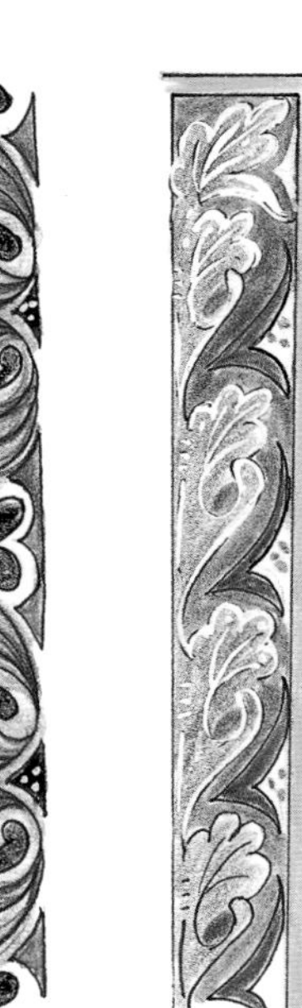

Interlaced patterns recall those found in Celtic illumination.

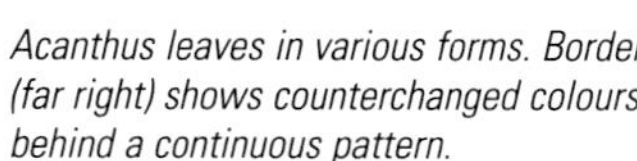

Acanthus leaves in various forms. Border (far right) shows counterchanged colours behind a continuous pattern.

Stylized flowers and leaf shapes used as extra decoration on outer edges of borders (see page 113).

Simple variations of the 3D box shape can be altered to suit border length and fitted around corners. Colour is used to suggest form.

Acanthus leaves or geometric patterns are often enclosed within outline borders of flat gilding. Plan the repetition of the motif along the border length, making modifications to fit the corners.

This geometric border comprises a 3D Greek key pattern, using colour to suggest the form.

Romanesque

The decorated letters of the Romanesque period show a mixture of influences. The elements of earlier styles, such as the interlaced patterns of Celtic illumination, the iconic depiction of figures from Byzantium and the development of historiated initials (often depicting combat between humans and animals), only serve to emphasize the love of variety that is characteristic of Romanesque manuscripts.

Romanesque

Romanesque is a term that was coined in the 19th century to describe late 11th- and 12th-century Western architecture that used Roman principles of construction.

It is also used to describe manuscripts and other visual arts of the period, indicating a style influenced by the art of ancient Rome and, to a lesser degree, that of Byzantium. Romanesque emerged as the dominant style in Europe, developing out of the almost iconic style of painting and the elaborate borders found in Anglo–Saxon manuscripts of the late 10th century.

As the church grew wealthier and more powerful, monastic scriptoria thrived, producing service books and other necessary texts to supply the expanding number of new religious foundations. Among the most important centres for the production of illuminated volumes were Winchester and Canterbury in England and Mont St. Michel in northern France. Although the vast majority of books were made by and for the use of ecclesiastical establishments, there was also an increase in the making of both scholarly and technical works, such as herbals and bestiaries.

As well as making books look attractive, the painted and decorated letters and plain-coloured versals were functional. A large initial gave a visual lead into a more important text, and could even contain a narrative scene encapsulating the text on

► ***Winchester Bible***
MS 17, fol. 169r
England, Winchester, mid-12th century
The end of the book of Jeremiah and the opening of Baruch: This superb illuminated volume was produced over a period of 15 years, by a team of artists working in the cathedral scriptorium. The bright colour scheme used in the historiated initials is picked up in the heavy versal letterforms.

.ORATIO.

noster· completi sunt dies nostri quia uenit finis noster.
Velociores fuerunt persecutores nostri COPH
aquilis celi· super montes persecuti sunt nos· in
deserto insidiati sunt nobis· RES.
Spiritus oris nostri xpistus dominus captus est in peccatis
nostris cui diximus· in umbra tua uiuemus in gen
Gaude et letare filia edom quia ha SEN
bitas in terra hus· ad te quoque perueniet calix
inebriaberis atque nudaberis· TAV
Completa est iniquitas tua filia syon· non
addet ultra ut transmigret te· Visitauit ini
quitatem tuam filia edom· discooperuit peccata tua·
FINIT LAMENTATIO IEREMIE PROPHETE

INCIPIT ORATIO EIUSDEM:

ECORDARE
domine quid acciderit nobis
intuere et respice op
probrium nostrum·
Hereditas nostra uersa
est ad alienos. domus
nostre ad extraneos·
Pupilli facti sumus
absque patre· matres
nostre quasi uidue·
Aquam nostram pecunia bibimus· et lig
na nostra precio comparauimus.
Ceruicibus minabamur· lassis
non dabatur requies·
Egypto dedimus manum et assyriis.
ut saturaremur pane·
Patres nostri peccauerunt et non sunt·
et nos iniquitates eorum portauimus·
Serui dominati sunt nostri· et non fuit
qui nos redimeret de manu eorum·
In animabus nostris afferebamus panem
nobis a facie gladii in deserto·
Pellis nostra quasi clibanus exusta est
a facie tempestatum famis·
Mulieres in syon humiliauerunt· et
uirgines in ciuitatibus iuda·
Principes manu suspensi sunt· facies
senum non erubuerunt·
Adolescentibus inpudice abusi sunt·
et pueri in ligno corruerunt·
Senes de portis defecerunt· iuuenes
de choro psallentium·
Defecit gaudium cordis nostri· uersus est in luc
tum chorus noster· cecidit corona capitis nostri·
ue nobis quia peccauimus·
Propterea mestum factum est cor nostrum· ideo
contenebrati sunt oculi nostri·
Propter montem syon quia disperiit·
uulpes ambulauerunt in eo·
Tu autem domine in eternum permanebis· solium tuum
in generatione et generationem·
Quare in perpetuum obliuisceris nostri· et dere
linques nos in longitudinem dierum?
Conuerte nos domine ad te et conuertemur· in
noua dies nostros sicut a principio·
Sed proiciens repulisti nos· iratus es contra
nos uehementer. FINIT ORATIO IEREMIE:

INCIPIT PROLOGUS IN LIBRU
BARUCH NOTARII IEREMIE PROPHETE.

Liber iste qui baruch nomine prenotatur in hebreo
canone non habetur· sed tantum in uulgata editione. Si
militer et epistola ieremie prophete. Propter notitiam autem
legentium hic scripta sunt· quia multa de xpisto nouissimisque
temporibus indicant.

FINIT PROLOGUS

De oratione et sacrificio pro uita nabuchodonosor.

INCIPIT LIBER BARUCH NOTARII IEREMIE PROPHETE:

ET VERBA LIBRI QUE SCRIPSIT
baruch filius neerii· filii maasie· filii sedechie·
filii sedei· filii helchie in babylonia· in anno
quinto in septima die mensis· in tempore quo
ceperunt chaldei ierusalem et succenderunt eam igni·
Et legit baruch uerba libri huius ad aures ie
chonie filii ioachim regis iuda· et ad aures uni
uersi populi uenientis ad librum· et ad aures
potentium filiorum regum· et ad aures presbi
terorum· et ad aures populi a minimo usque
ad maximum eorum omnium habitantium in
babylonia· ad flumen sudi. Qui audientes
plorabant et ieiunabant· et orabant in con
spectu domini. Et collegerunt pecuniam secundum
quod potuit uniuscuiusque manus· et miserunt
in ierusalem ad ioachim filium helchie filii salon
sacerdotem· et ad reliquos sacerdotes. et ad
omnem populum qui inuenti sunt cum eo in ierusalem.

that page. Coloured headings in different sizes and plain capitals in the margin indicated subsequent chapters and verses.

The Romanesque alphabet on the following pages has been adapted from several different sources of English and French manuscripts of the 11th century, and demonstrates the variety of decorative possibilities of the period. The Romanesque period is not associated with repetition – variety is characteristic, and the drawing and painting is vibrant in its execution. The letters are based on built-up versals (*see page 131*) of Roman proportions, although some of the earlier uncial forms have been retained. Some letters are enormously elaborate; others less complex, with fewer elements. Plain capitals used as headings are quite heavy in weight, the forerunners of Lombardic forms, which appeared in the 13th century (*see pages 172–177*).

▼ ***Psalter***
Arundel MS 60, fols. 52b–53
England, Winchester, second half of 11th century
The crucifixion and initial to Psalm 51: This coloured line drawing with its vigorous acanthus scroll borders is reminiscent of French illumination of the same period. The work may have been carried out by a foreign scribe.

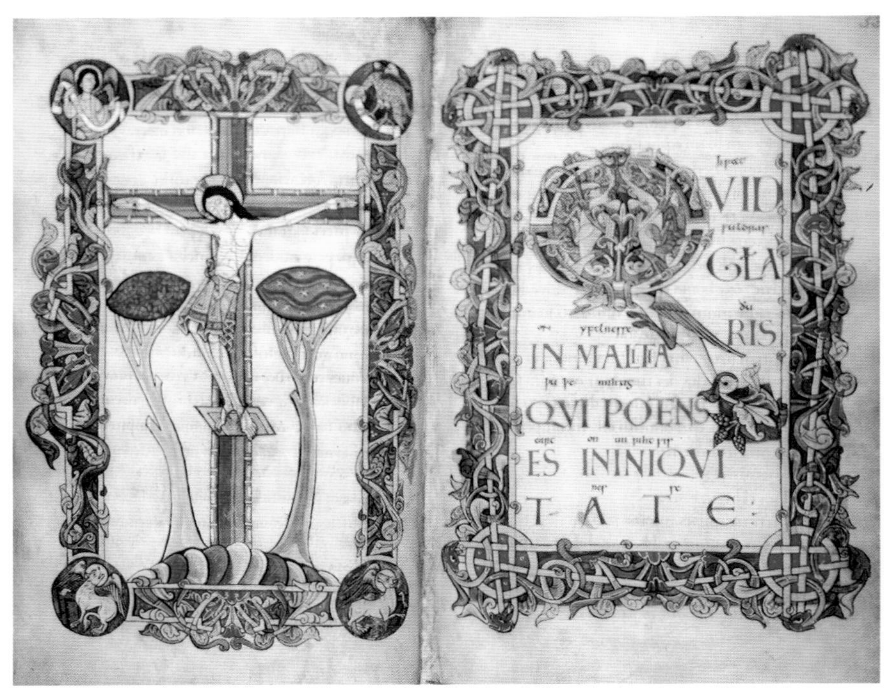

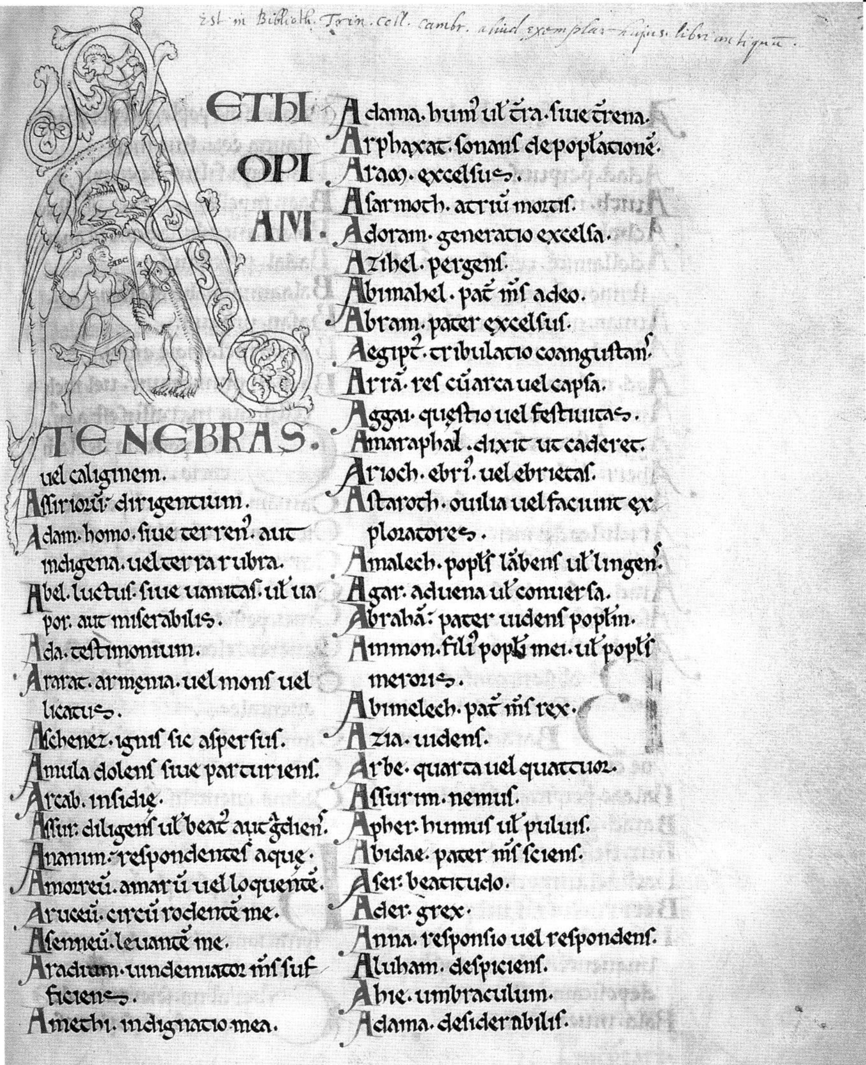

Est in Biblioth. Trin. coll. cambr. aliud exemplar huius libri antiquu.
ETHI
OPI
AM.
TENEBRAS.
uel caliginem.
Assiriorum: dirigentium.
Adam. homo. siue terren. aut
indigena. uel terra rubra.
Abel. luctus. siue uanitas. ul ua
por. aut miserabilis.
Ada. testimonium.
Ararat. armenia. uel mons uel
licatus.
Aschenez. ignis sic aspersus.
Amula dolens siue parturiens.
Arcab. insidie.
Assur: diligens ul beat aut gchens.
Ananum: respondentes aque.
Amorreu. amaru uel loquente.
Arucceu. circu rodente me.
Asenneu. leuante me.
Aradium. uindemiator mis suf
ficiens.
Amethi. indignatio mea.
Adama. hum ul tra. siue trena.
Arphaxat. sonans depoplatione.
Aram. excelsus.
Asarmoth. atriu mortis.
Adoram. generatio excelsa.
Azibel. pergens.
Abimahel. pat mis adeo.
Abram. pater excelsus.
Aegipt. tribulatio coangustans.
Arra. res cu arca uel capsa.
Aggai. questio uel festiuitas.
Amaraphal. dixit ut caderet.
Arioch. ebri. uel ebrietas.
Astaroth. ouilia uel faciunt ex
ploratores.
Amalech. popls lambens ul lingens.
Agar. aduena ul conuersa.
Abraha: pater uidens poplm.
Ammon. fili popli mei. ul popls
meroris.
Abimelech. pat mis rex.
Azia. uidens.
Arbe. quarta uel quattuor.
Assurim. nemus.
Apher. humus ul puluis.
Abidae. pater mis sciens.
Aser: beatitudo.
Ader. grex.
Anna. responsio uel respondens.
Aluham. despiciens.
Abie. umbraculum.
Adama. desiderabilis.

▲ ***Commentaries of St. Jerome***

MSO.4.7, fol. 75r (detail) England, 12th century

The lively outline drawing of the initial shows a man teaching a bear the alphabet. The heavy coloured versals are characteristic of manuscripts of this period.

Romanesque Initial "X"

This letter is decorated with tones of rich red and green – the characteristic colours of this period and style. The acanthus leaves are also typical and occur in various different forms throughout this alphabet. PVA medium (or glue) mixed with distilled water is used instead of gesso for the flat gilding on this letter.

Tools and materials

- *HB pencil*
- *Tracing paper*
- *300 gsm (140 lb) hot-pressed watercolour paper*
- *4B pencil for carbon transfer or red ochre carbon paper (*see pages 78–80*)*
- *PVA mixed with distilled water in a 50:50 solution, tinted with a tiny amount of watercolour (*see page 52*)*
- *Ruler*
- *Ruling pen*
- *Old brush (size 0) for applying PVA solution*
- *Transfer gold*
- *Glassine*
- *Dogtooth agate burnisher*
- *Piece of soft washed silk*
- *Large soft brush*
- *Sable brushes, sizes 0, 00, 000*
- *Ox-gall liquid to mix with paint if necessary*

Gouache paints

- *Permanent green deep*
- *Cadmium yellow pale*
- *Ultramarine*
- *Zinc white*
- *Scarlet lake*
- *Alizarin crimson*
- *Opaque white*
- *Vandyke brown*
- *Distilled water for mixing*

1 Trace the letter onto tracing paper using an HB pencil.

2 Transfer the outline to the watercolour paper. You can use a 4B pencil on the back of the drawing, or red ochre carbon paper, or a light box (see pages 78–80). Tidy up any ragged lines lightly with a pencil afterwards. You need only draw the outline at this stage, not all the details.

3 Stir the PVA solution thoroughly. Working on a flat surface, use a ruling pen to outline the gilded area (see page 73), then use an old brush to fill the area with a thick, even layer of PVA solution. When it is completely dry (one hour or more), add a second layer. Leave it to dry.

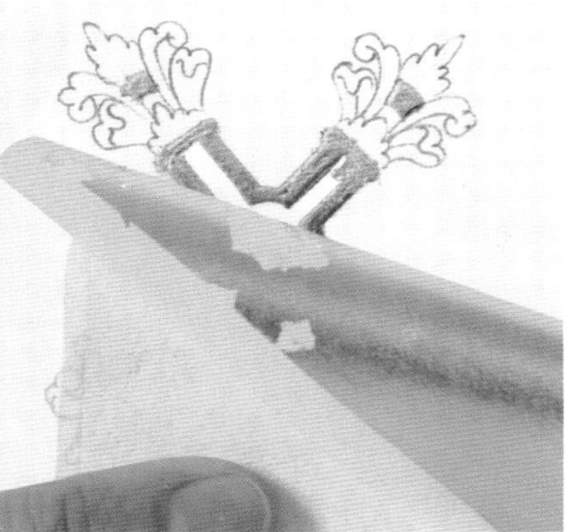

4 With a sheet of transfer gold at hand, breathe on the PVA solution to activate it. Lay the gold, pressing it down onto the glue to make sure it adheres. Burnish the gold gently through the backing paper.

5 Apply two or three layers of transfer gold to cover completely. When you are satisfied with the coverage, burnish the gold gently in a circular motion through glassine. Take care not to press too hard. Polish it lightly with the washed silk for a brighter shine.

6 Remove any excess gold carefully, using a large soft brush.

7 Mix a small quantity of a dilute wash of green (permanent green deep + cadmium yellow), then add a little ultramarine + zinc white. Paint in the lower leaf areas with the size 0 sable brush.

8 For the darkest red areas, mix equal quantities of scarlet lake + alizarin crimson, slightly thinner than normal. Apply using the size 0 brush. Use this mix well-diluted for the other leaf areas.

9 Add the leaf details in darker green – the same mix as in step 7, with less water and a little more ultramarine in the mixture.

10 Paint in the highlights on the leaf edges, ribs and dark red leaves with opaque white, using a size 000 brush.

11 Finally, using a size 00 brush, outline everything with a strong mix of scarlet lake + alizarin crimson + a little Vandyke brown. This will tidy up any rough edges and finish off the piece neatly.

12 The finished letter. If you have problems achieving smooth edges, trace some of the complex shapes onto spare watercolour paper and practice your painting technique. It requires control to make the bristles of the brush go exactly where you want them.

Romanesque Round letters

A typical polychrome letter using watercolour paint, with a basic drawing in sepia waterproof ink. Thin raw sienna wash was first applied everywhere except the blue areas.

Ultramarine, Winsor green and burnt sienna applied in thin washes let the drawing show through.

Tidy outline edges with ivory black/Vandyke brown mix if needed. Watercolour is preferable to gouache.

Romanesque Wide letters

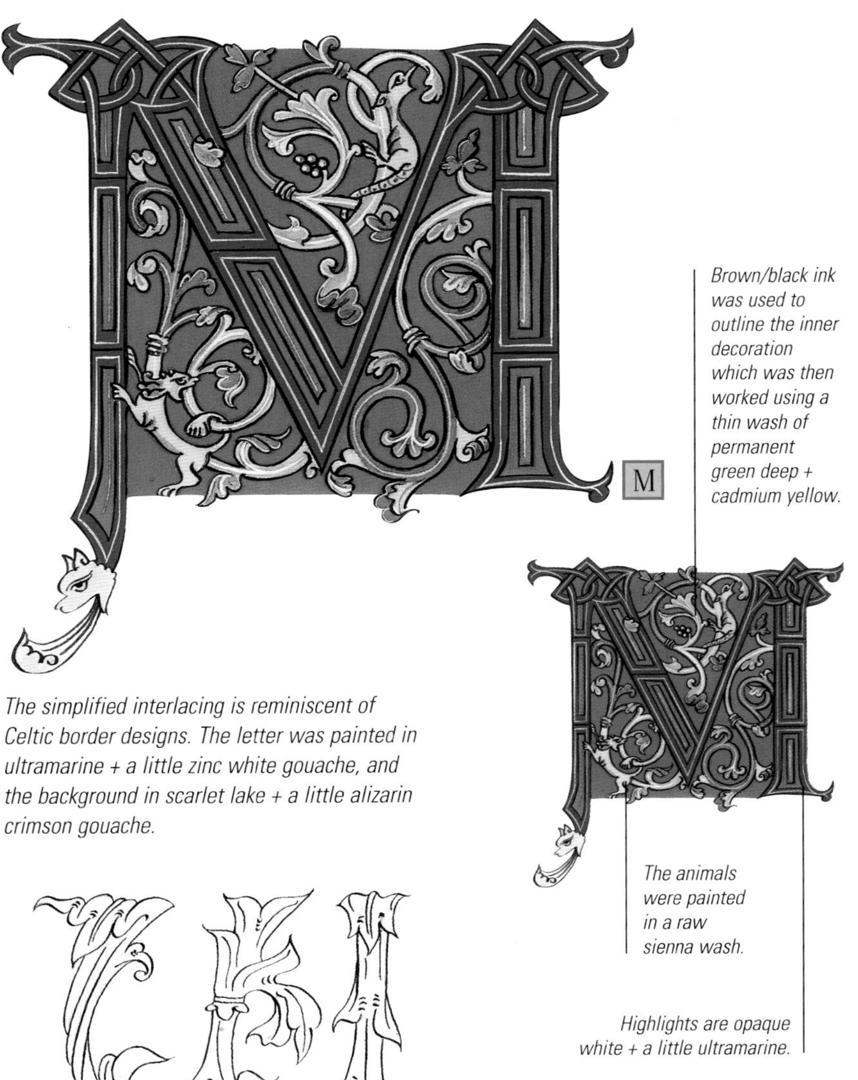

The simplified interlacing is reminiscent of Celtic border designs. The letter was painted in ultramarine + a little zinc white gouache, and the background in scarlet lake + a little alizarin crimson gouache.

Brown/black ink was used to outline the inner decoration which was then worked using a thin wash of permanent green deep + cadmium yellow.

The animals were painted in a raw sienna wash.

Highlights are opaque white + a little ultramarine.

Romanesque Rectangular/straight letters

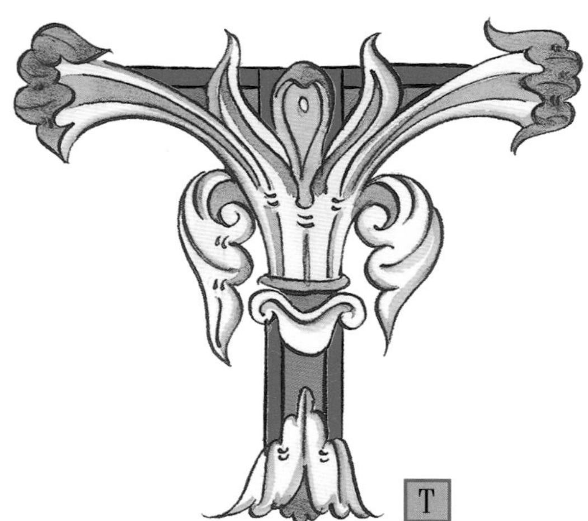

*A stronger mix of the red gouache was fed into a pointed nib to draw this vibrant letter, although this could be done with a brush. Some letters, such as this T (*see also U, below, N and K, opposite, W, page 147, and numbers, pages 152–153*), are made entirely of stylized forms of acanthus leaves. Other letters and numbers use acanthus leaves as small decorative motifs within the letter.*

A light wash of scarlet lake + a little purple lake was laid first.

Permanent green deep + zinc white + a little ultramarine.

The palest tone is where a damp brush was drawn over the outline to pull out the colour.

Romanesque Rectangular/diagonal letters

The lighter tone of red of the decorated inset panels is a mid-toned wash of scarlet lake + a little purple lake. The design is drawn in over the wash in the full strength red, with the gouache fed into a pointed nib with a brush. The letter X, which is the project on pages 142–145, is also included in this group.

The central knot recalls earlier Celtic designs (see pages 89–103*).*

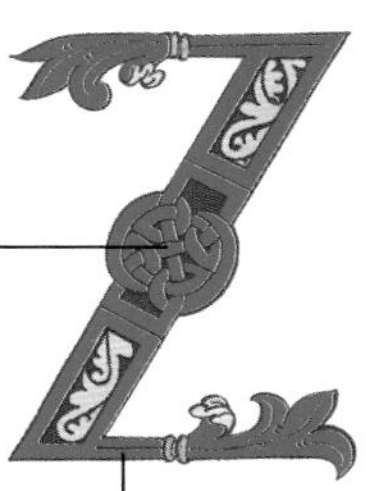

The outline was drawn in with a brush after the gold was laid.

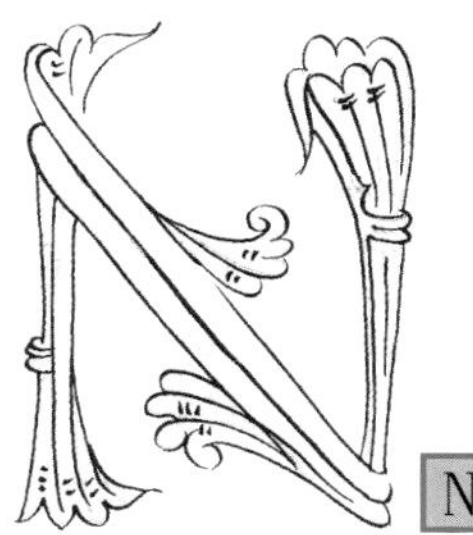

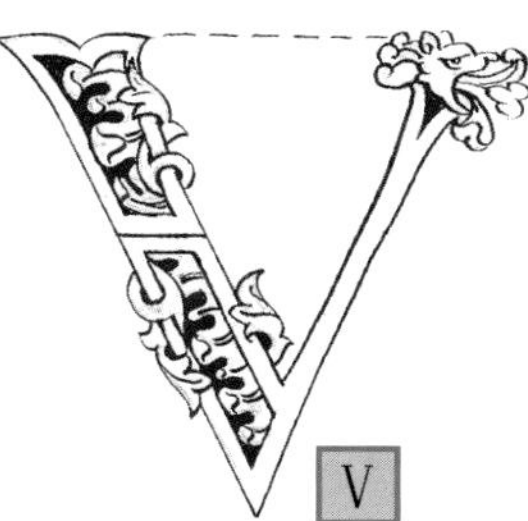

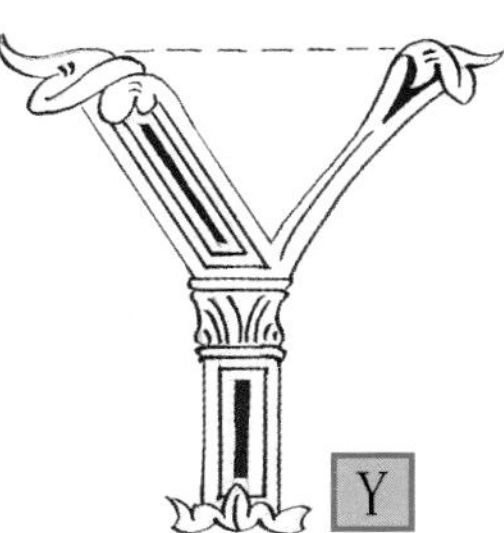

Romanesque Narrow/straight letters

The interlaced design at the head and foot of this letter I derives from the earlier Celtic styles, but the acanthus leaves and the gold are pure, exuberant Romanesque.

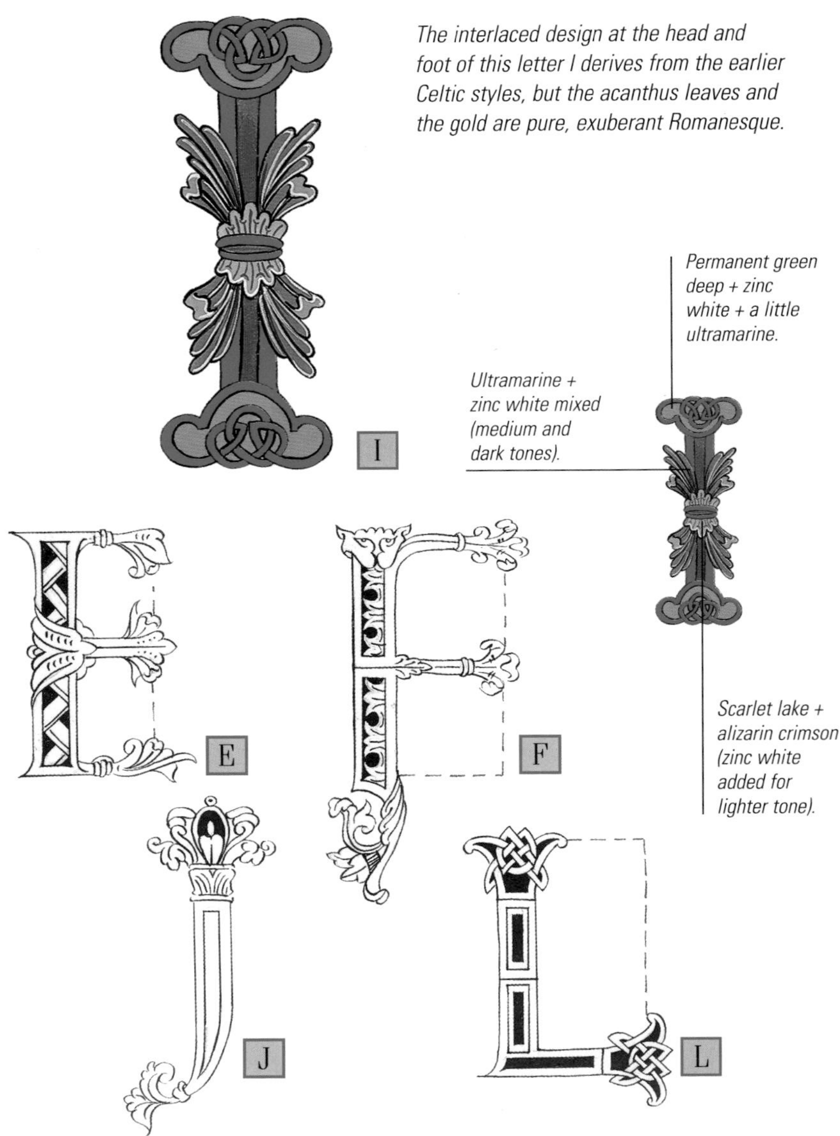

Romanesque Narrow/curved letters

P

*The branched stem is also left unpainted, but with a fine line decoration in a rich green. B (*below*) is similar.*

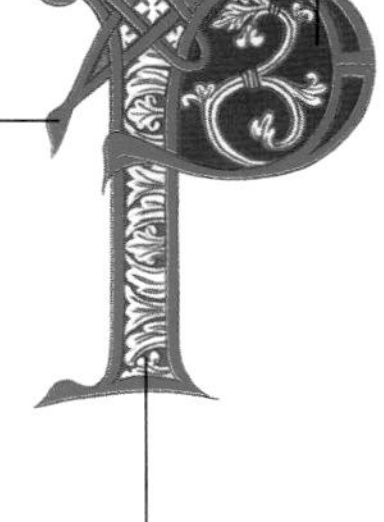

The letters are not always filled with gold or a colour. Sometimes they are left open to show the colour of the vellum or paper.

The inset panel shows another form of acanthus leaf decoration.

*Where there are dotted lines indicated on the outline letters on these two pages (*see also pages 146, 149*), they show the area to be filled with decoration. This also applies to the bowls of R and D. Use them to experiment with your own decorative ideas from the examples given on pages 146–153.*

B

R

S

Romanesque Numbers

6

*These numbers have been created specially for this book, based on a variety of typical decorative motifs, including the amusing animal masks (*see also pages 146 and 158*) found in both English and French manuscripts of the mid-to-late 11th century. The basic shapes come from modern numerals devised to accompany the elegant versals on page 131.*

*The colours used on the loose vine stem and acanthus leaves are the same as for I (*see page 150*).*

*As with the letters on the preceding pages, the painting style of the numbers can vary from polychrome (*see Q and M, pages 146, 147*) to simple, lively coloured outlines. 1 and 2 could follow the colour scheme of T on page 148.*

The pink acanthus leaves wrap around the gold shape of the numeral. Fine white and darker pink lines define the curved forms of the leaves.

The gold knots add a sparkle to the dark blue background.

1
2
3
4
5
7
8
9
0

Foundational Capital and lower-case letters

These pages show a basic foundational hand and numerals, as well as some suggested variations, which are suitable for text incorporated into more complex projects (*see pages 69–71 and 81–83*). Study the letters carefully to observe their shapes and how they are formed, using the numbered strokes. Letter height is given in the nib width "ladders", and this remains constant whichever size nib you choose.

The pen angle diagrams indicate the angle at which the nib is held to the horizontal writing line, in order to achieve the naturally occurring thicks and thins typical of the letter style. Look to see where these are. Practice is needed to keep this angle consistent as you write. Try this exercise to help you: Use either the diagram or a protractor to check the angle and "set" your pen nib against it in relation to the writing line, then make a letter shape using your whole arm to move the pen, rather than just your fingers. Check the thicks and thins, and adjust your pen angle as needed.

Edward Johnston (1872–1944) devised the foundational hand based on his studies of 9th- and 10th-century manuscripts, in particular the Carolingian script of the Ramsey Psalter (British Library, Harley MS 2904). Modern foundational varies slightly from the original manuscript, as rules have been imposed to improve consistency of style; Johnston's interpretation has also been further simplified and refined in the alphabets shown here. It is suitable for use with the decorated Romanesque capitals on the preceding pages.

Written at a constant 30° pen angle (except diagonals), letters are formed with frequent pen lifts, starting and finishing with thick serifs. Classical Roman capitals are now used with foundational script, but in the 10th century, the capitals would have been uncials or versals.

Calligraphy by Ian Garrett

Based on a round "o", lower-case letters are written at an x-height of 4 nib widths, with branched arches. Ascenders and descenders are both 3 nib widths.

Foundational Extra characters

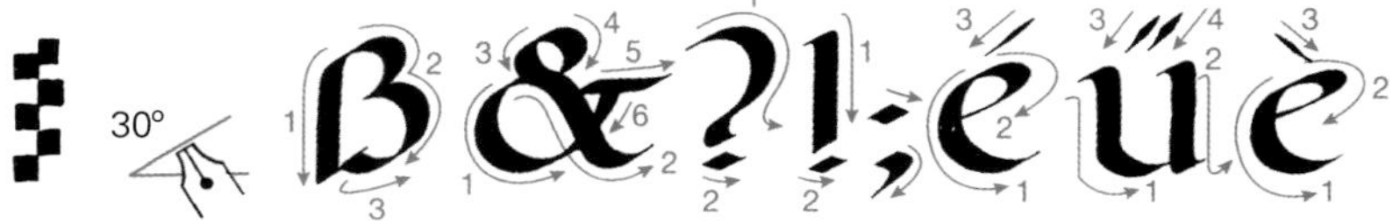

As for the lower-case letters, symbols are based on a round "o", and written at an x-height of 4 nib widths, with branched arches.

Foundational Lightweight

nbncndnenfn
nhńinjnknln

Five nib widths x-height and slab serifs throughout give this variation elegance rather than strength.

abcdefghijklm

nopqrstuvwxyz

ß&?!;éűè

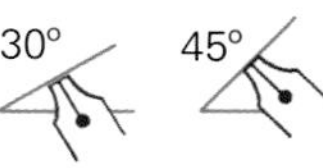

Foundational Numbers

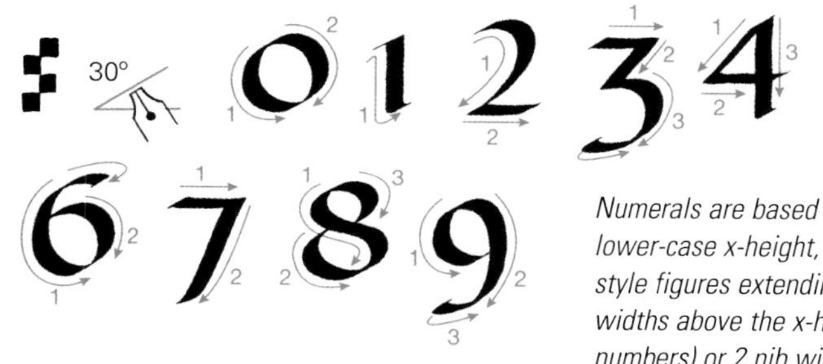

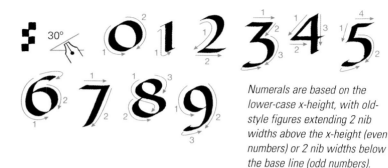

Numerals are based on the lower-case x-height, with old-style figures extending 2 nib widths above the x-height (even numbers) or 2 nib widths below the base line (odd numbers).

Foundational Cnut Charter hand

anbncndnenfn
gnhninjnknlr

Compressed sloping letters, springing arches, and pen manipulation on many strokes. Based on an early 11th-century manuscript. Note the inward pull on "u", "h", "m" and "n."

abcdefghijklm

nopqrstuvwxyz

ß&?!:éűè

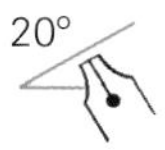

Borders and Motifs

As with Ottonian borders and motifs, the Celtic influence can also be seen in Romanesque manuscripts (*see also pages 138–153*). Knots and strapwork are incorporated with sinuous organic forms, acanthus leaves and fabulous beasts into intricate patterns. Gold is not so often used, allowing the vigorous, pen-drawn shapes in rich colours to assume greater importance.

Animal masks in many different designs are included as an integral and amusing part of letters and borders. Their mouths bite the letters, or parts of other animals in the design, reminiscent of the Celtic zoomorphic forms.

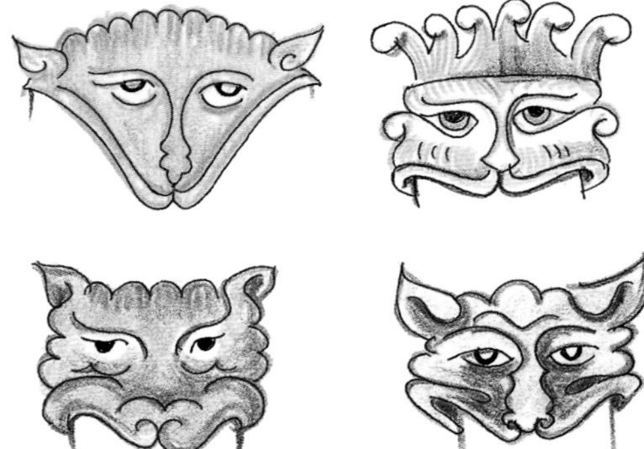

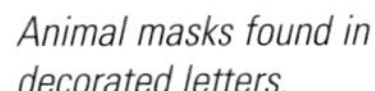

Animal masks found in decorated letters.

*Strange beasts are used to form whole letters (*see page 133*), as well as for terminal decorations.*

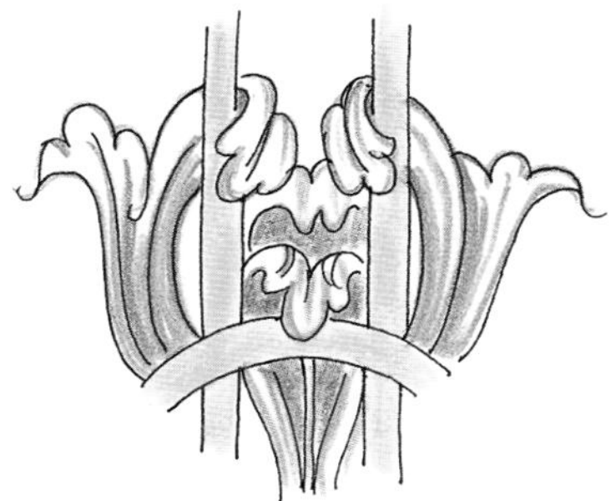

Acanthus leaves within and twining around gold borders.

Acanthus leaves.

Acanthus leaves, in various different forms, are important motifs used to fill borders of flat gilding. They also sprout vigorously from the ends of letters and the stems that fill the counter spaces (see pages 138–153).

Much of the decoration has a very vigorous "organic" quality.

*Examples below show some of the acanthus leaf variations used for borders and infills of letter shapes. Simple geometric patterns are also used as infills. Colours can be either bright or subtle, sometimes contained by strips of flat gilding – shown in these sketches as yellow – to make the page twinkle. Corners can be treated as separate, self-contained motifs (*see this page, far right*).*

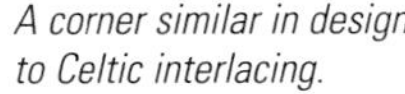

A corner similar in design to Celtic interlacing.

Acanthus leaves used in corners.

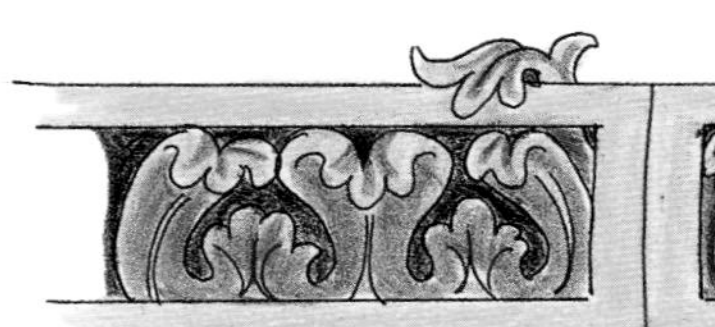

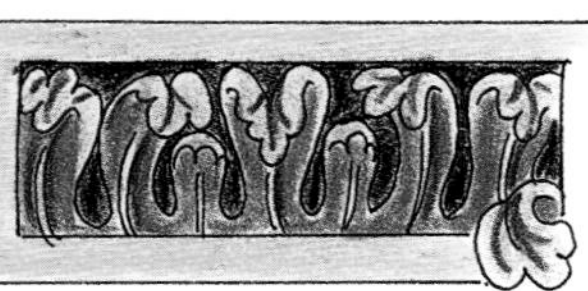

Most border and letter infills are based on acanthus leaves.

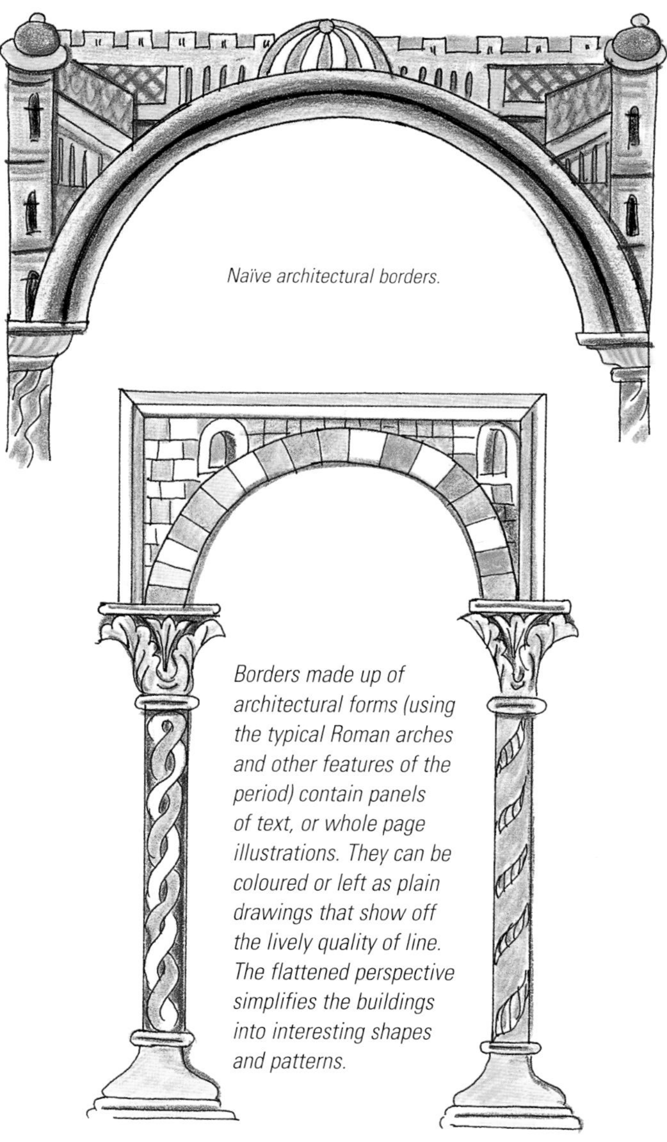

Naïve architectural borders.

Borders made up of architectural forms (using the typical Roman arches and other features of the period) contain panels of text, or whole page illustrations. They can be coloured or left as plain drawings that show off the lively quality of line. The flattened perspective simplifies the buildings into interesting shapes and patterns.

Gothic

England, France and Flanders (Belgium) continued to be important centres of manuscript production, but guilds of secular craftsmen gradually began to take over the work from the monasteries as the demand for books grew. The use of raised gold and white highlight decoration was characteristic, although the style changed with a growth of interest in realism. The strange, symbolic grotesques of the 12th century gave way to the naturalistic flowers found in the borders of late 15th-century books.

Gothic

The Italian painter and art critic Giorgio Vasari (1511–1574) first used the term *Gothic* to describe what he considered the barbaric style of Western art produced between Roman antiquity and the Renaissance.

It now indicates a period starting in the late 12th century and ending, according to region and how quickly Renaissance ideas were absorbed, sometime between 1300 and the end of the 16th century.

Manuscripts from the early Gothic period show close affinity to the styles of earlier centuries (*see Celtic, pages 86–109, Ottonian, pages 110–135 and Romanesque, pages 136–161*), but the leaves, twisted stems and animal motifs show a greater degree of sophistication. The Gothic love of the grotesque gives us strange creatures, neither man nor beast, which lurk in the margins.

High Gothic manuscripts from the first half of the 15th century featured extensive use of gold and very decorative initials and borders, which overflowed with flowers, leaves and animals. Sometimes, initials and borders held narrative scenes relating to the text. Heraldry was developing at this time, so a patron's portrait and coat of arms were often incorporated into a scheme. By the end of the 15th century, the Renaissance influence was clearly visible in the highly naturalistic flora and fauna that inhabited the flat-gilded borders.

► ***The Bedford Hours***
Additional MS 18850, fol. 54b
France, Paris, c.1423

This luxurious Book of Hours has 31 large miniature paintings, each of which is surrounded by deep borders containing smaller scenes linked together by an elaborate scheme of acanthus leaves and other flora and fauna. Raised gold backgrounds contain the painted Lombardic letters that introduce the verses for meditation. Their twisted stem decoration echoes earlier illumination styles.

Inlaudibus.

A Puissant noble
et excellent prince
Jehan filz du Roy
de france duc de
berry et dauver
gne. Conte de poitou. destampes. de
boulongne et dauvergne. Lau
rens de premier fait Clerc et vostre
moins digne secretaire et serf de
bonne foy toute obeissance et subgec
tion deue. comme a mon tresredoub
te seigneur et bienfaitteur et ag
greablement recevoir le labeur de
mon estude et benignement excu
ser la petitesse de mon engin au re
gard de la grant besongne de vre
commandement Ja pieca entrepri
se et nouvellement finee. Cōbien
que par vostre especial mandemēt
Jaie soubz la confiance de vostre
naturele benignite et en espoir de
vostre gracieux ayde et confort. en
treprins le dangereux et long tra
veil de la translation dun tierscius

◀ **Boccaccio: Des cas de nobles hommes et femmes malheureux**
Royal MS 14 E.v, fol. 5
Flanders, Bruges, c.1480

The wide border of flowers, fruit and acanthus leaves contains the arms and badges of Edward IV. The counter spaces of the generously-shaped initial A are filled with a filigree pattern painted in shell gold. The script is a French Gothic style known as Bâtarde.

▶ **Breviary**
Latin MS 136, fol. 148
France, early 15th century

The spiky, vine leaf border is typical of late 14th- and early 15th-century manuscripts. The lively grotesques (hybrid figures of weird and wonderful shapes designed to amuse the reader, seen here in the form of dragons) in the margins can be found in Gothic manuscripts from the 13th century onwards. The text hand is more rounded and openly spaced than many Gothic scripts.

France and England continued to dominate manuscript production into the 13th and 14th centuries. A much wider range of books was produced during this period: as well as religious texts, there were scholarly volumes for students, Books of Hours for private worship, almanacs for reference and even romances. This increased demand led to a move away from production in monastic scriptoria toward a thriving commercial book trade, particularly in centres of learning such as Paris and Oxford.

The alphabet on the following pages is based on capitals found in High Gothic manuscripts from Northern Europe (France and Flanders) in the mid-15th century. The English lettering artist Edward Johnston (1872–1944) dubbed the robust, amply proportioned versal letters "Lombardic". They provide a foil for the bold decorative style, lavish use of gold, and tightly compressed text letterforms used in books of this period. Most of the letterforms are round, with generous curves rather than sharp corners. Some uncial-like shapes are used, with serifs exaggerated to enclose the decoration. These capitals were rarely used as headings; their main function was to open chapters and indicate verses set either within the text or out into the margins.

Gothic Initial "Q"

This Gothic initial is painted on vellum using egg tempera. The background is raised and burnished gold on a plaster gesso base, enclosing a stylized vine stem. Trace only the letter shape, the enclosing rectangle and the vine pattern onto the vellum: you can add the details of the white overpainting very lightly in pencil before painting if you are not confident about putting them in freehand.

Tools and materials

- *HB pencil*
- *Tracing paper*
- *Piece of prepared vellum* (see pages 26–32)
- *4B pencil for carbon transfer or red ochre carbon paper or a light box* (see pages 78–80)
- *Fine pointed nib (Gillott 659 or mapping pen)*
- *Black waterproof ink*
- *Kneaded putty eraser*
- *Distilled water*
- *Plaster gesso mixed ready for use* (see pages 54–56)
- *Old brush (size 0) for applying gesso*
- *Round-bladed scalpel*
- *Piece of soft washed silk*
- *Dogtooth agate burnisher*
- *Glassine*
- *Transfer gold*
- *Double-thickness loose gold leaf*
- *Tweezers*
- *Large soft brush*
- *Pencil burnisher*
- *Egg yolk* (see page 46)
- *Sable brushes, sizes 0, 00, 000*
- *Ox-gall liquid*
- *Piece of plate glass with sanded edges, or other hard surface*

Ground pigments

(see page 45 for mixing instructions for egg tempera)
(Designer's gouache may be used as an alternative if ground pigments are not available.)

- *Scarlet lake*
- *Ultramarine*
- *Titanium white*
- *Zinc white*
- *Ivory black*

1 Trace the outline of the letter onto tracing paper using an HB pencil.

2 Transfer the outline shape to the vellum using your preferred method. Go over the outline with black waterproof ink. Remember to wash the nib out frequently as waterproof ink quickly clogs, especially in fine nibs. When the ink is dry, carefully lift off any surplus pencil marks with the eraser.

3 Tape the vellum onto glass or another flat surface. Damp the area to be gilded with a brush dipped in distilled water. Apply the gesso using a spooning action (see page 56) to flood the area with an even layer. Keep the gesso clear of the outlines. Leave on a level surface to dry.

4 Scrape away any untidy edges or bumps in the gesso with the round-bladed scalpel, letting just the weight of the blade do the work without pressing hard. Gently polish the plaster with silk to reduce friction, and then burnish the surface with the dogtooth agate burnisher.

5 Cover half the letter with glassine, then breathe on the gesso surface and apply a layer of transfer gold to cover the gesso completely (which may take several attempts to achieve). Press the gold down gently. Cover the gilded part of the letter with glassine and then repeat the method to gild the other half.

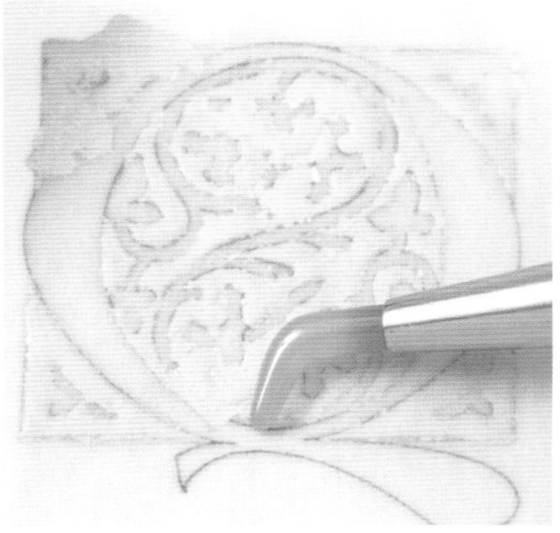

6 Leave the gesso to settle for about half an hour, and then burnish it gently through glassine, using the dogtooth burnisher carefully around the edges. It is best to burnish on a hard, smooth surface, such as glass or melamine.

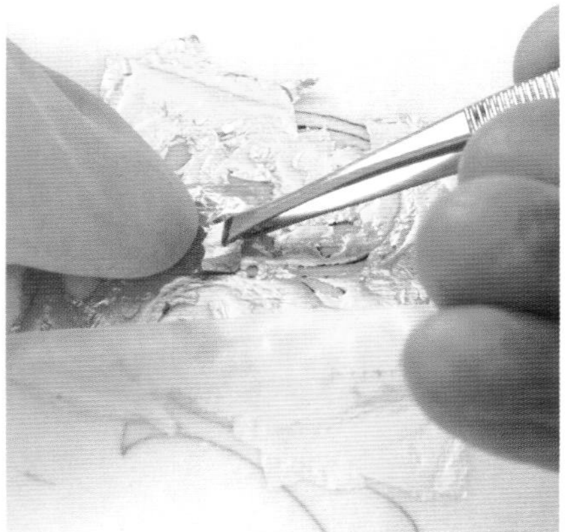

7 Make sure everything you need to apply gold leaf is ready at hand (see page 57). Breathe on the gesso again and then use the tweezers to carefully apply a layer of double-thickness gold to cover the background, pressing it down gently with the silk. Burnish through glassine as in step 6.

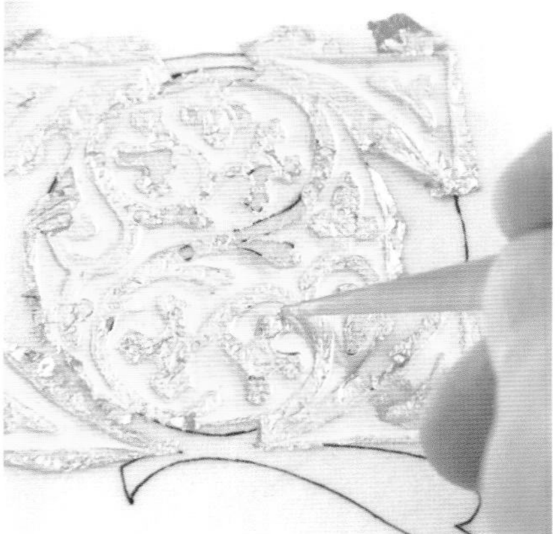

8 Repeat step 7 to add a second layer of gold. Allow the gesso to settle again, then burnish directly onto the gold, working gently at first. Polish the edges with a pencil burnisher, taking care not to dent the gesso.

9 *Remove any excess gold with a soft brush and give the surface a final burnish.*

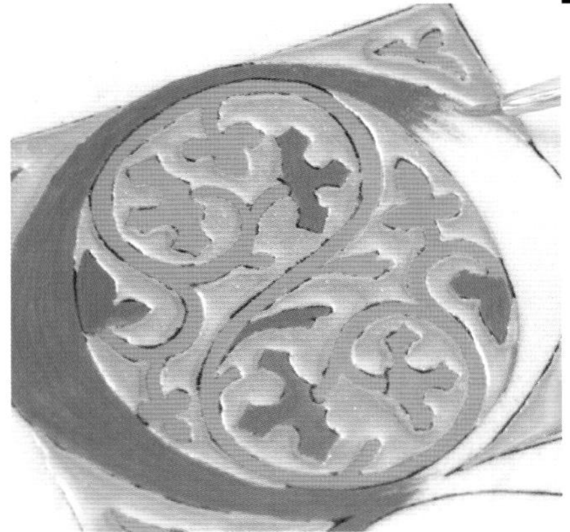

10 *Mix up the ground pigments with the egg yolk (*see page 46*). Paint the mid-tones first, using a size 00 brush to apply fine, interlocking strokes. Use scarlet lake + zinc white for the vines and some of the leaves, and ultramarine + zinc white for the letter shape and remaining leaves. Add more white for the lighter tones.*

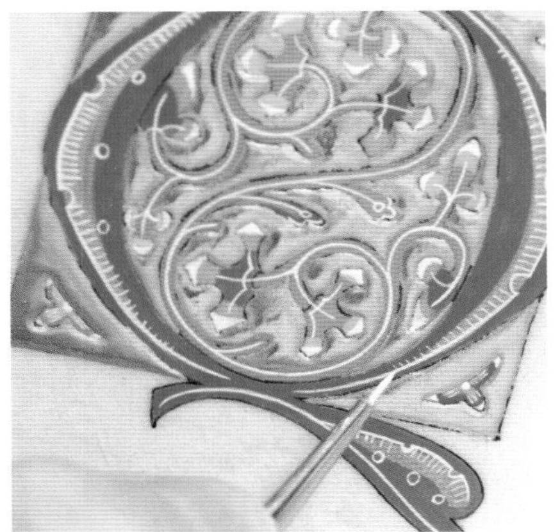

11 *Add the white decoration on the letter with a size 000 brush, using titanium white over a thin wash of white or a very light tone of the letter colour. Tidy up ragged edges by outlining everything with ivory black. Adding a drop of ox-gall liquid will help when painting up to a gold edge.*

12 *The finished letter. Note that when you are painting outlines around the gold, they are ideally done freehand, but you can try using the brush ruling method for the straight lines (*see page 73*).*

Gothic Round letters

T

The gold details are overpainted in shell gold onto the red border.

The acanthus leaves on the letter shape are in mid and light blue (see also page 178).

The curving vine stems used throughout this alphabet are reminiscent of those found in Ottonian capitals. The colour scheme is a simple one of mainly red and blue tones, but the raised gold provides a sumptuous background to these Gothic letters. The letter Q, which is the project on pages 168–171, is also part of this group.

C

D

E

G

O

Gothic Wide letters

W

Fine details are painted in titanium (or opaque) white over a thin wash of zinc white.

W was not found in the Latin alphabet, but this generously shaped W follows roughly the same proportion rule as described on pages 121 and 197, except that it is based on two Us side by side to give a family likeness within this alphabet.

M occupies a similar amount of space to W, with the straight stem in the centre rather than at the right-hand side, so you can see the difference between the two letter shapes.

Where the raised gold also forms the outer background area (unlike T, opposite), the area is sometimes broken up with small flowers or diamonds, using the same colour scheme as the letter.

M

Gothic Rectangular/curved letters

You need a size 00 sable brush and a steady hand for these fine details. When the shell gold paint is dry, burnish these delicate patterns through glassine with an agate burnisher to bring up a soft shine. *(See also pages 172, 176.)*

The fine gold details on the blue background are painted in shell gold. *(See also T on page 172.)*

J is a relatively modern addition to the alphabet. In Latin, the letter I was used instead. This letterform has been designed to fit into the group of rectangular letters with curves, although it is narrower than the other letters.

The colour of the vine leaves alternates from red to blue, as the stem twines to fill the space. The shapes of the leaves can be varied according to the space available.

S

The white highlighting on S enhances the sinuous form of the letter and the vine stems that it encloses.

U has a pattern of gold diamonds formed by a trellis of lines (these could be red or blue). The flowers contained within the pattern follow the alternate red and blue scheme common to this style.

The internal vine stems pattern can be as simple as in this letter, or quite complex, as Y.

A

H

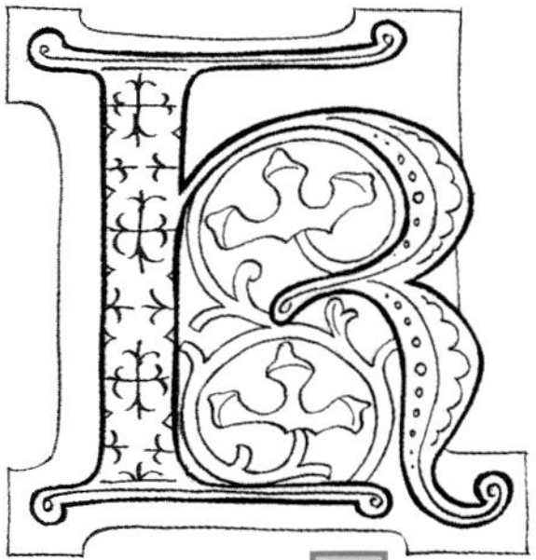

K

N

U

Y

Gothic Rectangular/straight letters

The outer gold border can be pierced with cutout shapes (see also pages 173 and 175).

All the letters and numbers in this Gothic alphabet are designed to make enclosed shapes. Here the top cross bar of F has been extended downwards and almost meets the foot of the letter, which has been drawn out sideways. The L uses this technique as well.

This stylized flower motif recurs frequently in the decoration of the letter body. It sometimes has four petals (see also pages 173, 174, 175, 177).

Gothic Rectangular/diagonal letters

Where the sides of the letter are open, unlike the Z or V on this page, the gold area is contained by the black outline. (See also I on page 176.)

The strong, straight diagonal of X is balanced and softened by a sinuous curve and short, branched vine stems in the alternate red and blue colour scheme. V has acanthus leaves on the letter body (see also T on page 172) *enclosing a pattern of diamonds, which would be painted in alternate colours. Z was not part of the Latin alphabet, but has been designed in the same style.*

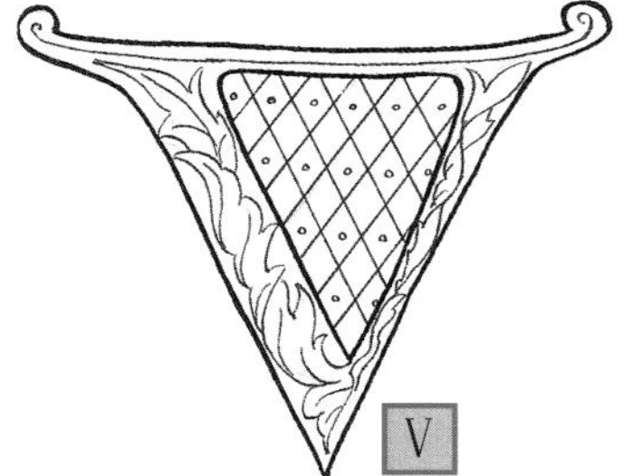

Gothic Numbers

Where numerals occurred in old manuscripts, the Roman forms were used. These numbers have been designed specially for this book, to follow the flamboyant and richly decorated letterforms on the preceding pages.

8

*The decorative patterns enclosed by the number shapes can be as varied and complex as you wish. Some of the internal spaces lend themselves particularly to curving vine stems, but others can accommodate the alternate red/blue diamond pattern shown in 2 (*opposite*), U (*page 175*) or V (*page 177*).*

*Rather than growing out of the number as in most cases (*see opposite*), here the vine stem makes a complete loop within the internal spaces.*

Filigree decoration painted in shell gold on the blue background adds the finishing touch.

Acanthus leaves painted in mid and light tones of green (not commonly used for letters in manuscripts) appear to wrap around the darker green of the numeral.

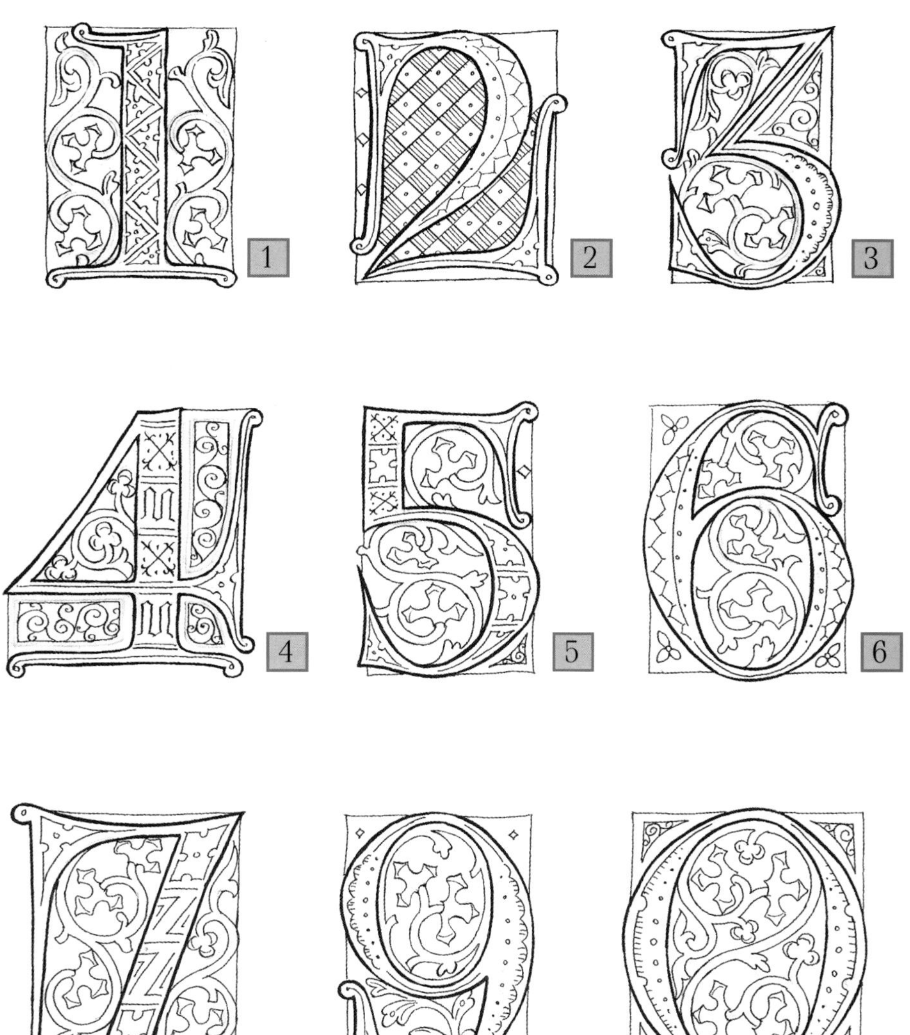
1
2
3
4
5
6
7
9
0

Gothic Capital and lower-case letters

These pages show a basic Gothic hand and numerals, as well as some suggested variations, which are suitable for text incorporated into more complex projects (*see pages 69–71 and 81–83*). Study the letters carefully to observe their shapes and how they are formed, using the numbered strokes. Letter height is given in the nib width "ladders", and this remains constant whichever size nib you choose.

The pen angle diagrams indicate the angle at which the nib is held to the horizontal writing line, in order to achieve the naturally occurring thicks and thins typical of the letter style. Look to see where these are. Practice is needed to keep this angle consistent as you write. Try this exercise to help you: Use either the diagram or a protractor to check the angle and "set" your pen nib against it in relation to the writing line, then make a letter shape using your

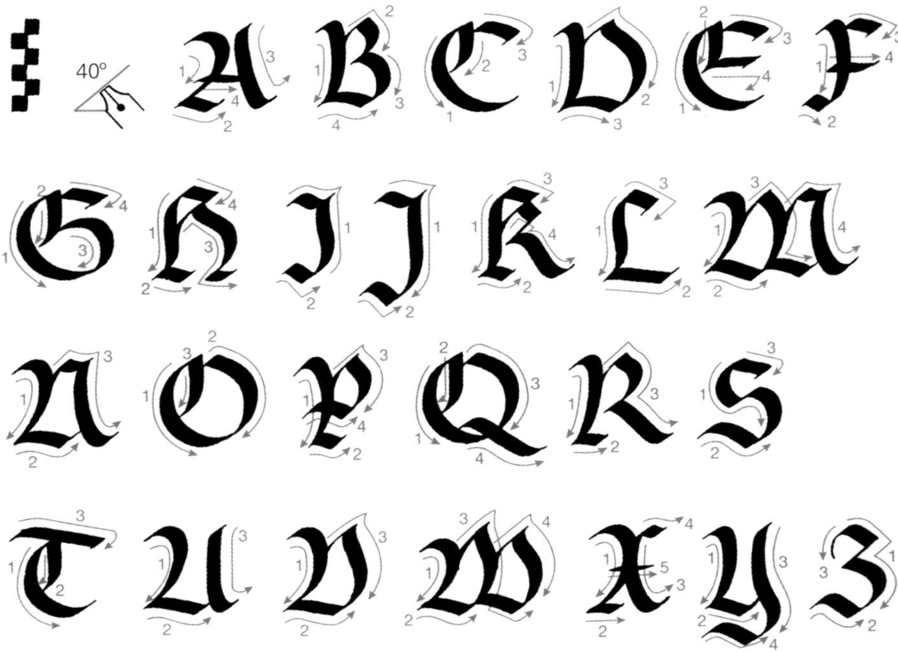

whole arm to move the pen, rather than just your fingers. Check the thicks and thins, and adjust your pen angle as needed.

Gothic has dense, angular strokes and diamond heads and feet. Narrow counters in lower case make it very textural and difficult to read. The pen is held at 40–45°, and letters are made with many pen lifts and manipulated angles. The capitals (6 nib widths high) are wider and rounder, with the addition of hairlines and flattened diamond shapes for decoration. In Gothic manuscripts, versals were often used for capitals.

This style evolved from the Caroline minuscule, and by the 13th century, it was well established as a prestigious bookhand, continuing in its many forms until the 16th century.

Calligraphy by Ian Garrett

Lower-case letters are generally written at 4–5 nib widths x-height, with narrow counters of 1½ nib widths.

Gothic Extra characters

As for lower-case letters, symbols are generally written at 4–5 nib widths x-height, with narrow counters of 1½ nib widths.

Gothic Modern quadrata

bncndnenfngnhinjnknl
lnonpnqnrnsntnunwnx
znanbncndnenfngnhni

From the same historical period (13th century) but less rigid than the letterform above, with "diamond" tops and bottoms. Write at a 45° angle and at 4 nib widths.

abcdefghijklmn

opqrstuvwxyz

ß&!?;éüè

45°

Gothic Numbers

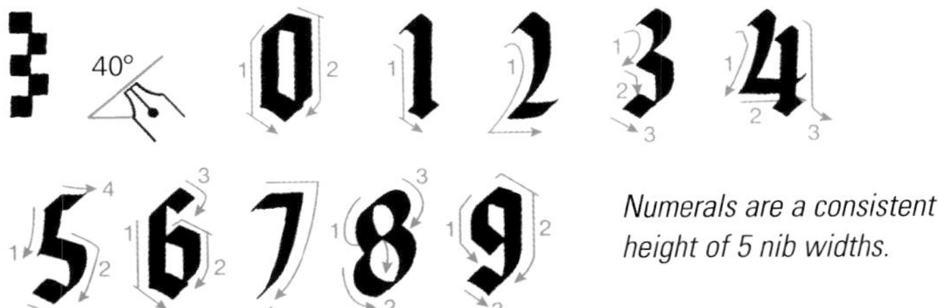

Numerals are a consistent height of 5 nib widths.

Gothic Rotunda

nbncndnenfng
hnijnknonlomn

This rounded letterform is based on a 15th-century Italian style. This less angular, more open Gothic style is very legible. Note the various pen angles and that the x-height is slightly lower.

abcdefghijklm

nopqrꝛstuvwxy

zʒß&!?;ẽüé

0° 20° 30°

Borders and Motifs

Gothic borders burst with exuberant decoration. The style changes from the relative simplicity of 13th-century manuscripts through to those of the late 15th century, showing Renaissance influence in the more naturalistic depiction of flora and fauna, but the basic motifs remain largely the same. Vine stems with raised gold leaves, acanthus leaves, flowers, human figures in dress of the period and strange beasts almost threaten to take over the pages, particularly in Books of Hours. Gold (shown as yellow on these pages) is used raised and burnished, often with indented patterns in the surface. It is also used as a gold paint made of powdered metal for highlights on coloured grounds and in patches to contrast with the brilliant polish of the raised gold.

Where lines of text drop short, the spaces are filled with a whole range of patterns at the same body height as the writing. Stylized stems, leaves, flowers, geometric patterns and fantastic elongated beasts were all used as infills. Checked patterns of colour and gold form both backgrounds to illustrations and fill the counter spaces of letters *(see pages 168–171)**.*

Fantastic beasts are either painted or, in earlier Gothic manuscripts, simply line drawings.

Squares or diamonds: gold alternated with red and blue, and highlights in white.

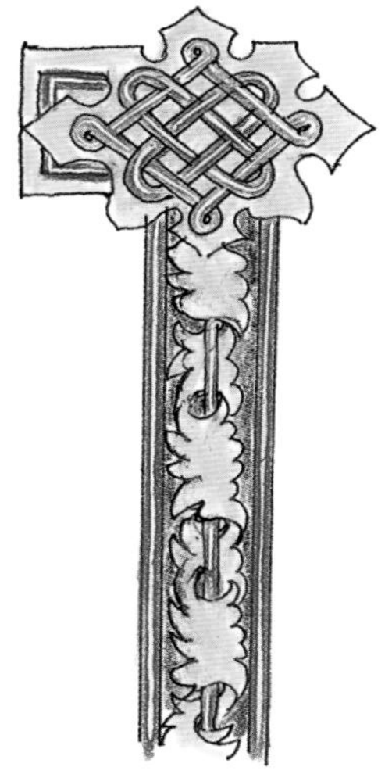

Border infill with both shell and raised gold decoration. A Celtic-style knot forms the corner.

Filigree stems, vine leaves and painted flowers.

Vine stems are pen-drawn curves and spirals, making whole borders of filigree patterns with leaves and flower buds of raised and burnished gold. Naturalistic flora and fauna are intertwined among the stems. Colours follow those used in the letterforms – tones of blue and red – but accents of sharp greens and shell gold lift the designs.

Painted border with raised gold vine stem and leaves.

Natural flora with both shell and raised gold decoration.

Filigree stems, acanthus leaves in paint and shell gold, tiny leaves or buds in raised gold and flowers.

Renaissance: White Vine

The flowering of the Renaissance brought about a rediscovery of Classical texts. Scholars and scribes drew their influences from the elegant manuscripts of the 10th and 11th centuries, apparent in the intricate, interlaced designs and rich use of gold.

Renaissance: White Vine

The term *Renaissance* has become inextricably linked with the 200 years between the mid-14th and mid-16th centuries. It was coined by Italian Humanist scholars, such as Francesco Petrarch (1304–1374), Poggio Bracciolini (1380–1459) and Niccolò Niccoli (1364–1437), working in Florence and Rome.

It signified the rebirth of learning and a revival of Classical art that was very different from the Gothic period that had gone before. The reformation of book design and the scripts in which books were written were important elements in this reappraisal.

Although the texts the Humanists studied were from antiquity, the manuscripts themselves only dated back to the Carolingian period (*see Ottonian, pages 110–135, and Romanesque, pages 136–161*). Compared to the elegance and clarity of these beautiful books, the Gothic style was judged too difficult to read. Scholars began to develop a supremely legible round hand accompanied by White Vine initials and borders in a conscious attempt to emulate the earlier volumes.

The origins of the elaborate foliated branch work can be seen in the flattened vine scroll of Ottonian manuscripts, but the result is distinctly new. The vine stems are

▶ ***Duns Scotus: "Quaestiones on the sentences of Peter Lombard"***
Additional MS 15273, fol. 8
Italy, Naples, c.1480–1485
Heraldic emblems of the manuscript's original owner are set within the complex White Vine scroll border, along with assorted animals and putti (cherubs). The large miniature shows a monastic scribe at work. The patches of flat colour enclosed by the vine are not arranged symmetrically, but are balanced visually across the design.

SAMARITA
NVS ILLE
PIISSIM
VS SPOLIA
tum uidens hominem, & atrociter sauciatum miserationis affectu com
patiens medicinam attulit efficacem: qua curatis ipsius uulneribus ac ple
na reddita sanitate, in sui principium a quo descendens ab hierusalem de
uiauerat, finaliter reducatur. ... e ista saucii sanatione salubri, ac de
uii reductione finali tanq̃ de pedibus sedentis super solium excelsum ma
gister in hoc opere finali determinat ut sicut ex primo & secundo claru
it deum esse alpha tam in se ens int omnia primum q̃ omnium aliorū
originale principium: sic ex tertio & quarto appareat ipsum esse & o
tam in se finem ultimum q̃ creaturę suę per seipsum in seipsum fina
liter reductiuum. Hanc autem reductionem finalem praecedit curatio
semiplena & plena curatio comitatur. Secundum hanc distinctionē
igitur potest diuidi quartus iste, dicendo q magister primo agit de ho
minis saucii curatione salubri. Secundo de hominis deuii reductione fi
nali: Curatur enim homo salubriter in susceptione deuota sacramentorū
ueracium: & reducitur finaliter in perceptione iocunda prgmiorum cę
lestium. Sacramenta enim disponunt & praeparant: premia uero perfi
ciunt & consumant. Vel potest dici q primo agit de curatione semi
plena, seu dispositiua & secundo de curatione plena, seu perfectiua: &
utraq diuisio redit in idem. Nam curatio semiplena fit per gratiam
sacramentorum quę sunt medicinę salubres: plena curatio, seu fina
lis reductio fit per collationem prgmiorum quę sunt iocundę refectio
nes. In prima igitur parte agit de sacramentis per quę curatur lā
guidus a morbo culpae. In secunda de prgmiis per quę liberatur a lā
gore pęnę. Et incipit secunda in principio distinctionis xliii. Post
haec & c. Prima diuiditur in duas primo nanq determinat de sacra
mento in generali secundo in speciali. Secunda in principio distinctio

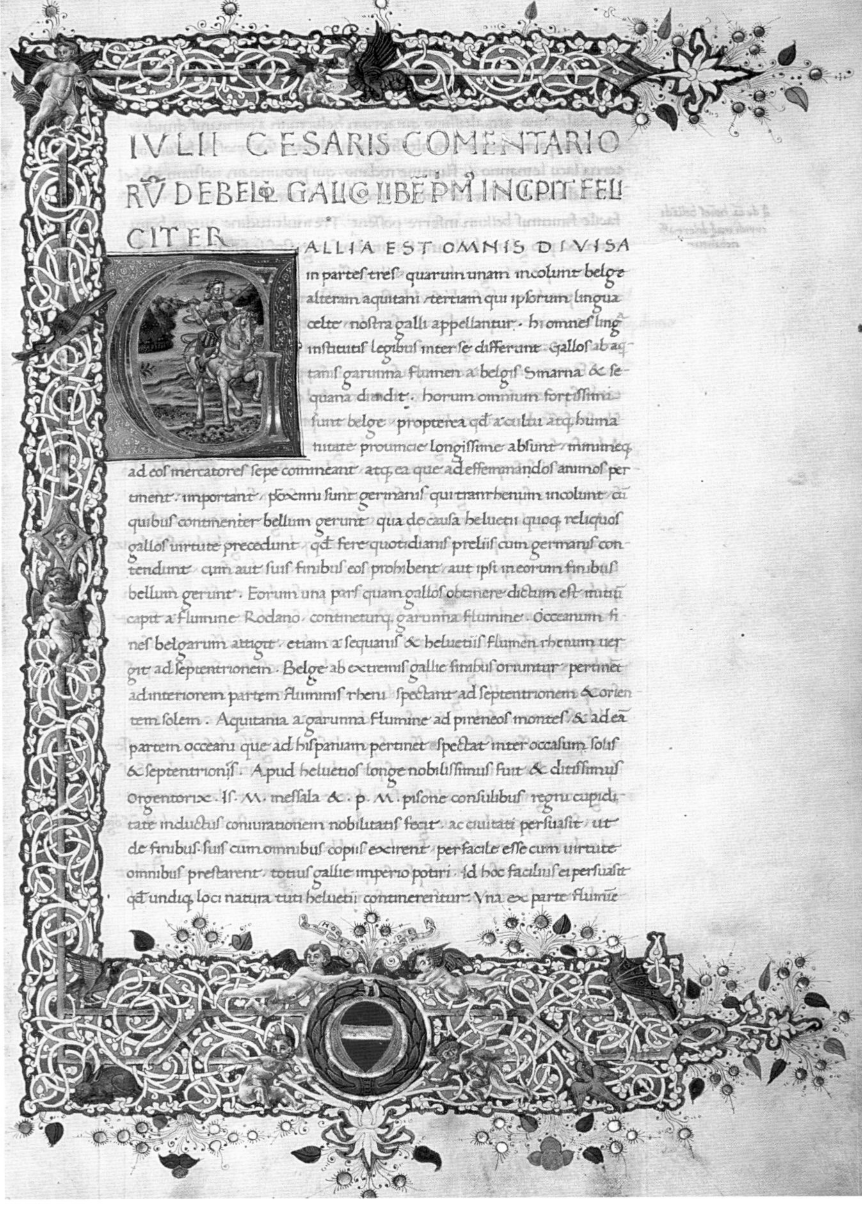

IVLII CESARIS COMENTARIO
RV̄ DE BELL' GALLICO LIBER PM INCIPIT FELI
CITER

GALLIA EST OMNIS DIVISA
in partes tres quarum unam incolunt belge
alteram aquitani tertiam qui ipsorum lingua
celte nostra galli appellantur. hi omnes ling
institutis legibus inter se differunt. gallos ab aq
tanis garunna flumen a belgis Smarna & se
quana dividit. horum omnium fortissimi
sunt belge propterea qd a cultu atq huma
nitate provincie longissime absunt minimeq
ad eos mercatores sepe commeant atq ea que ad effeminandos animos per
tinent important. proximi sunt germanis qui trans rhenum incolunt cu
quibus continenter bellum gerunt qua de causa helvetii quoq reliquos
gallos virtute precedunt qd fere quotidianis preliis cum germanis con
tendunt cum aut suis finibus eos prohibent aut ipsi in eorum finibus
bellum gerunt. Eorum una pars quam gallos obtinere dictum est initiu
capit a flumine Rodano continetur garunna flumine Occeanum fi
nes belgarum attingit etiam a sequanis & helvetiis flumen rhenum ver
git ad septentrionem. Belge ab extremis gallie finibus oriuntur pertinet
ad inferiorem partem fluminis rheni spectant ad septentrionem & orien
tem solem. Aquitania a garunna flumine ad pireneos montes & ad ea
partem occeani que ad hispaniam pertinet spectat inter occasum solis
& septentrionis. Apud helvetios longe nobilissimus fuit & ditissimus
Orgentorix. Is M. messala & p. M. pisone consulibus regni cupidi
tate inductus coniurationem nobilitatis fecit ac civitati persuasit ut
de finibus suis cum omnibus copiis exirent perfacile esse cum virtute
omnibus prestarent totius gallie imperio potiri. Id hoc facilius ei persuasit
qd undiq loci natura tuti helvetii continerentur. Una ex parte flumie

separate and wind themselves around solid Roman capitals with great vigour. They are usually left unpainted, as blank vellum and groups of dots in threes break up the patches of intense colour. Sometimes these dots are of shell gold that has been burnished and indented to catch the light.

The decoration is essentially two-dimensional and is not always symmetrical; the stems grow and branch from one or possibly two bases and the colours are used to balance the design. Patches of shell gold provide contrast with the brilliant lustre of the raised and burnished gold of the letter.

The style of the Florentine Humanists was spread by their own great enthusiasm as well as by the cultivation of booksellers and collectors in other parts of Italy and Europe. Many of the best scribes of the period were not professionals as might be expected, but churchmen and notaries.

◀ ***De Bello Gallico***
MS Ludwig XIII 8 (83.MP.151), fol. 2
Italy, Florence, c.1460–1470

The entwined vine stems enclose the text only on three sides, the open space giving a more airy feel to the page, compared to the previous illustration. Characteristic animals, putti and heraldry embellish the rich pattern, complementing the simplicity of the text hand. The gold initial shows Caesar on horseback.

▶ ***Expositio Psalmorum Davidis: Augustine of Hippo***
Additional MS 14779, fol. 2
Italy, Naples, c.1478

This explanation of the Psalms was written out by Rodolfo Brancalupo. It is a fine example of the Humanist book script used by Bracciolini earlier in the century, which was based on the 12th-century Caroline manuscripts that the Renaissance scholars believed were of classical origin. The x-height of the lower-case letters is large in relation to the nib width, giving a very open appearance to the text. The display letters are a combination of square capitals, rustics and some uncials.

Renaissance: White Vine Initial "N"

Raised gilding is used here as a foil to the intense jewel colours, and the softer sheen of shell gold contrasts with the brilliant polish of the gold letter. Check through the procedure of making and applying gesso (*see pages 54–56*) and techniques for raised gilding and shell gold (*see pages 57–61*) before you begin.

Tools and materials
- *HB pencil*
- *Tracing paper*
- *Red ochre carbon paper (*see page *79) or graphite paper*
- *Sepia waterproof ink*
- *Fine pointed nib (Gillott 659 or mapping pen)*
- *Plaster gesso mixed ready for use*
- *300 gsm (140 lb) hot-pressed watercolour paper*
- *Round-bladed scalpel*
- *Glassine*
- *Clean, sharp scissors*
- *Tweezers*
- *Transfer gold*
- *Double-thickness loose gold leaf*
- *Dogtooth agate burnisher*
- *Pencil burnisher*
- *Shell gold*
- *Sable brushes, sizes 0, 00, 000*
- *Large soft brush*
- *Piece of soft washed silk*

Gouache paints
- *Scarlet lake*
- *Alizarin crimson*
- *Zinc white*
- *Ultramarine*
- *Winsor blue*
- *Oxide of chromium*
- *Lemon yellow*
- *Vandyke brown*
- *Ivory black*
- *Opaque white*
- *Distilled water for mixing*

1 Copy the design onto tracing paper and transfer it to the watercolour paper using carbon transfer or red ochre trace-down sheet (see page 79). Go over the drawing using a fine-pointed nib and sepia ink.

2 Working on a flat surface, dampen the area for gilding with a clean brush dipped in distilled water, then flood the area with plaster gesso (see page 56), teasing it out into the corners. Leave it to dry overnight on a flat, level surface.

3 Gently scrape the surface of the gesso with the scalpel to level out any bumps – do not press, just let the weight of the blade do the work – then polish the plaster with silk. This will reduce the surface friction when you burnish the gesso directly.

4 Breathe on the gesso surface and apply a layer of transfer gold over the whole letter. Burnish the gold through glassine with the dogtooth agate burnisher, then burnish gently directly on the gold. Make sure the whole letter is completely covered.

5 *Have everything necessary for gilding ready at hand (*see page 57*). Breathe on the gesso and apply a layer of loose-leaf gold in one or more pieces to cover the whole letter, pressing it down with the silk. Burnish through glassine, using the point of the agate to tuck the gold over the edges.*

6 *Gently burnish the gold directly before repeating step 5 to add a second layer of loose-leaf gold. Set the edges using a pencil burnisher first through glassine, then burnish directly on the gold working carefully around the letter.*

7 *Remove the surplus gold with a soft brush.*

8 *Next, paint in the areas of shell gold using a size 00 brush. First use a dilute wash, and then paint a second thicker layer of crosshatched strokes. Allow the paint to dry thoroughly, then smooth the surface through glassine before burnishing it directly with a gentle, circular motion.*

9 Mix the gouache so that it flows easily from the brush, but retains its colour intensity. Paint in the red (scarlet lake + zinc white + a little alizarin crimson), then green (oxide of chromium + lemon yellow + zinc white) and finally the blue (ultramarine + Winsor blue + zinc white).

10 Mix a dilute wash of Vandyke brown and ivory black to shade the right and underside of the stems (the light comes from above left) and add details to the flowers. Use a thicker mixture of these colours and a size 000 brush to outline everything, tidying up any rough edges as you work.

11 With opaque white and a size 000 brush, add spots (not too small) in groups of three in the red, blue and shell gold areas. On the green patches, use a concentrated mixture of shell gold in the same way. When dry, polish these spots with a pencil burnisher, twisting it to indent them slightly.

12 The finished letter. Repair any small pinholes by dotting in a small amount of shell gold. Leave to dry, and then burnish.

White Vine Round letters

The O, C, D, G and Q forms in this alphabet are all based on a circle. For the C and G, the top and bottom "arms" of the letters are slightly flattened. D occupies the same visual area as O.

C

Letters can be squared up into a neat rectangle. Use a ruling pen to draw on a border with shell gold at step 7. Burnish and then outline with the brown/black mix at step 9.

D

G

Make a colour rough before you begin, aiming for an even balance of red, green and gold across the letter.

O

Q

White Vine Wide letters

Note that M has a scalloped border.

Note that the M is not an upside-down W; the centre section is the same width as a V. The W is two Vs side by side.

Be patient and do not rush to burnish the gold too hard too soon. You may scrape the gold and damage the plaster beneath.

Aim for the appearance of even colour distribution across the design – sometimes the first attempt does not always work.

White Vine Rectangular/straight letters

Balance the colours across the design so that they are evenly distributed but not necessarily symmetrical. The patches of shell gold should be placed away from the polished gold letter.

All rectangular letters occupy the same visual area as an O. H is the defining letter in this group; note that its crossbar is slightly above centre. The crossbar of the T is the same width as the H. Note that the vine pierces the T as well as wrapping around it. The curve of the U follows that of the lower half of an O.

Shading the underside of the vine stems gives a 3-D effect.

White Vine Rectangular/diagonal letters

*These letters also relate proportionally to the area of a letter O but are characterized by their diagonal lines. Z is the same width as a T. K is actually narrower (*see pages 200–201*) but is included here for its characteristics, rather than the space it occupies. N (*see pages 192–195*) also belongs in this group.*

K

A V

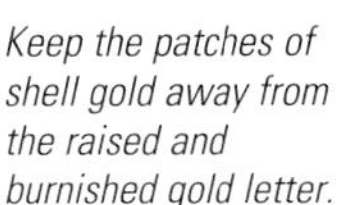

Keep the patches of shell gold away from the raised and burnished gold letter.

X

Y

Z

White Vine Narrow/straight letters

Narrow letters are effectively half the width of the rectangular letters on pages 198 and 199. The bottom bar of the E is slightly wider than those at the top and centre. The curve of the J is flattened as in the C and G on page 196.

The vine twists on L have been adapted for use on E and F in this group.

Repair any small pinholes in the surface of the gold leaf by dotting in a small amount of shell gold mixed with distilled water (see pages 61–62). Leave to dry, then burnish.

White Vine Narrow/curved letters

The dots always appear in groups of three, unless the space is very small.

B

*These four letters are also half the width of the rectangular letters on pages 198 and 199. The upper and lower "arms" of the S are flattened as for the C and G (*see page 196*). The bowls of the B (the lower is slightly larger), P and R are circular in shape and are related to the O.*

This branched vine pattern has been adapted to suit the other letters in this group, with the addition of a second stem on S.

P

R

S

White Vine Numbers

7

Plan colour schemes for single (or combinations of) numbers with coloured pencils on your original sketch or a photocopy. If you get the balance of colour right on the rough, you can gild and paint the finished piece with confidence.

A very simple vine shape pierces the number (see also I and F on page 200).

Decorative numbers like these (based on the alphabet form) were not used in original manuscripts. Plain Roman numerals (II, VI, X, etc.) were more often found and were used to indicate chapters or verses, as manuscripts were generally written in Latin.

Rectangular boxes or scalloped edges can be used for numbers too. Adapt the designs to fit around two or more numbers as necessary.

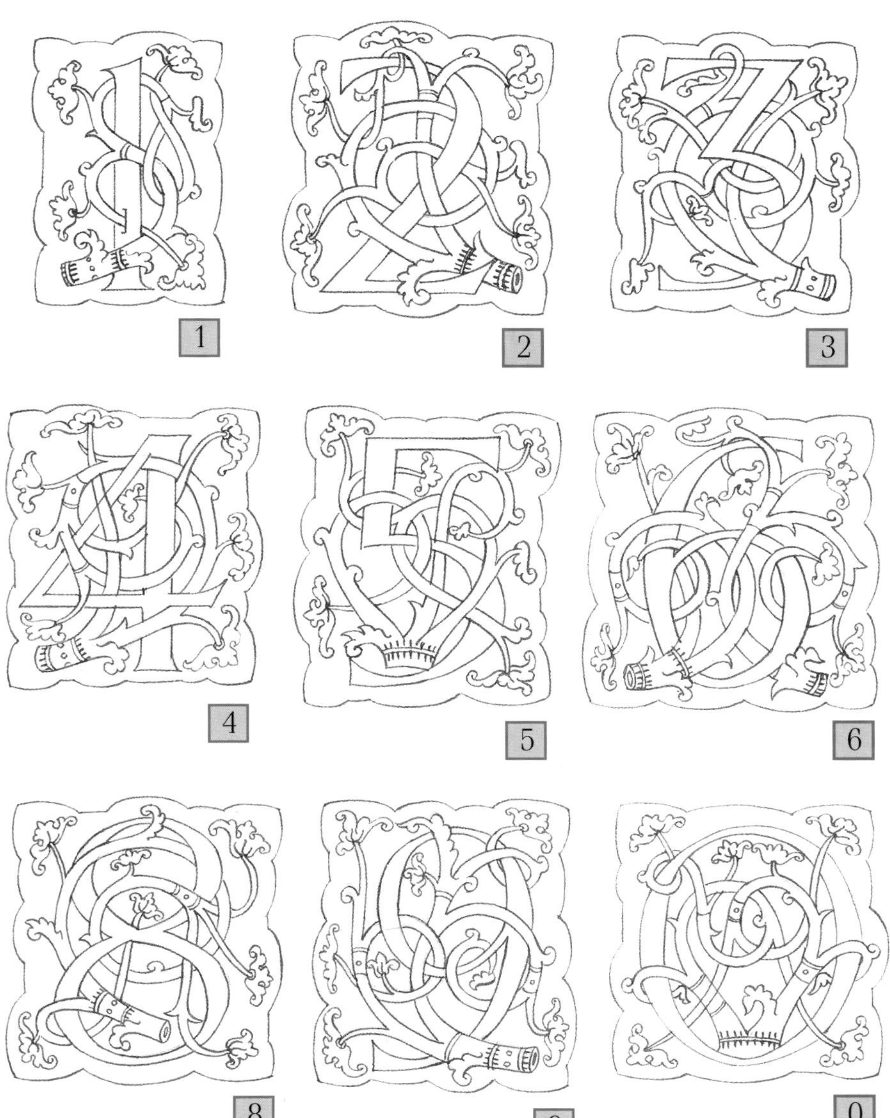

1 2 3 4 5 6 8 9 0

Humanist Square capitals

These pages show a basic Humanist hand and numerals, as well as some suggested variations, which are suitable for text incorporated into more complex projects (*see pages 69–71 and 81–83*). Study the letters carefully to observe their shapes and how they are formed, using the numbered strokes. Letter height is given in the nib width "ladders", and this remains constant whichever size nib you choose.

The pen angle diagrams indicate the angle at which the nib is held to the horizontal writing line, in order to achieve the naturally occurring thicks and thins typical of the letter style. Look to see where these are. Practice is needed to keep this angle consistent as you write. Try this exercise to help you: Use either the diagram or a protractor to check the angle and "set" your pen nib against it in relation to the writing line, then make a letter shape using your whole arm to move the pen, rather than just your fingers. Check the thicks and thins, and adjust your pen angle as needed.

The beauty of Roman inscriptional letters and the written square capitals of 5th-century manuscripts were important influences on the Humanist scribes. These elegant square capitals are based on those that were the specialty of the Paduan scribe, Bartolomeo San Vito (1435–1518). They were rarely used for whole passages of text, but were reserved for title pages, initial letters and colophons, the letters sometimes alternately coloured and gold.

The capitals are written at a height of 7 nib widths, with a fairly flat pen angle, between 15 and 20°. Some pen manipulation (marked *) and additional pen strokes are needed to make the serifs and to balance the weight of diagonals. Generous letter spacing and good legibility is characteristic.

Calligraphy by Margaret Morgan

18°
A B C D E
F G H I J K
L M N O P
Q R S T U V
W X Y Z ß
& ? ! ; É Ű È

Humanist Lower-case letters

The Humanist scribes revived the Carolingian hand of the 9th century and adapted it for their transcriptions of Classical texts. This new script was further refined, becoming the model for early typefaces used in printing.

These lower-case letters (or minuscules) are based on a 15th-century bookhand with a round "o" and broadly formed arches on "h", "m", "n" and "u". The pen angle is fairly flat (about 18°), as for the square capitals opposite, and the serifs are made in the same way, as separate strokes. Changes in pen angle (*) are needed to maintain the visual continuity of line width in all the letters. In diagonal letters (for example, "v" and "w"), it can help to write the top left-hand serif first, to help place the first diagonal more accurately.

Humanist Extra characters and numbers

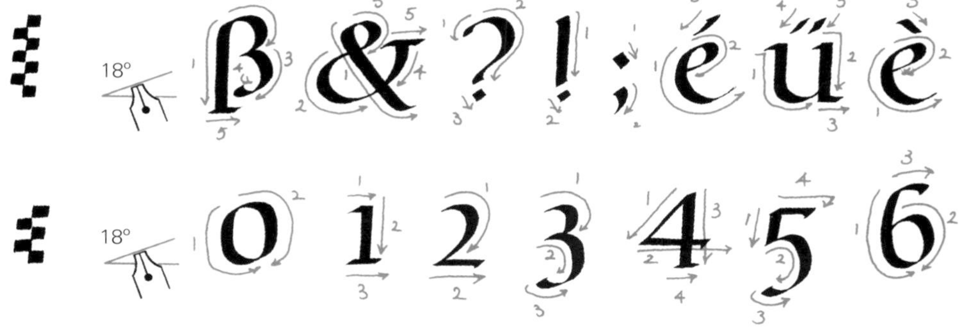

Numerals are based on the lower-case x-height, but the old-style figures extend 2 nib widths above x-height (even numbers) or 2 nib widths below base line (odd numbers).

Humanist Heavyweight

anbncndnenfng
hninjnknlnmno

Three nib widths of a larger nib (no. 1). Internal spaces are kept similar to the original by stretching the letter laterally. This gives a very strong visual texture.

abcdefghijklmn
opqrstuvwxyz
ß&?!;éűè

Borders and Motifs

Renaissance scribes drew their influence from the manuscripts of the 10th and 11th centuries, reinventing the vine stems and leaf motifs into even more organic manifestations, to writhe and twine their way through raised gold letters and borders. These intertwined forms also hark back to the early Celtic style of decoration. The colour scheme does not vary – red, blue and green, with contrasting patches of shell gold.

The vine, which is shaded to suggest three-dimensional form, is the most dominant motif, although naturalistic animals, plump putti (cherubs) and heraldic shields are frequently incorporated.

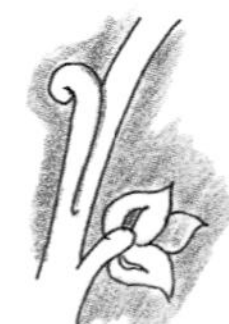

Details of vine stems and decorative leaves at the ends of stems.

A deer with golden antlers peers out from this deep border (see also page 189).

This swan-like bird is reminiscent of the Celtic zoomorphic forms, as it bites the vine that surrounds it.

*Cameo portraits, heraldic devices or other motifs relevant to the text or patron of the manuscript are contained within laurel wreaths or decorative cartouches set into the border (*see also page 189*).*

Vine stems extend out of the letter's counter space (the yellow indicates the body of the gold letter) to form a self-contained border strip.

Vine stems and leaves enclosed within raised gold borders.

Animals and portrait cameos may occur within borders.

Renaissance: Neo-Classical

The Renaissance in northern Italy generated a different decorative style, based on letters found in ancient Roman inscriptions in stone with architectural and other Classical motifs. The painting style is also different, using sketchy, interlocking strokes of darker colour over a light base wash, in a much greater range of colours.

Renaissance
Neo-Classical

Alongside the Humanist manuscripts in the White Vine style (*see pages 186–209*), a new and more classical style was developed in the north of Italy, by antiquarians with a passion for Roman culture. They looked at ancient Roman inscriptions in stone and made collections of authentic Latin texts.

This movement not only involved scribes such as Bartolomeo Sanvito (1435–1518) and Felice Feliciano (1433–1479), but also artists such as Andrea Mantegna (1431–1506) and Marco Zoppo (1433–1478). The effect of these painters on the style of book illumination is quite distinct. Large faceted capitals are shaded to look like those carved in stone, set about with motifs from ancient Rome. Shields, spears, banners, vases and skulls from memorials to the Republic's military heroes are combined with less bellicose images that include acanthus leaves, cornucopia, dolphins, medallions and swags of leaves.

The style of painting was quite different from the White Vine style, moving away from the use of flat colours, although these can still be used effectively (*see page 220*), to sketchy, hairline strokes often laid crosshatched over a wash of complementary colour. This increased the luminosity on the page. The artists painted as realistically as possible, using highlights and shadows to create a three-dimensional effect, reflecting the developments in the art of the period.

▶ ***The works of Virgil, opening of The Aeneid***
King's 24, fol. 59
Italy, Rome, c.1499
An example of the work of Bartolomeo Sanvito, showing the typical elements of this style: architectural borders with Classical motifs such as vases and swags of leaves, as well as large, decorated and faceted capital letters. The hairline strokes that make up the luminous colours can be seen clearly. The script is slightly sloped, related to the Italic hand of the later Renaissance manuscripts.

P·VIRGILII MARO
NIS AENEIDOS LI
BER PRIMVS·

ILLE ego q quondā gracili modulatus auena
Carmen: & egressus siluis uicina coegi
Vt quis auido parerent arua colono:
Gratum opus agricolis: at nūc horrentia martis:

ARMA VI
RVMQVE
CANO TRO
IAE QVI
PRIMVS AB ORIS

INTERPRETATIO EVSE
BII CAESARIENSIS ED
TA PER BEATVM HIERO
NYMVM; ET IPSIVS PRO
SPERIQ ADDITIONES
DE TEMPORIBVS.
PROLOGVS BEATI HIERONYMI.
EVSEBIVS
HIERONY
MVS VIN
CENTIO ET
GALIENO
SVIS SALVTEM.
VETVS ISTE DISER
TORVM MOS FVIT VT

◀ **Eusebius: Chronica (History of the World)**
Royal 14 C iii, fol. 2
Italy, Rome or Padua, c.1480–1490

St. Jerome and his lion: Another Sanvito manuscript, made for his friend and fellow scholar Bernardo Bembo, a treasure trove of superbly decorated capitals. The wonderful, freely written square capitals on this title page are bordered by tall pillars (reminiscent of Trajan's column in Rome), subtly painted in shades of sepia and highlighted with accents of shell gold that gleam warmly when they catch the light. The style of illumination owes much to the work of the painter Andrea Mantegna.

▶ **Petrarch: Trionfi (Poems)**
Additional MS 38125, fols. 33b–34
Italy, Milan, end of the 15th century

The faceted N sits in front of a rosette, cleverly painted to look like carved stone. It is set into a border rich in classical imagery and shell gold decoration. The illumination style is related to the paintings of Giovan Pietro Birago, who worked for the Sforza Dukes of Milan.

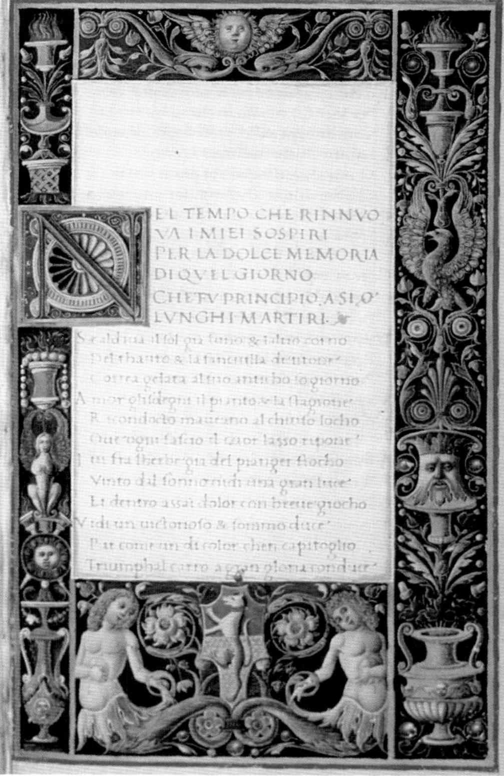

The work of one scribe in particular, Bartolomeo Sanvito, stands out from his contemporaries. His elegant square capitals and fluent Italic hand complement the exquisitely detailed *trompe l'œil* borders he painted. He was no mere copyist, but a knowledgeable collector of antiquities. He worked for Bernardo Bembo (1433–1519), and at Rome's Papal Court.

Many of the letters in this alphabet are based on those found in Virgil's *Eclogues and Georgics* and Eusebius' *History of the World*, both manuscripts written and probably decorated by Sanvito. The painted letters show variations in treatment and colour schemes of this elegant style.

Professional scribes who needed to write quickly to earn their money probably developed the Italic hand, or Humanist cursive, which was contemporary with this type of capital letter. The sloped script and joined letters took much less time to write than the precise and careful round hand with its many pen lifts.

Renaissance: Neo-Classical Initial "A"

This initial is painted in shell gold shaded with brown watercolour to simulate a letter carved in stone. The rich background is made with layers of hairline brush strokes of red over a wash of yellow. The decorative motifs are painted in a similar way to give a realistic feel. Working on vellum adds depth to the colour; the addition of gum water to the paint gives a soft sheen to the finished work.

Tools and materials

- *HB pencil*
- *Tracing paper*
- *Piece of prepared vellum* (see pages 26–32)
- *Dilute, waterproof, black ink*
- *Fine pointed nib (Gillott 659 or mapping pen)*
- *Masking fluid and old brush*
- *Sable brushes, sizes 1, 0, 00*
- *Soft plastic eraser*
- *Shell gold*
- *Dogtooth agate burnisher*
- *Glassine*
- *Piece of plate glass with sanded edges (optional)*

Watercolour paints

- *Yellow ochre*
- *Scarlet lake*
- *Ultramarine*
- *Alizarin crimson*
- *Cadmium yellow pale*
- *Oxide of chromium*
- *Vandyke brown*
- *Ivory black*
- *Winsor blue (to mix darker green)*
- *Distilled water for mixing*
- *Gum water for mixing* (see page 47)

Gouache paint for highlights

- *Opaque white*
- *Cadmium or spectrum yellow*

1 Trace off the design, tape it onto a light box and draw the backlit image onto the vellum. Alternatively, use the tracing down method described on page 78. Go over the design using a fine nib and dilute black waterproof ink.

2 Tape the vellum lightly onto a flat surface. A piece of plate glass makes an ideal surface because it can be easily manoeuvred and provides a hard surface for burnishing. Use an old brush to apply the masking fluid to the parts where you do not want the background colour.

3 When the masking fluid is completely dry (it becomes translucent), mix yellow ochre with distilled water, and apply a dilute wash with a size 1 sable brush. Use the paint sparingly, so that you do not overwet the vellum and make it cockle.

4 Mix up red (scarlet lake + a little cadmium yellow) with gum water and add a second layer of colour using hairline strokes that do not quite interlock. Add a third layer of red using crosshatched strokes that allow some yellow to show through.

5 When the paint is completely dry, remove the masking film with a soft eraser to reveal the design. Brush away the residue with a soft brush – using your fingers could transfer grease to the vellum surface.

6 Paint the initial with shell gold. Dilute it with distilled water and flood the area with a thin mixture first (not too wet). When it is dry, add a second thicker coat using crosshatched strokes to give an even covering. Put in the dots on the cornucopia and the red flowers.

7 Use the agate burnisher to polish the gold when it is dry, smoothing it first through glassine, then directly on the surface with a gentle circular motion.

8 Lay the first dilute washes (as in step 3) on the cornucopia (ultramarine + alizarin crimson), the leaves (cadmium yellow + oxide of chromium), and flowers (alizarin crimson).

9 Add the details of the design with a size 00 brush and stronger mixes of the colours used in step 8. Add some Winsor blue for a darker tone of green for the leaves. Mix scarlet lake with Vandyke brown and add a shadow to the right of all the elements in the design.

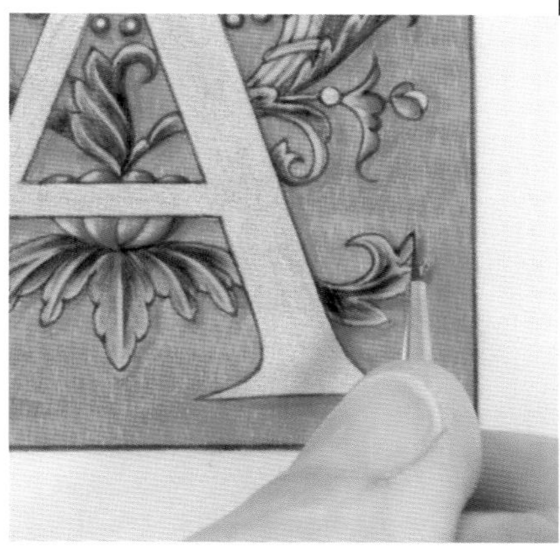

10 Mix Vandyke brown with a little ivory black and outline the whole design. This will tidy up any ragged edges. Use this paint to rule in the border (see page 73).

11 Shade the initial, assuming the light is coming from above. Use crosshatched strokes of the brown/black mix to build up the mid-tone on the right of the letter and the darker area at the base.

12 To complete the piece, add highlights with gouache paints. Use opaque white on the pink areas, and a mixture of white and cadmium (or spectrum) yellow on the rest.

Neo-Classical Round letters

*The flat gouache colours used here offer an alternative look, and masking fluid is not necessary (*see painting techniques, page 40*).*

D

The letter is painted in tones of cobalt blue. The darkest tone has some ultramarine.

Background of scarlet lake.

The leaves are painted in cadmium yellow + yellow ochre. Add Vandyke brown for darker tones and the outline. Use zinc white to mix lighter tones.

C

G

O

Q

Neo-Classical Wide letters

The background to this letter is painted in a mix of Hooker's green light + Winsor blue over a yellow ochre wash. The letter itself is painted in alizarin crimson + a little burnt umber. The colours of the leaves and flowers are the same as on the letter A in the main project, pages 216–219.

*The rectangular edges can be treated in different ways. Here, small half-moon shapes are cut out of the edge (*see also page 224*).*

Highlights were painted over the colour in shell gold, and then burnished.

A ruled border of burnished shell gold has been outlined with brown paint. Rule the lines using either of the techniques on page 73.

M

Neo-Classical Rectangular/straight letters

The background colour is the same as the letter A in the main project, pages 216–219.

Dolphins are painted in cerulean blue + a little light red.

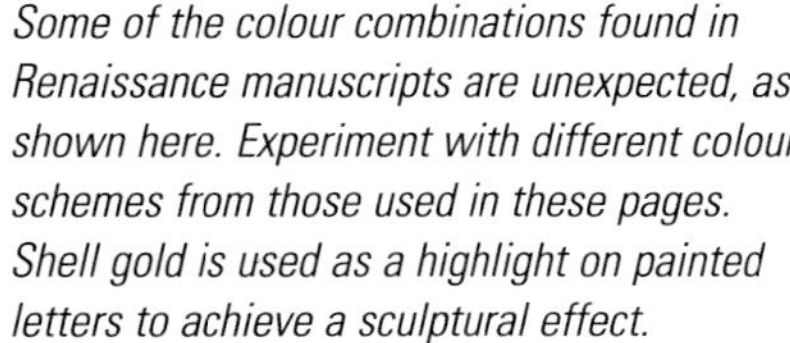

Some of the colour combinations found in Renaissance manuscripts are unexpected, as shown here. Experiment with different colour schemes from those used in these pages. Shell gold is used as a highlight on painted letters to achieve a sculptural effect.

The letter is painted in cerulean blue + permanent rose + Chinese white (for darker shading add more red).

Neo-Classical Rectangular/diagonal letters

*This background colour provides a rich contrast to the letter. Shadows have been painted in a mix of ultramarine + burnt umber. This group of letters also includes the letter A (*see pages 216–219*).*

The background colour is ultramarine + Winsor blue over a wash of permanent mauve. Strokes of permanent rose were then applied.

Scarlet lake over a yellow ochre wash makes up the letter.

V

K

N

X

Y

Z

Neo-Classical Narrow/straight letters

E

The flowers are painted in a wash of scarlet lake, shaded with alizarin crimson and opaque white gouache highlights.

The leaves are in cadmium yellow with opaque white gouache highlights.

The shadows are a mix of ultramarine + burnt umber.

F

I

Here, the background has been painted in ultramarine + Winsor blue over a cerulean blue wash, before a second layer of strokes of permanent rose. The letter has been shaded with shell gold, as for the letter A in the main project, pages 216–219.

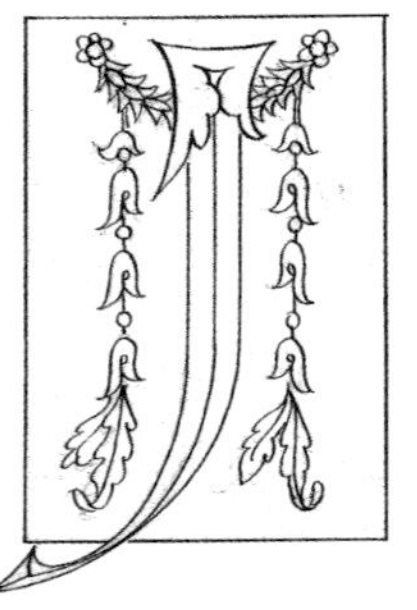

J

L

Neo-Classical Narrow/curved letters

R

Here, a strong mix of alizarin crimson in hairline strokes (two layers) over two washes of yellow ochre and scarlet lake achieves this deep, rich background colour.

The shadows are made from alizarin crimson + burnt umber.

This group of letters shows another different treatment, adapted from an early 16th-century manuscript attributed to Ludovico Arrighi (1475–1527). Masking fluid was laid over the letter, flowers and larger leaf areas, but the underlying drawing is still visible through the layers of background colour, so you can easily see where to add the painted shell gold filigree decoration.

Flowers are painted in cobalt blue + Chinese white.

Shell gold is used for the letter (as well as for the ruled border and flower centres). It is burnished to catch the light.

B

P

S

Neo-Classical Numbers

3

*This range of numbers has been devised specially for this book and is based on the numerals that accompany the versal alphabet (*see page 131*). Illuminated numbers were not found in original manuscripts but are useful for adding to birthday and celebration cards. There is a rich vocabulary of motifs (*see pages 232–235*) which you can use to devise your own versions.*

Follow the styles and colours on the preceding pages. This shows a vignetted colour background as another alternative.

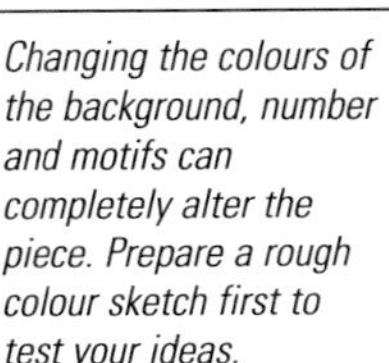

*As an alternative, use flat gouache colours to surround the numbers (*see page 225*) or add interest with one of the borders shown on pages 220 to 225.*

Changing the colours of the background, number and motifs can completely alter the piece. Prepare a rough colour sketch first to test your ideas.

1
2
4
5
6
7
8
9
0

Italic Capital and lower-case letters

These pages show a basic Italic hand and numerals, as well as some suggested variations, which are suitable for text incorporated into more complex projects (*see pages 69–71 and 81–83*). Study the letters carefully to observe their shapes and how they are formed, using the numbered strokes. Letter height is given in the nib width "ladders", and this remains constant whichever size nib you choose.

The pen angle diagrams indicate the angle at which the nib is held to the horizontal writing line, in order to achieve the naturally occurring thicks and thins typical of the letter style. Look to see where these are. Practice is needed to keep this angle consistent as you write. Try this exercise to help you: Use either the diagram or a protractor to check the angle and "set" your pen nib

against it in relation to the writing line, then make a letter shape using your whole arm to move the pen, rather than just your fingers. Check the thicks and thins, and adjust your pen angle as needed.

Based on an oval "o", the compressed letterforms of formal Italic alphabets have springing arches (branching two-thirds up the stem). They are written at a 5° slant, with a pen angle of 35–45°, and minimum penlifts to each letter. Italic is the most versatile hand for the modern calligrapher, and can be used for formal scrolls and certificates, or for more expressive forms of calligraphy. Italic capitals, based on classical Roman capitals, are compressed and sloped.

Calligraphy by Janet Mehigan

Lower-case letters are written at 5 nib widths x-height, with springing arches. Ascenders and descenders are 3 nib widths.

Italic Extra characters

As for lower-case letters, symbols are written at 5 nib widths x-height, with springing arches. Ascenders and descenders are 3 nib widths.

Italic Narrow

bncndnenfngnhninj
nlnmnonpnqnrnsn

Five nib widths and sloped. Write at 45° pen angle. Smooth oval arches spring from about ⅔ up the x-height stem. Write slowly.

abcdefghijklmno
pqrstuvwxyzß&
!?;èüé

45°

Italic Numbers

Numerals are the same height as capital letters, at a consistent 7 nib widths high.

Italic Flourished

Standard 5 nib widths and 30° pen angle. Write with rhythm and confidence. Allow extra space between lines and write using your whole arm movement. Fun to try.

30°

Borders and Motifs

The motifs used by the Humanist scribe/illuminators reflect their passionate interest in all things Classical. Roman inscriptions and architectural styles provided a rich source of ideas for their richly decorated manuscripts. The technique of painting, using sketchy, hairline strokes and overlaying colours, lends itself to the naturalistic rendering of their subject matter. Colour schemes are richer and much more varied, in some cases using eye-catching colour combinations, which do not appear in earlier manuscripts, giving pages a very sophisticated feel.

*The style of drawing is accurate, factual and restrained compared to the Romanesque period, but colours and painting technique (*see pages 212–215*) give a great vitality to the decoration. Yellow in the sketches represents the shell gold that was used in manuscripts of this period.*

Acanthus leaves and this type of floral rosette can be seen in ancient Roman architecture.

This simplified acanthus-style motif comes from an architectural frieze.

Laurel leaves, with their imperial connotations, are used in many ways. Here, they are shown in the form of a swag.

Heroic imagery, such as shields, spears and this armour, recall Rome's military might.

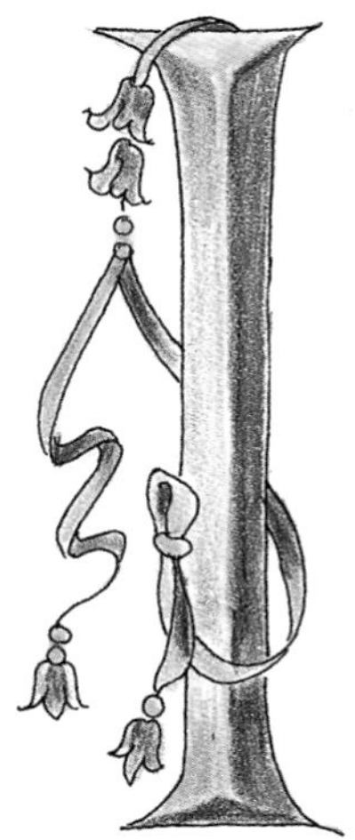

Monumental capital letters painted to look like faceted inscriptional letters carved in stone. The stark effect is softened by the draped ribbon banner (see also pages 216–223).

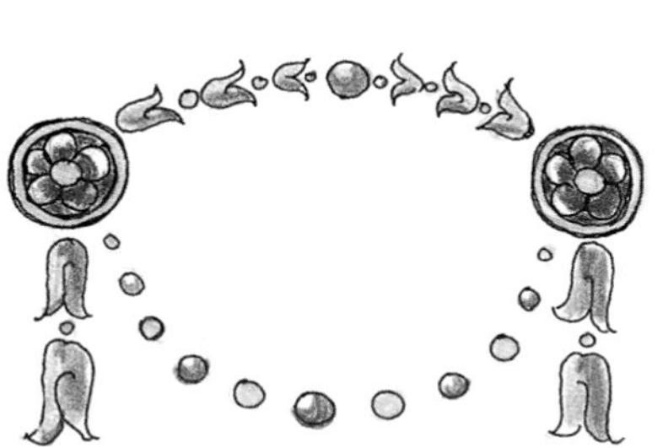

Floral rosettes and linked strings of flower buds and beads, decorated with highlights of shell gold.

A golden cartouche containing a floral motif resembles a piece of jewellery.

The discovery of the laws of perspective by Renaissance artists influenced manuscript illuminators. Borders are full of recognizable architectural features and decorative details, shaded to give a three-dimensional look (see also page 214).

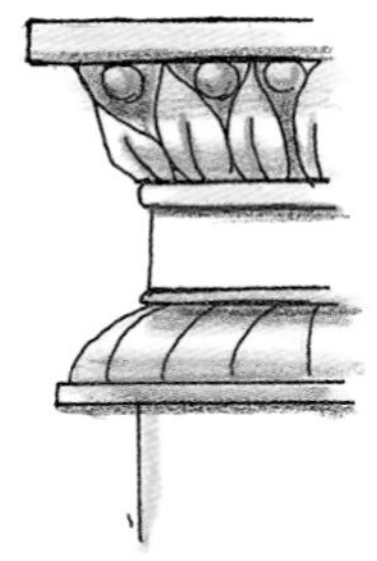

Moulded architrave detail.

A clever combination of colour tones and shell gold feathers form the beginnings of an arched border.

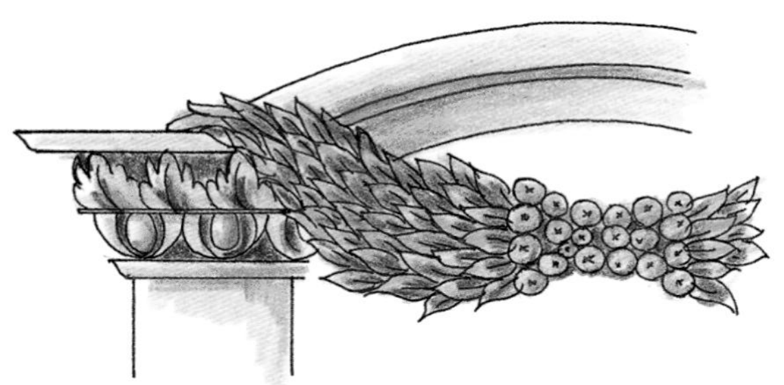

Acanthus leaves and a traditional egg-and-cup moulding form the capital of a border pillar. The arch supports a huge swag of laurel leaves and golden apples.

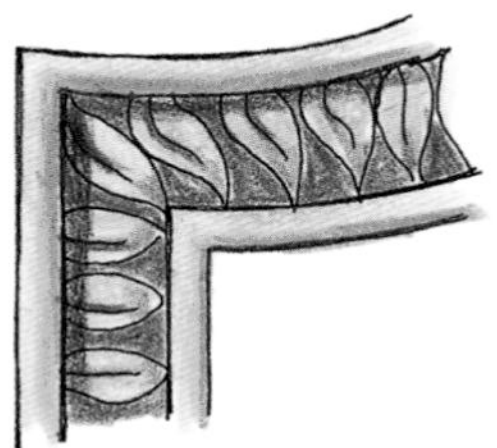

A repeated laurel leaf motif is contained within a double border of shell gold.

A golden urn, supported by acanthus leaves, modelled with overpainting in sepia.

The essence of Neo-Classical borders is that of symmetry. The decoration on each side of the page is not always exactly the same, but has a feeling of balance and order (see also pages 213, 214 and 215).

Symbols of plenty, such as cornucopia combined with flower buds against a hatched background.

This beacon on a column decorated with flowers and acanthus leaves is reminiscent of later Gothic manuscript illumination.

Chapter 4

Contemporary Gallery

The following pages show examples of work by some contemporary calligraphers. The pieces have been chosen to illustrate how traditional techniques and materials can be used in a modern idiom, and in some cases, very unconventional ways. The work not only reflects the historical development and centuries-old aspects of the craft, but also shows something of calligraphy and illumination's exciting present and future.

HOLY
HOLY
HOLY

▶ ***Manny Ling***
All My Words Are You
Panel: 14 x 40 cm (5½ x 15¾ in)
Transfer (U.S.: patent) bronze and gold leaf on spraymount.

Bands of gouache wash are painted onto stretched watercolour paper, and then the text is added with metal nibs.

The bronze (at the head and foot of the panel) and gold leaf were added in a very unconventional way – spraymount was sprayed directly onto the leaf and pressed onto the paper, and the gold then "dabbled" in places to give a textured finish.

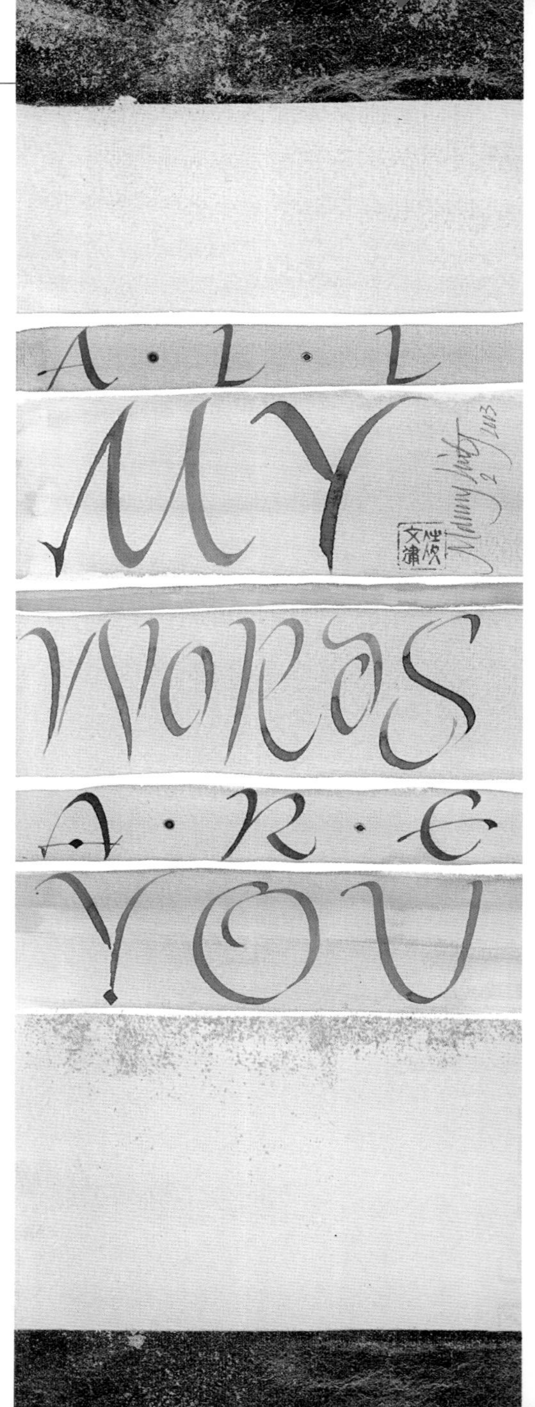

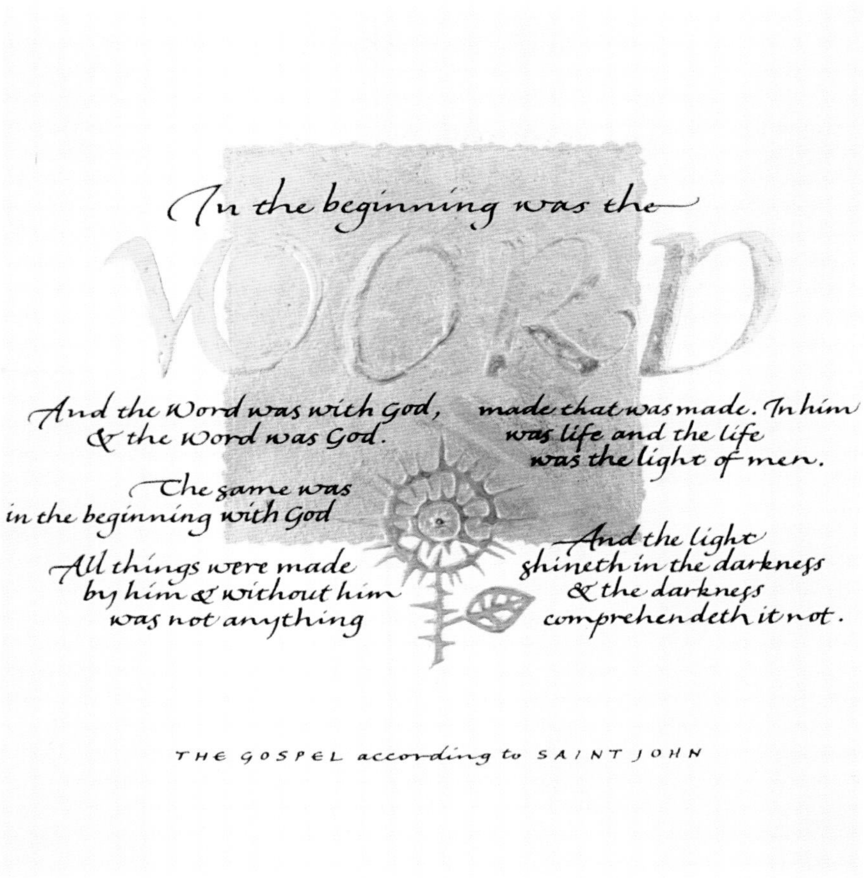

In the beginning was the
WORD
And the Word was with God,
& the Word was God.
The same was
in the beginning with God
All things were made
by him & without him
was not anything
made that was made. In him
was life and the life
was the light of men.
And the light
shineth in the darkness
& the darkness
comprehendeth it not.

THE GOSPEL according to SAINT JOHN

▲ **Margaret Morgan**
In The Beginning
Panel: 18.5 x 19 cm (7 x 7½ in)
Raised and flat gilding, text in Chinese stick ink.
"WORD" and the crown of thorns symbol were laid first in plaster gesso on Arches HP watercolour paper. When dry, two layers of gum ammoniac were painted in a square and everything gilded with transfer (U.S.: patent) gold and double-thickness 24 carat loose-leaf (U.S.: transfer) gold. The writing was added last.

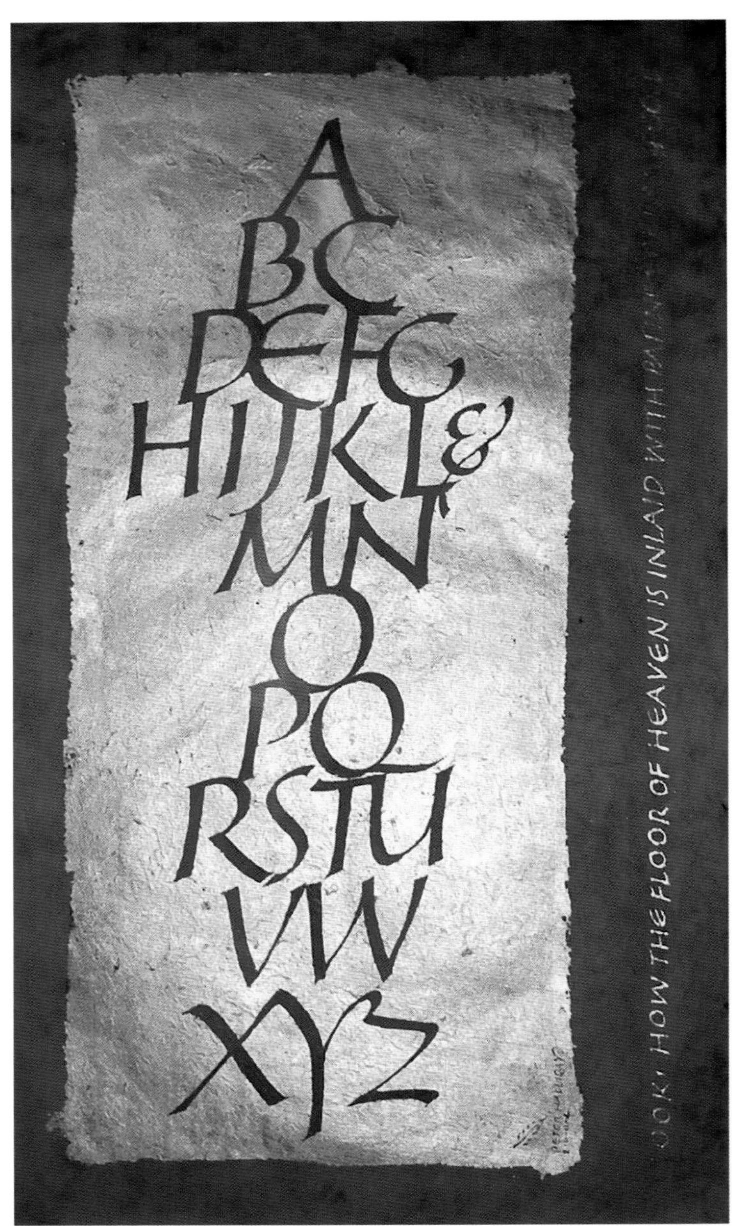

▶ **_Peter Halliday_**
Alphabet
Panel: 28 x 45 cm
(11 x 17¾ in)

Transfer (U.S.: patent) gold is pressed onto a base layer of oil pastel laid thickly on Nepali lokta paper, with the alphabet scratched out (sgraffito) using metal nibs to scrape through the gold to reveal the colour beneath. The quotation at the side is gold leaf on a PVA base.

▶ **Mary Noble**
Absorbed
Panel: 25 cm (9¾ in) square
Lettering written in various dilute mixes of gouache with metal nibs draws the eye into the central square, which has gold leaf pressed onto oil pastel. On Khadi handmade paper.

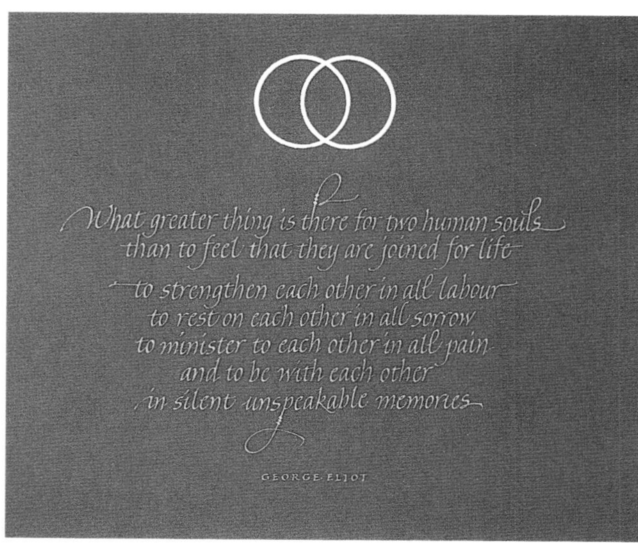

◀ **Marlene Gray**
What Greater Thing Is There
Panel: 25.5 cm (10 in) square
Transfer (U.S.: patent) gold leaf on acrylic gold size and text written in gouache with metal nibs on Ingres paper.

Valerie Dugan
Gold
Panel: 20 x 20 cm (8 x 8 in)

A modern take on a very traditional motif. Gold leaf on gum ammoniac with decorative acanthus-style leaf pattern painted in watercolour on vellum.

Janet Mehigan
B for Butterfly
Panel: 17 x 7 cm (6½ x 2¾ in)

Stretched vellum panel with a brilliant burnished gold capital letter on plaster gesso base. The nettle leaf and butterfly are painted in egg tempera over watercolour washes; the text is written in gouache with metal nibs.

Margaret Morgan
Holy Holy Holy
Panel: 11.5 x 18 cm (4½ x 7 in)
Flat gilding on PVA medium

Rough garden twine was used to draw the angel directly onto the paper and metal nibs were used to write the text. Where the PVA settled thickly in the angel shape, it has given a slightly raised effect.

HOLY
HOLY
HOLY
Lord · God · of · Sabaoth

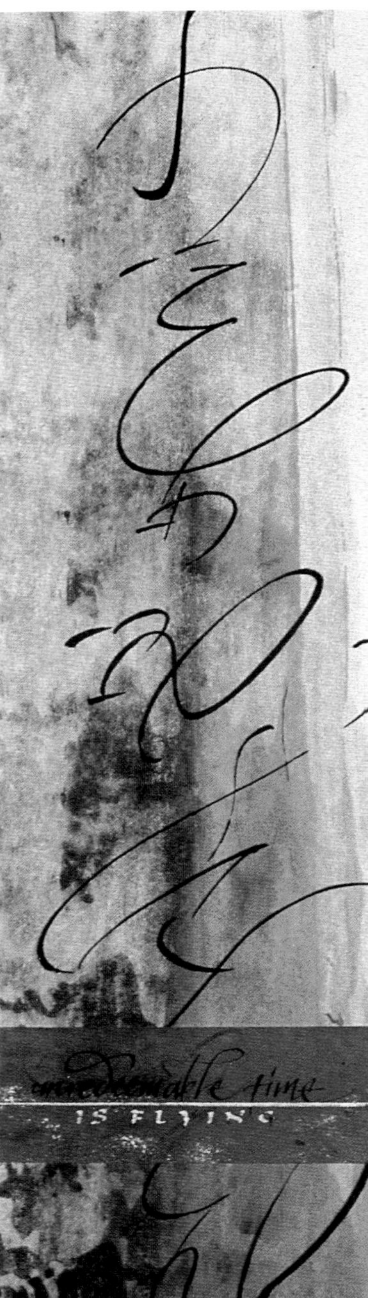

► **Peter Halliday**
Panel to commemorate the opening of the Science Learning Centre (West Midlands) at the University of Keele, 2005 (detail).
Panel: 87.5 x 60.5 cm
(34½ x 23¾ in)

The base is covered with Nepali lokta paper, painted with acrylic paint, and edged with gold leaf. There are two further layers of mirrored glass using gold leaf and sgraffito letters, and a layer of glass with quotations painted in coloured acrylic. The final layer is toughened glass with the dedication engraved into it.

► **Mary Noble**
Time Is Flying
Panel: 11 x 39 cm
(4¼ x 15½ in)

Free brush lettering in black ink, written over rollered stripes of Plaka (casein-based paint). The strip at the base of the panel is Japanese tissue, stuck with gelatine over the quotation in gold leaf on an acrylic medium and black ink.

► **Lin Kerr**
Pythagoras QED
Panel: 76 x 50 cm
(30 x 20 in)
Flat gilding on gum ammoniac.

The vertical gold strip is Dutch metal on a PVA base, dusted with pumice and gum sandarac before the text was written in gouache, directly over the metal. Additional text was added with hand-cut rubber and industrial metal stamps. The proof of the theorem is graphically illustrated in the mosaic squares, which are painted in pairs of complementary colours and tiny squares of gold leaf on gum ammoniac. On handmade Fabriano Roma paper.

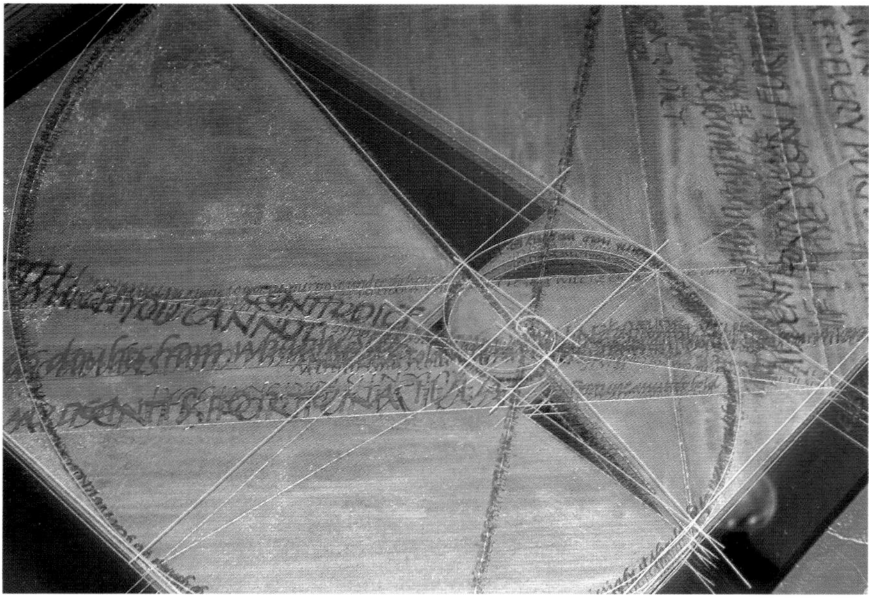

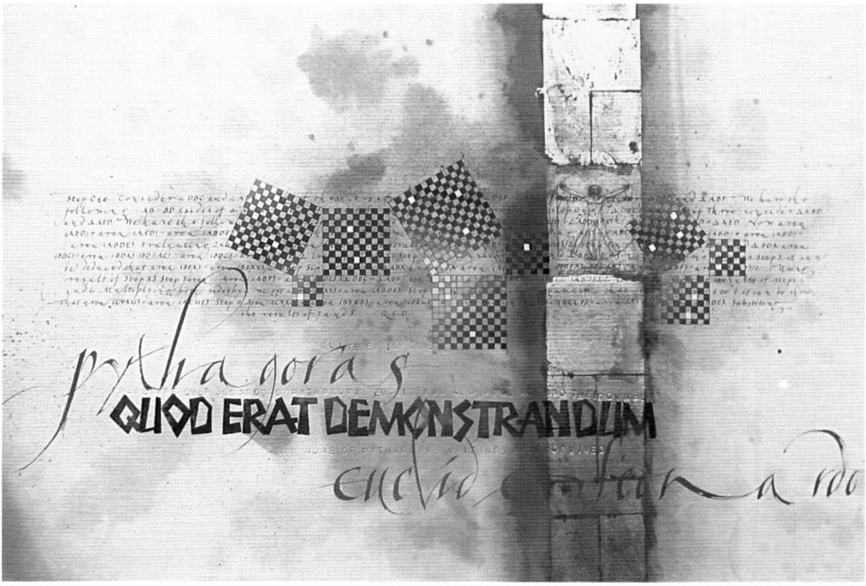
pythagoras
QUOD ERAT DEMONSTRANDUM

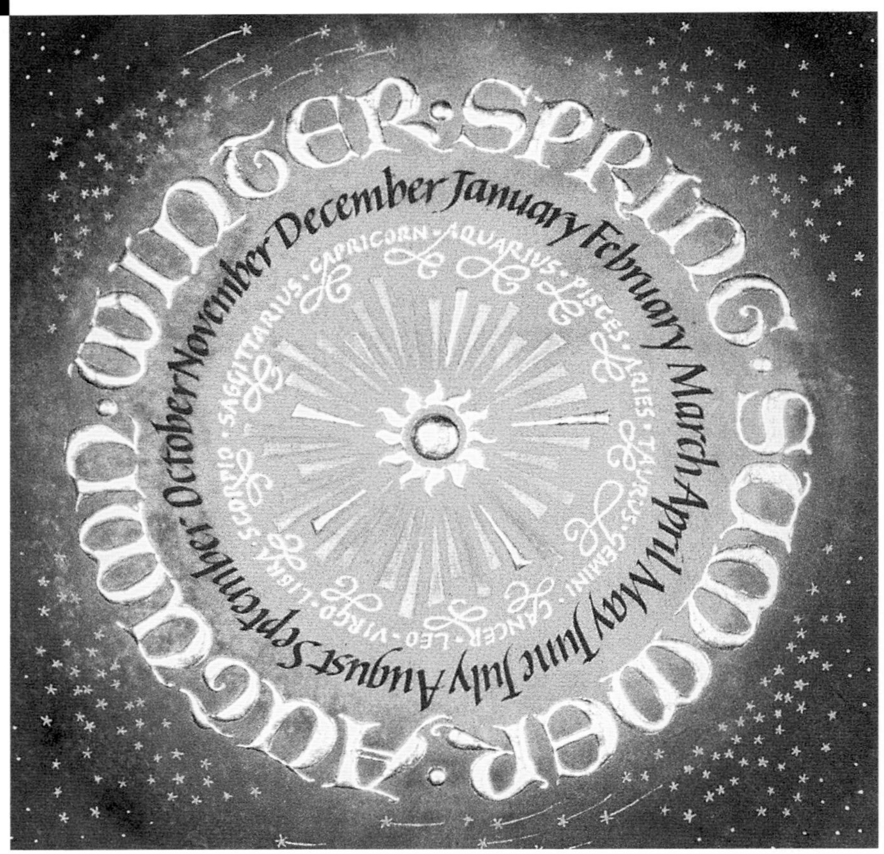

▲ ***Lorna Bambury***
The Seasons
Panel: 21.5 cm (9¾ in) square
Raised and flat gilding.

Lettering and decoration in raised and burnished gold, different colours of shell gold and gouache, using both quills and metal pens on a panel of stretched, dyed vellum.

The work of the originator of the "easy gesso" recipe on page 54.

► ***Nadia Hlibka***
She Bears All Things
Panel: 46 x 61 cm (18 x 24 in)
A synthesis of calligraphy and conceptual painting, which also includes gilding.

24 carat gold over acrylic medium on metal collage, with lettering in gouache over and under gel transfer. Acrylic, charcoal and coloured pencil are also involved in this intriguing, multilayered work.

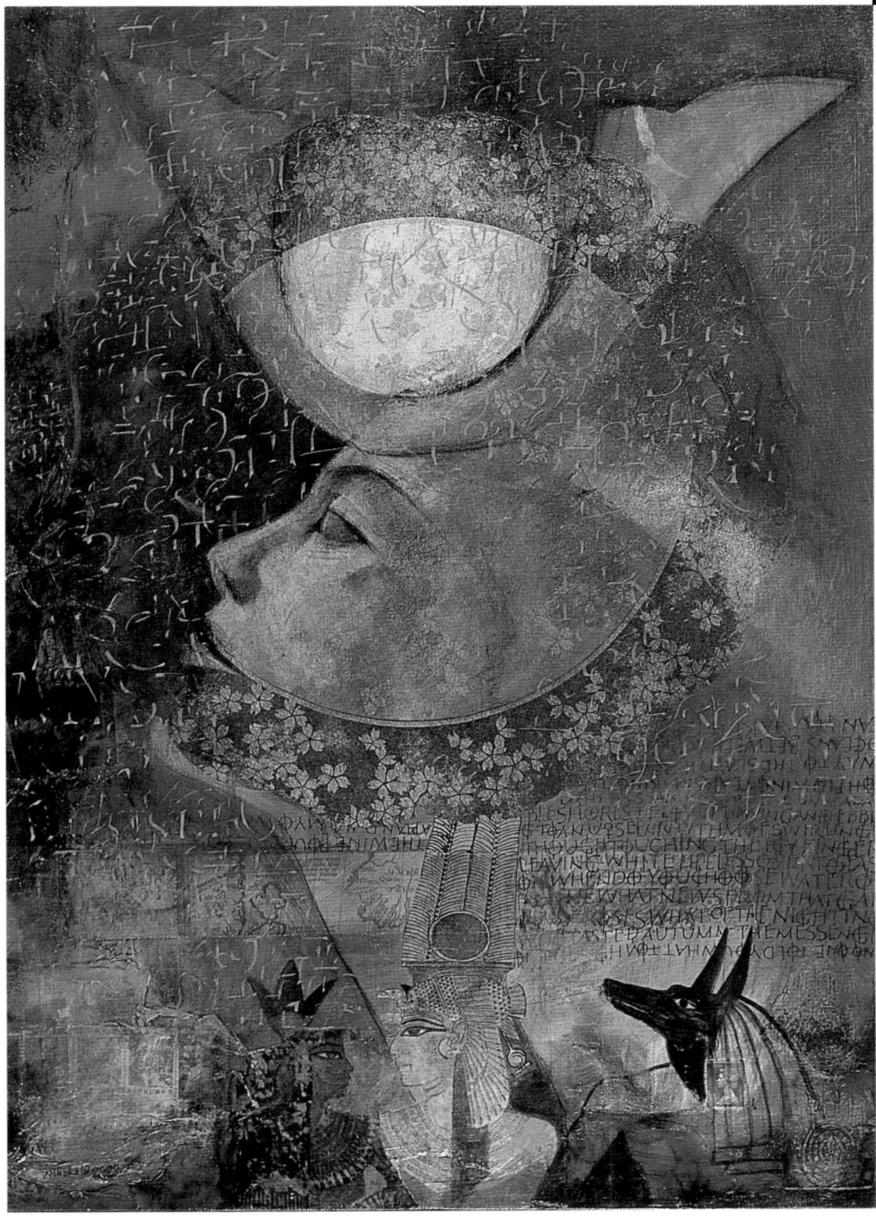

Glossary

Analogous Describes colours that are next to each other on the colour wheel.

Angle (of pen) The angle of the pen nib in relation to the writing line.

Ascender Part of some lower-case letters that extends above the x-height.

Base line The line on which the letters are written (writing line).

Blackletter (typographic term) Refers to Gothic letterforms.

Bleed Occurs when ink or paint spreads on contact with absorbent papers.

Body height Main part of the letter. *See also x-height.*

Broad-edged nib Produces thick and thin strokes by writing at a constant angle, not by applying pressure.

Burnish To polish gold leaf or shell gold.

Burnisher Tool used to burnish gold leaf. Made of agate, psilomelanite or hematite.

Capital Upper case, large or majuscule letter.

Carpet page Whole page of complex decoration, often cross-shaped, found in Celtic gospel books.

Chisel-edged nib *See Broad-edged nib.*

Colophon Tailpiece at the end of a manuscript often treated decoratively.

Complementary colour Colours that are opposite each other on the colour wheel, made by mixing two primary colours together.

Counter Space enclosed within a letter.

Counterchange Alternation or reversal of colours, often in a checkered pattern.

Cursive Informal style of writing with letters linked together.

Descender Part of some lower-case letters that extends below the writing line.

Exemplar A model alphabet or piece of work for students to copy.

Filigree Fine line decoration.

Gesso Can be used to refer to any adhesive medium used as a base for gilding, but most commonly for plaster-based medium.

Glassine Transparent, non-stick paper used in gilding.

Gouache Opaque watercolour, body colour.

Grain The direction in which the fibres lie in a sheet of machine-made paper.

Gum ammoniac Crystallized plant resin, soaked in water to make an adhesive size, or base, for flat gilding.

Gum arabic Type of gum, added to pigments and powdered gold as a binder.

Gum sandarac Crystallized plant resin. Finely ground, it can be used on paper or vellum in preparation for writing. Useful on absorbent papers to prevent bleed.

Half uncials Book script, found in manuscripts produced from the 5th to 8th centuries. Insular half uncials refers particularly to the style used in Anglo–Saxon and Irish manuscripts of the 7th and 8th centuries.

Hand Script or style of writing, for example, Italic hand.

Historiated A letter or border containing recognizable figures or scenes, which may relate to the text.

Humanist Used to refer to scholars and scribes of the Renaissance period, particularly in Italy.

Illumination Originally meant the use of gold in a manuscript. Now refers to all kinds of manuscript decoration.

Initial First letter of a word, sentence or paragraph. Can be written large, in colour, or decorated to denote relative importance.

Interlinear (line) space The space between two lines of writing.

Italic Script of Italian origin, forward sloping and cursive.

Laid Type of paper surface with slightly raised lines on the surface.

Layout Arrangement of heading, text, decorated capitals and any other elements in a piece of work.

Letterform An individual letter, also the inherent shape of the letter (e.g., round or oval) determined by the pen angle.

Lombardic Heavy Gothic capital.

Lower case (typographic term) Small letters or minuscules.

Majuscules Capital letters or upper case.

Manipulation (of pen) Changing the pen angle when writing, to achieve visual balance of stroke weight.

Margins White space around text in a book or panel of writing.

Minuscules Small letters that have ascenders and descenders; lower case.

Nap Slight surface texture of vellum, raised by abrasion.

Nib width Width of stroke of broad-edged nib. Used to assess height of a letter. *See also Weight and x-height.*

Ox-gall liquid Wetting agent that improves the flow of paint. Add sparingly to mixed paint to improve flow from pen.

Parchment Animal skin prepared for writing, usually sheep skin.

Paste-up Assembling of cut-up elements of a piece of work, stuck down onto paper to finalize the layout.

PVA Polyvinyl acetate, a modern glue used as a base for flat gilding.

Pen angle *See Angle.*

Pen lift Made at the end of each stroke of a letter.

Serif The small stroke that starts or finishes a letter.

Shade (of colour) Made by adding black, or the complementary, of any given colour.

Size An adhesive base for gilding. Also, glue added to paper pulp or to the surface of the finished sheet, which makes the surface less absorbent to ink or paint.

Square capitals Capital letters of the 5th and 6th centuries. Revived and adapted by Humanist scribes of the Renaissance.

Stem Main upright stroke of a letter.

Stroke Component of a letter, made without lifting the nib from the paper surface.

Terminal decoration Decorative forms at the end of letter strokes.

Tint (of colour) Made by adding white to an opaque colour. With watercolour, achieved by adding water only.

Tone (tonal value) Gradations of colour from light to dark.

Tooth Slight surface texture of paper, which prevents the nib from slipping.

Under-drawing Preparation of decorated letter or border, in pencil and/or pen, prior to gilding and painting.

Upper case (typographic term) Capital letters or majuscules.

Vellum Animal skin prepared for writing, usually calfskin.

Versal Used originally for capital letters written at the beginning of each verse or paragraph. Capitals built up of several pen strokes, usually used as headings, decorated initials or colophons in manuscripts.

Weight Relationship of the width of the stroke (nib width) to the letter's height.

Writing line Base line, usually ruled in pencil, on which letters are written.

x-height (typographic term) The body or main part of the letter, not including ascender or descender.

Zoomorphic Stylized animal forms found in Celtic illumination.

Resources

Layout, tracing, cartridge and watercolour papers; pencils; brushes; and most of the basic range of equipment mentioned in Chapter 1 is readily available in most art shops. These are some of the suppliers of more specialized items (some are mail order only). Try the Internet for other sources.

BookMakers International Ltd
8260 Patuxent Range Road, Suite C
Jessup MD 20794, U.S.A.
Tel: +1 301 604 7787
Fax: +1 301 604 7176
Email: bookmakers@earthlink.net
Web: www.bookmakerscatalog.com
Supplies, tools and equipment for hand bookbinding and book arts.

Falkiner Fine Papers
76 Southampton Row
London WC1B 4AR, U.K.
Tel: +44 (0)20 7831 1151
Email: falkiner@ic24.net
Large range of special papers (sample books available); cut pieces of vellum; pens, nibs, inks, ink sticks and ink stones.

John Neal, Bookseller
1833 Spring Garden Street, P.O. Box 9986
Greensboro NC 27429, U.S.A.
Tel (toll-free U.S.A. and Canada):
+1 800 369 9598
Tel: +1 336 272 6139
Fax: +1 336 272 9015
Email: info@johnnealbooks.com
Web: www.johnnealbooks.com
Books, tools and materials for calligraphy, illumination and bookbinding. Publisher of Letter Arts Review *and* Bound & Lettered. *Ships internationally.*

L. Cornelissen & Son
105 Great Russell Street
London WC13 3RY, U.K.
Tel: +44 (0)20 7636 1045.
Email: info@cornelissen.com
Web: www.cornelissen.com
Gold leaf, shell gold, burnishers and other gilding sundries. Also stockists of pens, nibs, brushes, paints and inks. Gum arabic and gum ammoniac in crystalline form.

Paper & Ink Arts
3 North Second Street
Woodsboro MD 21798, U.S.A.
Tel: +1 800 736 7772
Fax: +1 888 736 7773
Web: www.paperinkarts.com
Supplies and books for calligraphers, illuminators and other artists. Ships internationally.

Penmandirect
Martin Taylor, 1 Towneley Road West
Longridge, Lancashire PR3 3AB, U.K.
Tel: +44 (0)1772 784444
Email: penmandirect@supanet.com
Mail order calligraphy supplies (U.K. only).

Talas
20 West 20th Street, 5th Floor
New York NY 10011, U.S.A.
Tel: +1 212 219 0770
Fax: +1 212 219 0735
Email: info@talasonline.com
Web: www.talasonline.com
A professional source of bookbinding, conservation, preservation and restoration supplies since 1962.

T. N. Lawrence & Son Ltd
208 Portland Road, Hove
Sussex BN3 5QT, U.K.
Tel: +44 (0)845 644 3232
Email: artbox@lawrence.co.uk
Web: www.lawrence.co.uk
Large range of papers as well as other artists' materials.

Wm. Cowley
Parchment & Vellum Works
97 Caldecote Street, Newport Pagnell
Buckinghamshire MK16 0DB, U.K.
Tel: +44 (0)1908 610038
Email: enquiries@williamcowley.co.uk
Suppliers of whole skins, a range of cut pieces and offcuts of calfskin vellum, sheepskin and goatskin parchment.

W. Habberley Meadows Ltd.
5 Saxon Way, Chelmsley Wood
Birmingham B37 5AY, U.K.
Tel: +44 (0)121 770 0103
Web: www.habberleymeadows.co.uk
Gold leaf and gilding sundries.

Wright's of Lymm Ltd.
(Trading as C. F. Stonehouse & Sons)
Warrington Lane, Lymm
Cheshire WA13 0SA, U.K.
Tel: +44 (0)1925 752226
Email: info@wrightsoflymm.co.uk
Web: www.wrightsoflymm.co.uk
Gold leaf, burnishers and other gilding sundries.

Calligraphy Societies

These societies have an international membership. Regular journals and newsletters keep members up to date. Check the Internet for your own national or regional calligraphic society or guild.

Australian Society of Calligraphers Inc.
P.O. Box 190
Willoughby NSW 2068, Australia
Web: www.australiansocietyofcalligraphers.com.au

Calligraphy & Lettering Arts Society (CLAS)
54 Boileau Road, London SW13 9BL
U.K.
Email: info@clas.co.uk
Web: www.clas.co.uk

IAMPETH
c/o Kathy Saunders, Treasurer
1818 Kennedy Road, Webster
New York NY 14580, U.S.A.
Email: candoit99@aol.com
Web: www.iampeth.com

New Zealand Calligraphers
P.O. Box 99–674
Newmarket
Auckland, New Zealand
Email: info@ nzcalligraphers.co.nz
Web: www.nzcalligraphers.co.nz

Society of Scribes
P.O. Box 933, New York NY 10150, U.S.A.
Tel: +1 212 452 0139
Email: info@societyofscribes.org
Web: www.societyofscribes.org

Society of Scribes & Illuminators
6 Queen Square, London WC1N 3AT, U.K.
Email: scribe@calligraphyonline.org
Web: www.calligraphyonline.org

Further Reading

The following is a list of some useful and interesting books on the subject of illuminated manuscripts, as well as some that deal with aspects of calligraphy touched on in this volume. A few of the books may be out of print, but it is worth seeking them out in libraries or searching the Internet for second-hand copies.

ILLUMINATION

The Art of Medieval Manuscripts, Krystyna Weinstein (Hamlyn, 1997)

The Bedford Hours, Janet Backhouse (British Library, 1990)

The Book of Kells, Bernard Meehan (Thames & Hudson, 1994)

Celtic Art: The Methods of Construction, George Bain (Constable & Co. Ltd, 1977, 1995)

The Craftsman's Handbook (Il libro dell'arte), Cennino Cennini, trans. D. V. Thompson, Jr. (Dover, 1960) (Originally written by an Renaissance craftsman about gilding and painting techniques.)

The Gilded Page: The History and Technique of Manuscript Gilding, Kathleen P. Whitley (Oak Knoll Press, 2000)

A History of Illuminated Manuscripts, Christopher de Hamel (Phaidon, 1986, 1994)

Illuminated Books of the Middle Ages, Robert G. Calkin (Thames & Hudson, 1983)

The Illuminated Manuscript, Janet Backhouse (Phaidon, 1979, 1987)

The Illuminated Page, Janet Backhouse (The British Library, 1997)

The Lindisfarne Gospels: A masterpiece of book painting, Janet Backhouse (British Library, 1995)

Masterpieces of the J Paul Getty Museum (Thames & Hudson, 1997)

Painted Labyrinth, Michelle P Brown (British Library, 2003)

Secreta: Three Methods of Laying Gold Leaf, Joyce Grafe (Oregon Historical Society Press, 1990)

Understanding Illuminated Manuscripts, Michelle P. Brown (Getty/British Library, 1994)

Writing and Illuminating, and Lettering, Edward Johnston (A & C Black, 1994)

CALLIGRAPHY

A Book of Formal Scripts, John Woodcock (A & C Black, 1992)

A Book of Scripts, Alfred Fairbank (Faber & Faber, 1977)

The Calligrapher's Bible, David Harris (Barron's Educational Series, 2003)

The Calligrapher's Handbook, Heather Child (Ed.) (A & C Black, 1985)

Calligraphy, Michael Gullick (Studio Editions, 1990)

Collins Calligrapher's Companion, Mary Noble & Janet Mehigan (Harper Collins, 1998)

Historical Scripts, Stan Knight (A & C Black, 1984)

Practical Calligraphy, John R. Nash & Gerald Fleuss (Hamlyn, 1992)

Index

Page numbers in italics refer to captions.

Acknowledgments

Quarto would like to thank the artists for kindly supplying their illumination reproduced in this book. Artists are acknowledged in the captions beside their work.

Quarto would also like to acknowledge the following: 89, 91, 140, 165, 166, 189, 191, 213, 214, 215 by permission of The British Library; 90 by permission of the Chapter of Lichfield Cathedral; 113, 115, 167 by permission of the Director and the University Librarian, The John Rylands University Library, The University of Manchester; 114, 190 by permission of The J. Paul Getty Museum, Los Angeles, California; 139 by permission of the Chapter of Winchester Cathedral; 141 by permission of the Master and Fellows of Trinity College Cambridge; 240 Peter Halliday's *Alphabet* is reproduced with the kind permission of Revd. Julian Barker.

While every effort has been made to credit contributors, Quarto would like to apologize should there have been any omissions or errors and would be pleased to make the appropriate correction for future editions of the book.

Author's Acknowledgements

Thanks to Mary Noble, Janet Mehigan and Ian Garrett for the script exemplars on pages 104–107, 128–131 and 228–231, and 154–157 and 180–181, respectively.

I am grateful to the scribes who have allowed their work to be published in this book: Lorna Bambury, Rosemary Buczek, Valerie Dugan, Marlene Gray, Peter Halliday, Nadia Hlibka, Manny Ling, Janet Mehigan and Mary Noble.

Thanks also to William Cowley Vellum and Parchment Works, Newport Pagnell for kindly supplying samples of vellum and parchment, and Martin Taylor of Penmandirect for the loan of nibs and penholders for photography.

In addition, my grateful thanks are due to all the tutors and colleagues who have encouraged me, sharing their invaluable knowledge and skills so generously, not to mention family and friends who have stoically put up with my fascination with the craft of calligraphy and illumination over many years.